EARLIER AMERICAN MUSIC

EDITED BY H. WILEY HITCHCOCK
for the *Music Library Association*

17

THE
AMERICAN SINGING BOOK

SIMEON PEASE CHENEY

THE
AMERICAN SINGING BOOK

BY SIMEON PEASE CHENEY

NEW INTRODUCTION BY KARL KROEGER

Director, Moravian Music Foundation

DA CAPO PRESS • NEW YORK • 1980

Library of Congress Cataloging in Publication Data

Cheney, Simeon Pease, 1818-1890.
  The American singing book.

  (Earlier American music; 17)
  Reprint of the ed. published by White, Smith,
Boston.
  Includes index.
  1. Vocal music. 2. Sacred vocal music.
3. Music, American. 4. Composers–United States–
Biography. I. Title. II. Series.
M1495.C5A5 1980   784.8   80-13923
ISBN 0-306-77322-8

This Da Capo Press edition·of
The American Singing Book
is an unabridged republication of
the first edition published in Boston
in 1879 by White, Smith & Company,
supplemented with a new introduction by
Karl Kroeger and a photograph reproduced
by the courtesy of the Vermont Historical Society.

Published by Da Capo Press, Inc.
A Subsidiary of Plenum Publishing Corporation
227 West 17th Street, New York, N.Y. 10011

Manufactured in the United States of America

EDITOR'S FOREWORD

American musical culture, from Colonial and Federal Era days on, has been reflected in an astonishing production of printed music of all kinds: by 1820, for instance, more than fifteen thousand musical publications had issued from American presses. Fads, fashions, and tastes have changed so rapidly in our history, however, that comparatively little earlier American music has remained in print. On the other hand, the past few decades have seen an explosion of interest in earlier American culture, including earlier American music. College and university courses in American civilization and American music have proliferated; recording companies have found a surprising response to earlier American composers and their music; a wave of interest in folk and popular music of past eras has opened up byways of musical experience unimagined only a short time ago.

It seems an opportune moment, therefore, to make available for study and enjoyment—and as an aid to furthering performance of earlier American music—works of significance that exist today only in a few scattered copies of publications long out of print, and works that may be well known only in later editions or arrangements having little relationship to the original compositions.

Earlier American Music is planned around several types of musical scores to be reprinted from early editions of the eight-eenth, nineteenth, and early twentieth centuries. The categories are as follows:

> Songs and other solo vocal music
> Choral music and part-songs
> Solo keyboard music
> Chamber music
> Orchestral music and concertos
> Dance music and marches for band
> Theater music

The idea of *Earlier American Music* originated in a paper read before the Music Library Association in February, 1968, and published under the title "A Monumenta Americana?" in the Association's journal, *Notes* (September, 1968). It seems most appropriate, therefore, for the Music Library Association to sponsor this series. We hope *Earlier American Music* will stimulate further study and performance of musical Americana.

H. Wiley Hitchcock

INTRODUCTION

When Simeon Pease Cheney published *The American Singing Book* in 1879, the venerable, oblong, end-opening tunebook so familiar to most Americans was nearly a thing of the past. Over 150 years earlier the Boston ministers, John Tufts and Thomas Walter, had published the first American "singing books" for the purpose of improving the quality of congregational singing. Organized by Tufts and Walter to assure some uniformity in congregational singing through instruction in musical notation, the singing school became an American institution which spread in the next century from New England south and west, as the frontier expanded, to encompass the whole of the developing country.

Itinerant singing masters rode their circuits like traveling peddlers, stopping at a town for a few weeks or months, organizing their school, selling their singing books, teaching the rudiments of musical notation along with a few hymn-tunes and simple anthems, and then moving on—perhaps to return the following year. The singing school became a popular institution, not so much as an aid to congregational singing (although in many cases some improvement resulted) but because it was a rare, clergy-approved, social contact for young people. Most singing schools held sessions between late fall and early spring, when little enough recreational activity was available to the youth. Singing school graduates were expected to join the choir at their local church and help lead the congregational singing.

But by the last quarter of the nineteenth century things had changed considerably. The church choir in many fashionable churches had been replaced by a solo quartet of strong, often professional, singers who sang the responses and anthems and dominated rather than led the congregation in the singing of hymns. Lowell Mason's work in establishing musical academies and conventions and obtaining a place for music in the public school curriculum had undermined the role of the itinerant singing master, from whom people began to seek individual instruction in *bel canto* rather than group lessons in psalmody. The rise and wide acceptance of the denominational hymnal, containing both tunes and the complete text of the hymns, steadily pushed aside the oblong end-opener. Finally, the gospel songs of the new Social Gospel movement effected a change in the basic repertory of many churches. The songs of Ira Sankey and P. P. Bliss replaced those of Lowell Mason and William Bradbury. Simeon Pease Cheney's elder brother, Moses Ela, a singing master in Vermont for over fifty years, accurately evaluated the situation in 1888 in a letter to a friend: "The old Singing Masters days are a thing that *was*. The old men have lost their prestige for the young control the music."[1]

---

[1] Moses E. Cheney to Harriet Cushman, July 25, 1888; quoted in Charles W. Hughes, "The Cheneys: A Vermont Singing Family," *Vermont History,* v.45, n. 3 (Summer, 1977), p. 164.

The American Singing Book was by no means the last end-opener to be published. A few were issued in the 1880s by Luther Emerson, the Perkins Brothers, C. E. Leslie, and a few others. But compared with the veritable flood of tune-books on the market between 1830 and 1870, those published in the last quarter of the century were only a diminishing trickle of a once mighty stream.

It is not surprising then, given the history of the singing school movement and the decline of the old and familiar ways, that there is a strong aura of nostalgia about *The American Singing Book*. The compiler set himself a double purpose: "I have aimed at a book of good music, Sacred and Secular, for classes, choirs and all places and purposes where such music is needed." But in the same sentence he included an antiquarian goal: "To set forth the various styles of sacred music particularly which have prevailed from the beginning of composing and printing the same in America to the present time; and the men who have been the leading devotees in the work—the toilers, singers, composers and book makers, who have gone to a higher life, from William Billings to I. B. Woodbury."[2]

Simeon Pease Cheney was born in Meredith, New Hampshire on April 18, 1818, the ninth of the eleven children of Rev. Moses Cheney, a farmer and Free Will Baptist preacher in central and southern New Hampshire.[3] Musical and literary talent abounded in the family heritage. Moses Cheney found time among his pastoral duties and farm chores to write a religious tract, *The Believer's Assistant,* and to compose hymns, some of which were published in the denominational hymnal of the Free Will Baptists.[4]

Little is known of Simeon Pease Cheney's early life, but we may assume that he received more than the common school and singing-school education available to the rural youth of the day. Encouraged by his father, and following his elder brother's example, he may have been something of an autodidact.[5]

Sometime around 1830 the Cheney family moved to Vermont, where they became involved in musical affairs. In 1839 Moses Ela, Simeon's elder brother, and E. K. Prouty organized a musical convention in Montpelier, Vermont, reputedly the first of its kind ever held. Four more conventions followed in the succeeding five years in various Vermont towns.[6] By the mid-1840s the name of Cheney was a familiar one in Vermont musical life.

Undoubtedly motivated by the success and growing fame of the Hutchinson Family Singers, the Cheneys in 1845 decided to put their musical talents to more remunerative work. Four brothers —Nathaniel, Moses Ela, Joseph, and Simeon—and the sister, Elizabeth, formed the Cheney Family Singers, an ensemble which made its official concert debut in New York City on October 13,

---

[2]Simeon Pease Cheney, *The American Singing Book*, p. 2.
[3]Charles H. Pope, *The Cheney Genealogy* (Boston, 1897), p. 306.

[4]Hughes, *op. cit.*, p. 156.
[5]*Ibid.*
[6]*Ibid.*, pp. 157-58.

1845.[7] The review of the concert in the *New York Evening Post* the following day was kind if not particularly enthusiastic:

> The concert room was crowded in every part at an early hour. The singers, in their various glees, serenades, songs, trios, and quartets were tumultously applauded. Their style of singing is very pleasing, but as far as regards their being equal to the Hutchinsons, some difference of opinion seems to prevail. However, every piece of music sung by them was well received, and several of them encored.[8]

The Cheneys toured as a singing group for about two years following their debut, and then disbanded, each member going his or her own way.

Simeon settled in Dorset, Vermont, where he farmed, taught singing schools, and directed the choir at the Dorset church with great success. Little is known about the middle years of his life; but in the early 1870s he was drawn to California where his sons, John and Albert, were living.[9]

Although thoughts of compiling a singing book had come to him earlier, it was only during his stay in California that the idea took form. "From that hour to the present, at hotels, boarding houses, riding in cars, anywhere and everywhere, when I had a leisure moment, I worked to that end, as best I could."[10] White, Smith and Company in Boston published Cheney's *The American Singing Book* in 1879. He seems to have underwritten at least part of the cost himself, for a few years later he wrote to a friend: "Within the last two years I have been robbed of $1000 & I have invested $500 in my book & I am *more* than poor." It was his intention "to hold forth with my book anywhere I can and try to get a few dollars in some way."[11]

Simeon Pease Cheney spent his last years in Franklin, Massachusetts, where he published a series of articles on "Bird Music" in the *Century Magazine*, collected after his death by his son, John Vance Cheney, in a volume entitled *Wood Notes Wild* (Boston, 1892). He died on May 10, 1890.[12]

The contents of *The American Singing Book* are as varied as the country it sought to serve. The 322 pieces in the book address themselves to nearly every occasion in which social music-making played a role: the church, the parlor, the musical society, and the singing school. Even the old-time repertory of the popular "Old Folks Concerts," begun in the 1850s by "Father" Robert Kemp, is included,[13] as well as songs sung by The Cheney Family Singers during their concertizing years in the 1840s. With such variety the book could have been a hodge-podge; in fact it is carefully planned and tightly organized.

There are four main divisions in the book: a section on the rudiments of musical notation including elementary singing ex-

[7]Pope, *op. cit.*, pp. 377-78.

[8]*New York Evening Post*, October 14, 1945; quoted in Hughes, *op. cit.*, p. 159.

[9]S. P. Cheney, *op. cit.*, p. 2.

[10]*Ibid.*

[11]S. P. Cheney to Harriet Cushman, March 10, 1881; quoted in Hughes, *op. cit.*, p.162.

[12]Hughes, *op. cit.*, p.164.

[13]Frank J. Metcalf, *American Writers and Compilers of Sacred Music* (New York, 1925), pp. 286-88.

ercises; a Tune Department, containing four-part harmonizations of hymn-tunes, set-pieces, and anthems for church use; a Biographical Department, which includes sketches of the lives and careers of forty "leading teachers, composers and book makers in America, with a characteristic tune of each"; and a Secular Department, consisting largely of glees, quartets, and choruses sung by The Cheney Family Singers.

Nearly every tunebook published in America after 1721 contained a section on the rudiments of musical notation. Some of these were lengthy and expository; others were mere outlines of the basic principles, leaving it to the singer master to fill in the instructional details. Cheney's rudiments are similar to those found in most nineteenth-century tunebooks from the 1820s on. They differ in two significant aspects from those found in eighteenth-century tunebooks. The old "moods of time," the system in which the time signature carried an implied tempo, are no longer employed. The standard European system is used, in which the temporal value of any note varies faster or slower in proportion to other note values according to a tempo established at the beginning of the piece. There is no standard tactus, and Italian terms are used to establish or vary the pace. The other divergence from earlier practice is that the four-syllable fasola system of solmization has been replaced by the tonic-sol-fa system, with seven basic syllables and syllable modification for chromatic tones.

The rudiments in *The American Singing Book* are short, concise, and to the point. There is no needless theorizing, nor even lengthy expositions of important matters. Detailed explanations are left to the singing master. Considerable attention is devoted to a series of progressive vocal exercises, aimed at increasing vocal range and flexibility, and familiarity with part singing. The student is led through progressively distant keys, a variety of time signatures, and increasingly subtle rhythmic demands; by the end, if each exercise has been mastered, the student should be a reasonably capable singer.

The Tune Department contains hymn-tunes, set-pieces, sentences, and anthems for use in church, the parlor, and the singing school. The hymn-tunes are arranged according to the poetic meter they are designed to fit, beginning with Long Metre, through Common Metre and Short Metre, to the various Particular Metres.[14] Each division is further subdivided between new or unfamiliar tunes (mostly by Cheney and his associates) and "Congregational Tunes," those familiar melodies which had been sung in church for decades, which the congregations often knew by heart, and upon which the congregational singing in most churches still depended.

As in most nineteenth-century tunebooks, the anthems, set-pieces, and sentences come at the end of the Tune Department. Most of these compositions are also by Cheney and his friends;

----

[14]Long Metre, Common Metre, and Short Metre were by far the most frequently used metrical patterns in Anglo-American hymnody. Each stanza consists of four lines, with the number of syllables in each line varying according to a standard pattern. Long Metre is a pattern of 8.8.8.8. syllables; Common Metre is 8.6.8.6., and Short Metre 6.6.8.6. These patterns may also be doubled (e.g., Common Metre Doubled is 8.6.8.6.8.6.8.6.). Any metrical pattern that did not conform to one of these standard arrangements was classified as Particular Metre, and could have any metrical configuration.

however, a certain class appeal accrues from the addition of choruses by Pietro Guglielmi and Felix Mendelssohn, as well as the
final chorus from Beethoven's oratorio, *Christus am Olberge,* Op.
85; an excerpt from the Gloria of Haydn's *Heiligemesse;* and the
Hallelujah Chorus from Handel's *Messiah.* In line with custom,
only the vocal parts are printed, with occasional instrumental cues
to aid the organist in achieving a smoother, more authentic performance.

Perhaps the most valuable part of Cheney's tunebook for
today's user is the Biographical Department (pp. 168-213, and
307). Cheney went to considerable trouble to include information
about many of the leading composers, church musicians, and tunebook compilers of an earlier era. He relied upon some standard
published accounts, such as those in John W. Moore's *Complete
Encyclopedia of Music* (Boston, 1852), George Hood's *History
of Music in New England* (Boston, 1846), and N. D. Gould's
History of Church Music in America (Boston, 1853). But in many
cases he sought out relatives and close acquaintances of the subjects of the sketches in order to include new and up-to-date information. In compiling the biographical notices Cheney had the
collaboration of his brother, Moses Ela, and his friend, James A.
Johnson. Only twenty-three of the forty (actually forty-one, since
one sketch is printed far out of place) biographies appear in Frank
Metcalf's still indispensable *American Writers and Compilers of
Sacred Music* (New York, 1925), making *The American Singing
Book* a unique source of information about the lives and
contributions of a significant number of early American church
musicians.

One must use the biographical information in this section
with care and discrimination. Compiled as an act of homage, the
entries do not pretend to critical scholarship. Anecdotes of doubt-
ful veracity abound, and later research has corrected or supplemented some of Cheney's data; but when working in the sacred
music of nineteenth-century America, the prudent researcher will
not ignore Cheney's tunebook.

Accompanying each biographical sketch is an example of the
man's music. In most cases, this tune represents the composer's
most popular and enduring one, not necessarily his best or most
representative. Nor have the earlier compositions escaped the
editor's pencil. In all pieces, the melody appears in the treble
rather than tenor; and in many, small emendations have been
made, particularly in the inner parts, to "correct" harmony or
give a better line. On the whole, however, considering the prevailing attitude toward them in the genteel society, the old tunes
are treated with considerable respect.

The Secular Department, a feature found in many late nineteenth-century tunebooks, reflects the changing role of the tunebook in its society. In earlier years sacred and secular music were
seldom mixed within a tunebook. Glee books contained music
for the secular chorus and parlor use, while tunebooks provided
repertory for the church choir and singing school. However,
toward the end of the century these distinctive roles were blended,
and a single collection of hymn-tunes, anthems, glees, and choruses
was designed to fill the needs of the widest possible market. Much
of the Secular Department in Cheney's tunebook contains music
sung by The Cheney Family Singers three decades earlier. The wide

variety of songs includes sentimental ballads, patriotic airs, humorous glees, and songs extolling the beauties of nature.

Of the 126 composers in *The American Singing Book,* most are represented by only one tune each. The compiler himself is credited with fifty-one hymn-tunes, anthems, and secular pieces, by far the largest number. Cheney's friend, James A. Johnson, a former assistant to Lowell Mason, supplied twenty-one tunes and anthems. Twelve tunes come from the collections of Charles Zeuner, a former leader of the Boston Handel and Haydn Society, who died by his own hand in 1857. Cheney's elder son, John Vance Cheney, composed two tunes; his brother Moses Ela and his younger son Albert contributed one each.

Perhaps the most interesting groups of pieces, from the historical point of view, are those which Cheney came upon during his stay in California several years before the tunebook's publication. Five works by Frank J. Lewis of Sacramento and one each by J. K. Van Slyke and "Professor" Yarndley of San Francisco appear in the collection, as well as one tune by G. F. Inman, of Cheyenne, Wyoming Territory. These compositions surely represent some of the earliest Anglo-American composers active in the West.

What of *The American Singing Book* as music? Did the compiler succeed in his effort to produce "a book of good music, Sacred and Secular, for classes and choirs and all places and purposes where such music is needed"? In comparison with other tunebooks published in the 1870s, the variety of its pieces by both contemporary and earlier composers, its naïve, cheerful optimism,

and its open, unbiased acceptance of "good" music from any era, mark it as exceptional. The hymn-tunes, anthems, and choruses in *The American Singing Book,* with their Victorian purity, calculated plainness, and "barbershop" harmonies, are well in tune with the taste of the 1870s. But in the 100 years since its publication, church music has undergone many changes in taste: gospel songs, the Oxford Movement, folk- and pop-influenced hymnody, to mention only a few. One must admit that many pieces in *The American Singing Book* would probably produce snickers among today's singers.

Some pieces, however, are worth resuscitation: Cheney's set-piece The Sabbath, and his anthems "Come Unto Me" and "Rejoice in the Lord"; James A. Johnson's "Benedictus," and D. A. French's "Come Thou Fount" all could be sung today with enjoyment. Some of the secular pieces, such as Cheney's "Come Sing with Do Re Mi," his "California Song" and "Winter," and a few pieces from the repertory of The Cheney Family Singers, might find their way onto school or community chorus programs with equal satisfaction.

Shortly after Simeon's death, his brother Moses Ela penned a brief eulogy in a letter to a friend: "Simeon was the greatest native melodist that this Country has seen. His physical & mental qualities were ever equal to his subject & to the occasion, & every rival shrank from immediate comparison."[15] Taking into con-

---

[15]Moses E. Cheney to Harriet Cushman, November, 1890; quoted in Hughes, *op. cit.,* p. 164.

sideration fraternal affection and Moses Ela's propensity to hyperbole, this statement contains a ring of truth, the evidence for which is found in Cheney's remarkable *The American Singing Book*.

The writer wishes to express his appreciation to the staff of the Vermont Historical Society for its prompt and thorough aid in supplying biographical information for this introduction, and to Miss Betty Bandel of South Burlington, Vt. for her general advice and assistance.

KARL KROEGER
Winston-Salem, N.C.
April, 1980

THE AMERICAN SINGING BOOK.

BY SIMEON PEASE CHENEY.

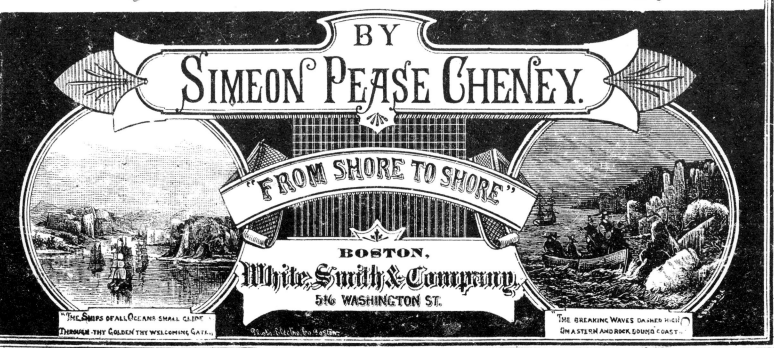

"FROM SHORE TO SHORE"

BOSTON,
White, Smith & Company
516 WASHINGTON ST.

"THE SHIPS OF ALL OCEANS SHALL GLIDE
THROUGH THY GOLDEN THY WELCOMING GATE."

"THE BREAKING WAVES DASHED HIGH
ON A STERN AND ROCK BOUND COAST."

Copy of Original Cover

THE
AMERICAN SINGING BOOK,

CONTAINS MORE THAN 300 PAGES OF A GREAT VARIETY OF EXCELLENT

Sacred and Secular Music, Old and New,

FOR ALL PURPOSES WHERE SUCH MUSIC IS USED.

A Valuable Feature in the Book is

THE BIOGRAPHICAL DEPARTMENT,

Containing Biographies of Forty of the Leading Composers, Book-makers, etc., of Sacred Music in America, from William Billings to I. B. Woodbury, which alone is worth the price of the Book.

The Publishers endorse this Book with great Confidence, believing it to be the most

ORIGINAL, IMPORTANT, AND INTERESTING SINGING BOOK

Ever published in this Country, and in every sense worthy of its Grand Title.

By SIMEON PEASE CHENEY.

BOSTON:
Published by White, Smith and Company.
516 Washington Street.

Gould, music printer, 18 P.O. Sq., Boston.

PREFACE.

"WHO READS A PREFACE?" EVERY-BODY WHO READS WELL.

LONG AGO I thought of compiling a Singing Book; but it was only about three years since, while teaching in California, that I fully determined to do it. I there had, on a special occasion of reflection upon the subject, a clear and sudden perception or vision of a book which so interested me, I immediately decided to make it a reality. From that hour to the present, at hotels, boarding houses, riding in the cars, anywhere and everywhere, when I had a leisure moment, I have worked to that end, as best I could. THE AMERICAN SINGING BOOK is the result. It is my first book, my little contribution to the great page of American Music History, now being made up.

I have aimed at a book of good music, Sacred and Secular, for classes, choirs and all places and purposes where such music is needed, and to set forth the various styles of sacred music particularly which have prevailed from the beginning of composing and printing the same in America to the present time; and the men who have been the leading devotees in the work—the toilers, singers, composers and book makers, who have gone on to higher life, from William Billings to I. B. Woodbury.

I have taken great interest in bringing forward our early psalm tune composers, and giving some permanence, as I hope, to their true position. Their natural, and in many cases their excellent compositions, compel me to believe them to have been men of no ordinary gifts. I agree fully with the following sentiment in the preface of *" The Continental Harmony* :

"Whatever may be said of the laws which governed our fathers in the arrangement of their musical ideas, none can reasonably deny the abounding evidence of inspiration found in their works." Their compositions *were inspirations,* hence original, hence they live.

So far as I know, the introduction of the biographies of men into a singing book with their music is a new feature; but I trust it will be an interesting and useful one. It certainly contains precisely the information I ever sought but never found in any book. This group of forty biographized men is arrayed with splendid talents. They were not merely "musicians" in the sickly sense in which they have often been called, but they were *grand men* with remarkable qualifications for the work of life. Among them were farmers, a great variety of mechanics, inventors, preachers, lawyers, teachers, poets and warriors. This Department has cost me much research and pains-taking. In its preparation I have been assisted by John W. Moore, James A. Johnson, Moses E. Cheney, Rev. Geo. Hood, H. P. Main and B. F. Otterson; all of whom are highly qualified for such work and devoted to "the cause."

To Rev. Dr. Hastings of New York, Mrs. Dr. Lowell Mason, Mrs. I. B. Woodbury and son, I am indebted for letters of information and printed documents which greatly assisted me. For contributions of new music, composed for my volume, and in some cases permission to use music from books, I am very grateful to the following gentlemen: G. J. Webb, O. Ditson, L. O. Emerson, W. O. Perkins, A. N. Johnson, W. S. Rogers, D. A. French, E. B. Clement, Leonard Marshall, Geo. F. Root, V. C. Taylor of Des Moines, John W. Moore, E. M. Bowman of St. Louis, Prof. Inman of Cheyenne. W. T., E. H. Bailey, Moses E. Cheney, Prof. Yarndly of San Francisco, also Caspar T. Hopkins and J. K. Van Slyke of the same city, Frank J. Lewis, John Vance Cheney and Albert Baker Cheney, all of Sacramento, Joseph Howard of East Orange, N. J., H. M. Hunter and George Briggs. But most of all am I under obligations to James A. Johnson of East Orange, N. J., for great and unabated interest in my work, for his compositions, arrangements and accompaniments, and able counsel in matters of taste. I most earnestly invite the attention of every-body to his forth-coming volume of Classical Music, "The Church Quartette," a book of Gems for Choirs and Musical Societies.

And my expression of gratitude would be incomplete without reference to the man whose skill, patience and honesty, have supported him through the peculiarly trying task of the type-work of this book. GEORGE GOULD, 18 Post-office Square, Boston, is a most excellent music printer. He not only has the mechanical knowledge and taste, but he is a practical musician, eighteen years an organist, with zeal, manhood, and professional pride to back him up.

To the *wonderful life* and *spirit* of California, I am indebted for the beginning of this work, quite a portion of which was accomplished there, and was probably the first work of the kind in the state. To L. K. Hammer of Sacramento, Jervis Joslyn of Cheyenne, W. T., D. L. Kent of Vermont, and Mrs. A. B. Tilton of New Hampshire, I here record my gratitude for special "aid and comfort."

My intention in this volume has been to have the *general* character of the music, a little above the taste of what are termed "common singers," but not beyond their reach. In the original conception of it, the thought of "making a dollar" never entered my mind; I only thought of making a *good book;* if I have failed, and the book becomes neither popular nor remunerative, still I shall not fail of a full reward for all the toil and thought I have bestowed upon it; it is already in my possession, in the rich knowledge I have gained, of men and women and music, in its protracted preparation.

The book contains more information concerning the history of Sacred Music in America, than any singing book ever published, with specimens of compositions that have prevailed from first to last, and is purely American in spirit, hence its title: while there are poetry and music from many nations, and as far back as "The Sweet Singer of Israel." Among the more than three hundred poets and musicians here represented, are the names of the most brilliant souls that ever walked this earth in flesh, and the words of him who "spake as never man spake."

The *new* music and poetry more especially represent New England and California; but I hope the book will be "good for all intermediate stations," become a fulfilment of its prophetic name, and its music be heard "FROM SHORE TO SHORE."

I dedicate THE AMERICAN SINGING BOOK to all who have been my pupils during the more than forty years of my Singing Master life, who remain in this world, wherever they may be; and implore the blessing of "Our Heavenly Father," "Our Elder Brother," and all the music-loving "Angel World," all whose words or music are written in this book, especially of the worthy *Biographized Band,* to rest upon it now and evermore.

So prays the humble author,

SIMEON PEASE CHENEY.

Maple Grove, Dorset, Vermont, Feb. 22, 1879.

RULES FOR STUDENTS IN VOCAL MUSIC.

The learner must at every step, have first a *clear* perception of what he is to sing, then he can *try* to sing it.

NOTES

represent the comparative length of tones. There are five in common use :

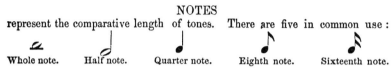

Whole note. Half note. Quarter note. Eighth note. Sixteenth note.

RESTS

show the comparative length of the suspension of tones, and correspond in number and length with the notes.

Whole rest. Half rest. Quarter rest. Eighth rest. Sixteenth rest.

A DOT

placed after a note or rest adds one half to its length.

 etc.

A second dot has half the value of the first, and a third dot has half the value of the second.

A HOLD

placed over or under a note or rest, gives liberty to prolong it at discretion.

MEASURES

are small divisions in time or rhythm, and are of two primitive kinds, double and triple ; their difference consists in the arrangement of the accent. If you sing a succession of monotones of equal length and force, as follows :

the ear is soon pained with the monotonous *sounds*, as the eye is with the monotonous *look*. But give an *accent* on every other tone, and the ear is *instantly relieved*, and you are singing in double measure.

If you give the accent on every *third* tone, you sing *triple* measure.

Double measure.   Triple measure.

So double measure in its simplest form, has two equal parts with an accent on the first ; triple measure has three equal parts with an accent on the first.

By uniting two double measures, quadruple measure is formed ; and by uniting two triple measures, sextuple measure is formed.

Quadruple measure.   Sextuple measure.

These four kinds of measure, double, triple, quadruple and sextuple are in common use. There are others with eight parts, twelve parts, and even more.

The line dividing measures is called the bar.

The double bar is used at the end of a line in the poetry of a psalm tune, dividing the music into strains. There is no necessity for it, and it often perplexes the beginner by dividing the parts of a measure ; it is not much used in this book.

There are not only four *kinds*, but there are also several *varieties* of measure, each of which is indicated by figures placed at the beginning of a tune, next to the signature, showing in a fractional form the contents of each measure.

DIFFERENT KINDS OF MEASURES AND THEIR VARIETIES.

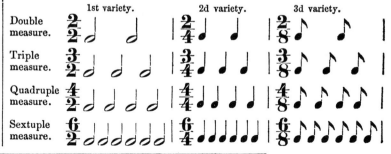

All kinds of measure have their principal accent on the first part. The second accent is less than the first. *Any part* of a measure *may* receive the accent.

When the accented part of a measure is divided and joined to an unaccented part, as follows,

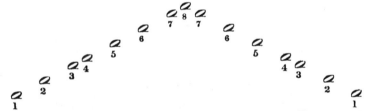

the note thus formed is called syncopated, and has the accent.

BEATING TIME

is a motion of the hand for each part of the measure, by which we are able to "keep time" more evenly.

Double measure has two beats, one down and one up.

Triple measure has three beats, one down, one left or right, and one up.

Quadruple measure has four beats, one down, one left, one right and one up.

Sextuple measure has six beats, two down, one left, one right and two up. But if the movement be rapid, only two beats are given, one down and one up, as in double measure.

THE SCALE

is a succession of eight tones by which we sing up and down in the realm of sound in regular steps, indicated to the eye as follows.

It will be seen there are five long and two short steps. They are called whole and half steps, or major and minor seconds. The latter are always between 3 and 4 and 7 and 8.

THE STAFF

with five lines and four spaces, shows the difference in the pitch of tones.

Reckoning from the lower line upward, we read, first line, first space, second line, second space, and so on.

If a higher tone be required than the upper line represents, the space above the staff is used; if one still higher, a short line is added. In that way any number of lines may be added above or below, and they are called added or leger lines above and added lines below. The number of lines in the staff is arbitrary. More or less than five *might* be used.

The lines and spaces are named from the first seven letters of the alphabet; but the order in the alphabet is reversed, and we read A, B, C, &c. *upward.*

The letters are variously arranged on the staff to accommodate different voices, and their position is established by a clef.

In singing books there have been commonly only two clefs used, the treble or G clef and the bass or F clef.

The G clef fixes G on the 2d line the F clef places F on the 4th line.

THE G CLEF

has been commonly used for three parts in sacred music, namely,

THE SOPRANO,

for the highest female voices;

THE ALTO,

for the lowest female voices;

THE TENOR,

the highest part for male voices. But when used for the Tenor, the whole staff is an octave lower than in the other two parts.

THE TENOR OR C CLEF

as used in this country, is more appropriate for the tenor part. It represents the same *order* of letters as the G clef, but an octave lower.

The Staff, the three clefs, the first position of the scale, with each clef, with the letters, numerals and syllables may be seen in the following diagram.

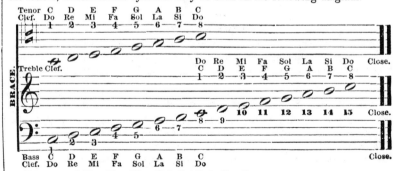

Pronounced Doe Ray Mee Fah Sol Lah See Doe.

The C midway between the treble and bass staffs, is called "Middle C." With the Tenor clef, C on the third space has the *same pitch* as "Middle C." It will be seen the *Clef* determines the order of *letters* on the staff; while the *scale* determines the order of *intervals*.

INTERVAL

is a common term for the difference of pitch between any two tones. From 1 to 2 is the interval of a second, from 1 to 3 a third, 1 to 4 a fourth and so on.

This scale is called "the natural scale." But *how difficult to be natural in any thing!* To be able to sing the tones of the scale in *perfect pitch* is a very rare and exquisite attainment. In other words, singing "in tune" is *very uncommon*. This position of the scale is called the scale of C, because it *begins* on C. In any position of the scale, the letter upon which the first tone is placed, gives name to the scale; it is also called the key of C, key of G, &c.

By repeating the scale, we can ascend or descend to any desired pitch.

The *first tone* of *every scale* is also the last tone of a scale below it; and the last tone of every scale is the first tone of a scale above it. Hence but seven letters and seven syllables are required. Two united scales then, only contain fifteen tones, as may be seen in the last diagram.

THE MINOR SCALE

has several forms. The following examples give the two in general use.

Minor Scale in common use.

Compound Minor Scale.

When six and seven are sharped in the ascending minor scale, as in the second scale of the example above, the last half is like the last half of the Major scale; so I venture to call it the *Compound* Minor Scale. The most striking difference between the major and minor scales is found in their *first thirds*. Language cannot describe the effect of that difference; it can only be heard and felt.

THE SHARP (♯)

placed before a note requires a tone a half step or minor second higher than the note represents. It does not "*raise*" any thing, it demands a new tone.

THE FLAT (♭)

requires a tone a half step or minor second lower than the note represents, before which it is placed. It does not "*sink*" or "*depress*" any thing. Like the sharp it demands a *new tone*.

THE NATURAL (♮)

is used to suspend or cancel the effect of the sharp and the flat.

When sharps or flats are found at the beginning of a tune, they indicate the scale or key it is written in, and are called "the signature"; but when introduced afterwards for harmonic or modulating purposes, they are termed accidentals or chromatics, and affect all tones on the letter upon which they are introduced, throughout *that measure*.

If we divide with flats and sharps the major seconds of the scale, we then have an entire scale of Minor seconds, called

THE CHROMATIC SCALE.

In ascending, the sharp is used because the sharped tone naturally leads to the tone next above it; while the flat naturally leads downwards, or to the tone next below it, hence is used in descending.

The Major Scale in the key of C

is the first to be introduced to the pupil, and he must work at it till he can instantly tell the letter, syllable and numeral of every line and space, with each clef, and sing with a good degree of readiness and accuracy. Then he is prepared for other positions of the scale.

All tunes in the major scale could be *written* in the key of C; but many would be too high or too low to be *sung* there. So, of necessity, the scale has a variety of positions on the staff. Every letter may become every numeral.

TRANSPOSITION OF THE SCALE.

By this is meant *moving* the scale and arranging the staff by the use of flats or sharps, so that the scale may always have the same order of intervals.

There are two equally natural ways of transposing: one by moving upward a fifth or downward a fourth, which will require in each new position a *sharp on the seventh;* and the other, by moving a fourth upward or a fifth downward, which will require a *flat on the fourth* of each new position.

The Scale transposed from C to G, a fifth upward.

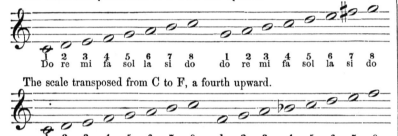

The scale transposed from C to F, a fourth upward.

If we build the scale on G, as above, we find the staff represents every tone in its true pitch except 7 or F; that being a minor second too low, gives wrong intervals between 6 and 7 and 7 and 8; so F is given up for F *sharp.* Then we have the same order of intervals in the G scale as in the scale on C, and F sharp is the signature of the scale on G. F sharp is the *natural* seventh of the scale on G, as *B* is the natural seventh of the scale on C.

In the scale on F, in the above example, all is right except B, which is too high, as F was too low; so B is exchanged for B flat; then the scale on F is also perfect. B flat is the natural fourth and the signature for the scale on F.

MAJOR AND MINOR SCALES.

To every signature belong a Major and a Minor scale, which are called *Relative* Major and Minor scales; and a note on a given letter in either scale has the same syllable but not the same numeral.

Relative Major and Minor Scales on C and A.

It will be seen the *Relative* scales are the intervals of a third apart; that 6 of a Major scale is 1 of its relative Minor; and that 3 of a Minor scale is 1 of its relative Major scale.

Now follow the Major and Minor scales with signatures in the regular order of

TRANSPOSITION BY SHARPS.

The syllables move with the numerals, and will be omitted.

C scale with relative minor A.   G scale with relative minor E.

D scale with relative minor B.   A scale with relative minor F sharp.

E scale with relative minor C sharp.   B scale with relative minor G sharp.

F sharp scale with relative minor D sharp.

To sharp a note on a letter already sharp, the *double sharp* is used.

To flat a note on a letter already flatted, the *double flat* is used. The former is a cross (×), the latter, *two flats* (♭♭).

TRANSPOSITION WITH FLATS.

B flat scale with relative minor G.

F scale and relative minor D.

E flat scale with relative minor C. A flat scale with relative minor F.

D flat scale with relative minor B flat. G flat scale with relative minor E flat.

DEFINITIONS OF MUSICAL TERMS.

A Tempo, Return to the original movement.
Ad libitum, or *Ad lib.*, As you please.
Adagio, Slow.
Allegro, Quick.
Allegretto, Rather quick.
Andante, Rather slow and distinct.
Andantino, Quicker than Andante.
Crescendo or *Cres.*, or ——◁ Increase.
Cantabile, Graceful, smooth and replete with **feeling**.
Dolce. sweetly.
Dal Segno, Return to the sign.
Da Capo, or *D. C.*, Go back to the beginning.
Al segno, Repeat from the sign.
Duet, For two voices.
Diminuendo or *dim.*, or ▷—— Diminish.
Forte or *f*, Loud.
Fortissimo or *ff*, Very loud.
Fine, The end.
Grave, Slow and solemn.
Legato, Smooth and connected.
Lento, In slow time.
Mezzo or *M*, Medium or middling.
Mezzo Forte or *MF*, Rather loud.
Moderato, Moderately.
Mosso, Movement.
Mosso Molto, In a quick, emotional style.
Maestoso, With majesty.

Piano or *p*, Soft.
Pianissimo or *pp*, Very soft.
Piu, More.
Piu Lento, Slower.
Poco, a little.
Piu Allegro, a little quicker.
Quartet, For four voices.
Ritard or *rit.*, Slower and slower.
Rallentando or *rall.*, Equivalent to *rit.* and *dim.*
Swell, or ◁——▷ Increase and diminish.
Staccato, or ▮▮▮▮ Distinct.
Semi-Staccato, or . . . . Less distinct than Staccato.
Sforzando or *fz*, or > Explosive.
Solo, For one voice.
Sempre, Always or throughout.
Sempre Pianissimo, Continue to sing very softly.
Segno, Sign.
Tutti, All.
Vivace, Quick and sprightly.

CLASS EXERCISES.*

THE SCALE ON C, THE FIRST POSITION.

* These Class exercises should be sung sometimes slow, sometimes quick, sometimes loud and sometimes soft; and frequently with one syllable, La, or any other.

1. O, the charm - ing Spring! How the birds do sing! Flow - ers ope their eyes, Look - ing to the skies.

2. re mi fa sol

3.

4.

5. Let us with a joy-ful mind, Praise the Lord, for he is kind; For his mercies shall endure, Ev - er faithful, ev - er sure.

6.

7. sol sol fi fi sol

Sharp 4

8.

We've sung with do re mi, We've sung with do se la; We've sung with la sol fi, And sung with re mi

fa. Now let our voi-ces ring, As our old song we sing. "Once on a time old John-ny Bull flew

in a rag - ing fu - ry, And swore that Jon - a - than should have no tri - als sir, by ju - ry; That no e - lec - tions

should be held a - cross the bri - ny wa - ters, And now, said he, I'll tax the tea of all his sons and daugh - ters."

Let us with a joyful mind. 7s.

MOZART.
TO BE SUNG AFTER LAST STANZA.

1. Let us with a joy - ful mind Praise the Lord, for he is kind; For his mercies shall en - dure, Ev - er faithful, ev - er sure. Hal - le - lu - jah, A - men.

2. He, with all - command - ing might, Filled the new-made world with light; For his mercies shall en - dure, Ev - er faithful, ev - er sure.
3. All things liv - ing he doth feed, His full hand sup - plies their need; For his mercies shall en - dure, Ev - er faithful, ev - er sure. *mf* *p*

4. Let us then with joy - ful mind, Praise the Lord, for he is kind; For his mercies shall endure, Ev - er faithful, ev - er sure. Hal - le - lujah, A-men.

mf *p*

Major scale on G, with

Relative Minor on E.

1

1 2 3 4 5 6 7 8 8 7 6 5 4 3 2 1
Do re mi fa sol la si do do si la sol fa mi re do

2 3 4 5 6 7 8 8 7 6 5 4 3 2 1
La si do re mi fa si la la si fa mi re do si la

2

CLASS EXERCISES.

The Lord is great! Ye hosts of heav'n a - dore Him, And ye who tread this earth - ly ball,

Common errors. Ther Lor dis grea, Ye hose zof eaven a - dore im, An je

In ho - ly songs re - joice a - loud be - fore Him, And shout his praise who made you all.

a - low be - fore im, An shou 'tis praise who may jew all.

Major scale on D with   Relative minor on B.

Do re mi fa sol la si do   do si la sol fa mi re do   La si do re mi fa   si la   la si fa mi   re do si la

The Golden Robin.

Words by ROSE STANDISH.

1. Blithesom - est of things, All day long he sings; When the au - tumn go - eth, Will he spread his wings, Will he spread his wings?

2. Let the clouds drop rain, Great trees heave and strain, Ne'er a note for - gets he, Of his sweet re - frain, Of his sweet re - frain.

3 Glad, blithe-heart-ed thing, Dar - ling of the spring, Go not from us un - til Au - tumn tak - eth wing, Autumn tak-eth wing.

Major scale on A with

Relative minor F#

1 2 3 4 5 6 7 8 8 7 6 5 4 3 2 1
Do re mi fa sol la si do do si la sol fa mi re do

1 2 3 4 5 6 7 8 8 7 6 5 4 3 2 1
la si do re mi fa si la la si fa mi re do si la

Do si la   re do si   mi re do   fa mi re

Hail, Co-lumbia, hap-py land! Yankee Doodle, doodle doo; And we'll rally round the flag boys, United, heart and hand; Three cheers for the red, white and blue.

Sol mi sol la si do re mi fa mi do re mi do la

What are the birdies talking a - bout? What do you spose they say? Trilling, chattering, singing, talking, Just at the break of day? Just at the break of day?

Major scale on E, with

Relative minor C♯

Do re mi fa sol la si do do si la sol fa mi re do La si do re mi fa si la la si fa mi re do si la

Do

La si do la mi fa la re fa mi do la fa si re do

'Mid pleas - ures and pal - a - ces though we may roam, Be it ev - er so hum-ble, there's no place like home.

Major scale on B with   Relative minor G♯

Do re mi fa sol la si do do si la sol fa mi re do   la si do re mi fa si la la si fa mi re do si la

Do si la

Be thou, O God ex - alt -ed high, And as thy glo-ry fills the sky, So let it be on earth displayed, Till thou art here as there obeyed.

sol la si do re mi

The tempest's roar, how loud ! The sky, how like a shroud ! How long and cold this night ! But lo! the morn - ing light.

Major scale on F, with ..... Relative minor D.

1. Do re mi fa sol la si do do si la sol fa mi re do La si do re mi fa si la la si fa mi re do si la

Let us with a joy-ful mind, Praise the Lord, for he is kind; For his mercies shall endure, Ev - er faith - ful, ev - er sure.

And glad - dens all the distant isles, all the dis-tant isles.

Major scale on B♭ with   Relative minor G.

Do re mi fa sol la si do do si la sol fa mi re do   la si do re mi fa si la la si fa mi re do si la

Do sol   Fi sol se la di re la mi

"For know   the best time to be hap‐py and sing, Is sum‐mer, is win‐ter, is au‐tumn, is spring."

"O'er that dear breast where love and   pi‐ty spring, May peace   e‐ter‐nal spread her downy wing, Spread her downy wing."

1. Good morning, neighbor Brown! Pray, what's the news up town? I know of noth-ing *new*, Pray, neighbor Jones, do *you?*

Major scale on A♭ with   Relative minor F.

2. Do re mi fa sol la si do do si la sol fa mi re do   la si do re mi fa si la la si fa mi re do si la

5. sol...... mi...... do sol la........ fa........ re.. la.. si...... sol...... mi.. si.. do...... la........ fa.. do.. re... si.... sol.. fa.. do

Moderato.

7. Come, Ho - ly Spirit, heavenly dove, With all thy quick'ning powers; Kin-dle a flame of sa-cred love In these cold hearts of ours.

Major scale on D♭, with   Relative minor B♭.

EXERCISES IN C.

EXERCISES IN C.

PLYMOUTH. L. M.

John Vance Cheney.   S. P. Cheney.

1. Un - to our God most high, we sing The songs of Zi - on ev - er - more; The songs they sang when Israel's king, Je - hovah's al - tars bowed before.

2. Ex - alt the Lord our God, he cried, Who on - ly do - eth wondrous things; And e'er he laid his harp a - side, The world did sing, and still it sings,

3. O bless-ed be his glorious name, Till sun and stars be dark a - gain; Let earth awide with glo - ry flame, For-ev - er, ev - er and A-men.

SAN FRANCISCO. L. M.

S. P. Cheney.

1. Kingdoms and thrones to God belong, Crown him, ye nations, in your song; His wondrous name and power rehearse, His honors shall en - rich your verse.

2. He rides and thunders thro' the sky; His name, Jehovah, sounds on high; Praise him aloud, ye sons of grace; Ye saints, re-joice - be - fore his face.

3. God is our shield, our joy, our rest; God is our king, proclaim him blest. When terrors rise, when nations faint, He is the strength of ev' - ry saint.

MAIR. L. M.

S. P. Cheney.

Allegretto.

1. All people that on earth do dwell, Sing to the Lord with cheerful voice: Him serve with fear, his praise forth tell, Come ye before him and re-joice.

2. Oh, en-ter ye his gates with praise; Approach with joy his courts unto: Praise, laud and bless his name always, For it is seem-ly so to do.
3. The gracious Lord, our God is good, His mer-cy is for-ev-er sure: His truth at all times firmly stood, And shall from age to age en-dure.

ASHFORD. L. M.

Charles Zeuner.

Why sinks my weak, desponding mind? Why heaves my heart the anxious sigh? Can sov'reign goodness be unkind? Am I not safe if God is nigh!

ZION'S HYMN. L. M.

CHAS. ZEUNER.

1. Je-sus demands the voice of joy, Loud thro' the land let triumph ring; His honors should your songs employ, Let glorious praises hail the king.

ZION'S CHANT. L. M.

CHAS. ZEUNER.

1. When we our wea-ried limbs to rest, Sat down by proud Euphrates' stream, We wept with doleful thot's oppressed, And Zi - on was our mournful theme.

MORRISTOWN. L. M.

A. A. HADLEY.

1. How sweetly flowed the gos-pel sound, From lips of gentle-ness and grace, When list'ning thousands gathered round, And joy and rev'rence filled the place.

2. "Come, wand'rers, to my Father's home; Come, all ye weary ones, and rest;" Yes, sacred Teach-er, we will come, Obey thee, love thee, and be blest.

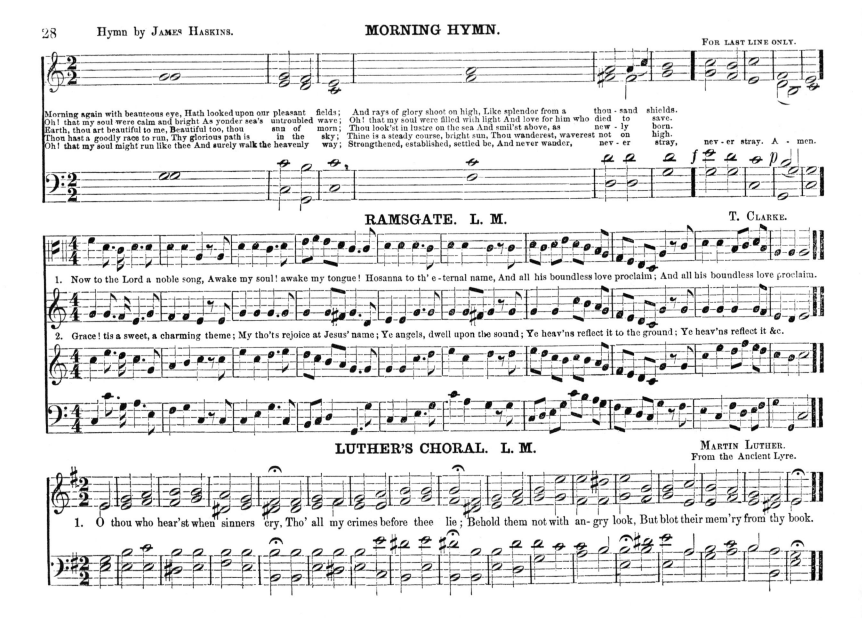

Hymn by JAMES HASKINS.

MORNING HYMN.

FOR LAST LINE ONLY.

Morning again with beauteous eye, Hath looked upon our pleasant fields; And rays of glory shoot on high, Like splendor from a thou - sand shields.
Oh! that my soul were calm and bright As yonder sea's untroubled wave; Oh! that my soul were filled with light And love for him who died to save.
Earth, thou art beautiful to me, Beautiful too, thou sun of morn; Thou look'st in lustre on the sea And smil'st above, as new - ly born.
Thou hast a goodly race to run, Thy glorious path is in the sky; Thine is a steady course, bright sun, Thou wanderest, waverest not on high.
Oh! that my soul might run like thee And surely walk the heavenly way; Strengthened, established, settled be, And never wander, nev - er stray, nev - er stray. A - men.

RAMSGATE. L. M.

T. CLARKE.

1. Now to the Lord a noble song, Awake my soul! awake my tongue! Hosanna to th' e - ternal name, And all his boundless love proclaim; And all his boundless love proclaim.

2. Grace! tis a sweet, a charming theme; My tho'ts rejoice at Jesus' name; Ye angels, dwell upon the sound; Ye heav'ns reflect it to the ground; Ye heav'ns reflect it &c.

LUTHER'S CHORAL. L. M.

MARTIN LUTHER.
From the Ancient Lyre.

1. O thou who hear'st when sinners cry, Tho' all my crimes before thee lie; Behold them not with an - gry look, But blot their mem'ry from thy book.

REPOSE. L. M.

S. P. Cheney.

I lay my body down to sleep, Peace is the pillow for my head, While well-appoint-ed angels keep Their watchful stations round my bed.

LUMMIS. L. M.

S. P. Cheney.

Allegretto.

1. Now to the Lord a no-ble song: Awake, my soul! awake, my tongue! Ho-san-na to th' e-ternal Name, And all his boundless love proclaim!

2. See where it shines in Je-sus' face, The brightest image of his grace: God, in the per-son of his Son, Has all his mightest works outdone.

WOODLAND. L. M.

S. P. Cheney.

1. Bless, O my soul! the liv - ing God; Call home thy tho'ts that rove abroad: Let all the powers within me join In work and worship so divine, In work and worship so di - vine.

2. Bless, O my soul! the God of grace: His favors claim thy highest praise; Why should the wonders he hath wrought, Be lost in silence, and forgot, Be lost in silence, and forgot?

PRATT. L. M.

S. P. Cheney.

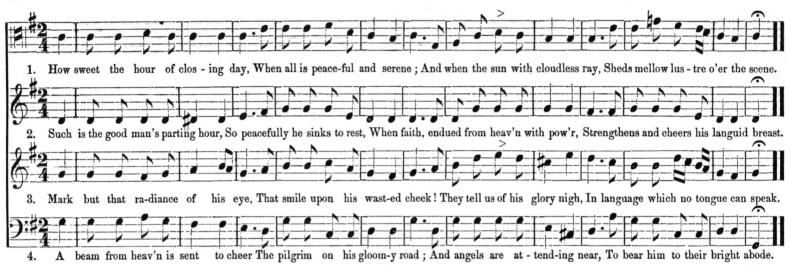

1. How sweet the hour of clos-ing day, When all is peace-ful and serene; And when the sun with cloudless ray, Sheds mellow lus-tre o'er the scene.

2. Such is the good man's parting hour, So peacefully he sinks to rest, When faith, endued from heav'n with pow'r, Strengthens and cheers his languid breast.

3. Mark but that ra-diance of his eye, That smile upon his wast-ed cheek! They tell us of his glory nigh, In language which no tongue can speak.

4. A beam from heav'n is sent to cheer The pilgrim on his gloom-y road; And angels are at-tend-ing near, To bear him to their bright abode.

TWILIGHT. L. M.

J. A. Johnson.
Composed for this book.

dim. ——— *cres.*

1. Still evening comes with gentle shade, Sweet harbinger of heav'nly rest From toilsome hours and anxious thot's Re-volv-ing in the pen-sive breast.

MEMPHREMAGOG. L. M.

Melody by Miss N. C. MITCHELL.

I know that my Redeemer lives, He lives, and on the earth shall stand ; And tho' to worms my flesh he gives, My dust is measured in his hand.

FIRMAMENT. L. M.

CHAS. ZEUNER.

The heav'ns declare thy glory, Lord, In every star thy wisdom shines; But when our eyes behold thy word, We read thy name in fairer lines, We read thy name in fairer lines.

CHAPEL STREET. L. M.

W. MATHER.

1. E - ternal source of ev' - ry joy, Well may thy praise our lips employ; Thy goodness crowns the rolling year, While in thy temple we ap-pear.

NAPA. L. M. 6 lines.

S. P. CHENEY.

1. I'll praise my Maker with my breath, And when my voice is lost in death, Praise shall employ my no-bler pow'rs; My days of praise shall

2. The Lord hath eyes to give the blind, The Lord sup-ports the sink - ing mind; He sends the lab'ring conscience peace; He helps the stranger

ne'er be past, While life and tho't and be-ing last, Or im - mor - tal - i - ty en - dures, Or im - mor - tal - i - ty en - dures.

in dis - tress, The wid - ow and the fa - ther-less, And grants the prisoner sweet re - lease; And grants the prisoner sweet re - lease.

dim & rit.

NEW YORK. L. M.

GEO. JAMES WEBB.

1. Be thou ex-alt-ed, O my God! Above the heav'ns where angels dwell; Thy pow'r on earth be known abroad, And land to land thy wonders tell.

2. My heart is fixed, my song shall raise Immor-tal hon-ors to thy name; Awake, my tongue, to sound his praise, My tongue, the glory of my frame.
3. High o'er the earth his mer-cy reigns, And reaches to the ut-most sky; His truth to end-less years remains, Till low-er worlds dissolve and die.

EMERY. L. M.

Composed for this book by F. J. LEWIS, Sacramento, Cal.

Firm.

1. A-wake, my soul, to joy-ful lays, And sing the great Redeemer's praise; He just-ly claims a song from me; His lov-ing kindness, O, how free.

2. Tho' numerous hosts of might-y foes, Tho' earth and hell my way op-pose, He safe-ly leads my soul a-long; His lov-ing kindness, O, how strong.

KING STREET. L. M.

CHAS. ZEUNER.

1. Lord, when thou didst ascend on high, Ten thousand angels filled the sky; Those heavenly guards around thee wait, Like chariots that at-tend thy state

ALDEA. L. M.

Contributed by V. C. Taylor, Des Moines, Iowa.

Allegro Moderato.

1. When the soft dews of kind-ly sleep My weary eye-lids gent-ly steep, Be my last tho't, how sweet to rest For-ev - er on my Savior's breast.

CHEYENNE. L. M. Double.

Composed for this book by G. F. Inman of Cheyenne, W. T.

1. Thee will I love, O God, and own My strength is in thine arm alone; Je - ho - vah is my rock, my tower, My Savior in the dark-est hour;

2. With forms of death on ev'-ry side, Beset with foes, my courage died; Hell compassed me with horrors dread, The snares of death were round me spread.

My God, my strength, my confidence, My buckler, helm, and high defence; On him I call, and bless his name; Ne'er shall my hope be put to shame.

In my dis-tress to God I prayed, I called up - on my God for aid; He heard my cry, it reached his throne; Thy will I love, O God, a - lone.

SABBATH EVE. L. M.

WILLIE KENT, 1878.

1. Sweet is the light of Sabbath eve, And soft the sunbeams lingering there ; For these blest hours the world I leave, Wafted on wings of faith and prayer.

2. Season of rest ! the tranquil soul Feels the sweet calm and melts in love ; And while these sacred moments roll, Faith sees a smil - ing heaven above.

CROWNINGSHIELD. L. M.

F. J. LEWIS.

Soft be the gent-ly - breathing notes That sing the dy-ing Savior's love, Soft as the evening zephyr floats, And soft as tuneful lyres a - bove.

TEMPLE CHANT. L. M.

CHAS. ZEUNER.

So let our lips and lives express The ho-ly gospel we profess ; So let our works and virtues shine, To prove the doctrine all divine.

BINGHAMPTON. L. M.

JAS. A. JOHNSON. 1873.

1. For thee, O God, our constant praise In Zion waits, thy cho - sen seat ; Our promised al - tars there we'll raise, And all our zeal - ous vows complete.

2. O thou, who to our humble prayer Did'st always bend thy listening ear, To thee shall all man-kind re - pair, And at thy gra-cious throne ap-pear.

3. Our sins, tho' numberless, in vain To stop thy flow-ing mer - cy try ; For grace shall cleanse the guilty stain, And wash a - way the crim - son dye.

MOORE. L. M.

S. P. CHENEY.

1. Jesus shall reign where'er the sun Does his successive journeys run, His kingdom stretch from shore to shore, Till moons shall wax and wane no more.

2. People and realms of ev'ry tongue, Dwell on his love with sweetest song ; And in-fant voi - ces shall pro-claim Their ear- ly blessings on his name.

3. Let ev'ry creature rise and bring Pe-cul-iar hon - ors to our king; Angels descend with songs a - gain, And earth re - peat the loud Amen.

HOPE. L. M.

E. B. Clement.

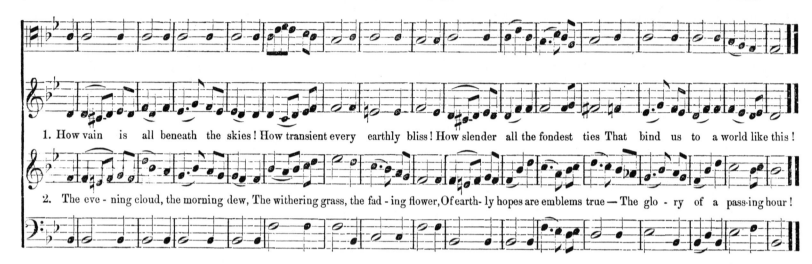

1. How vain is all beneath the skies! How transient every earthly bliss! How slender all the fondest ties That bind us to a world like this!

2. The eve - ning cloud, the morning dew, The withering grass, the fad - ing flower, Of earth- ly hopes are emblems true — The glo - ry of a pass-ing hour!

NEAPOLIS. L. M.

Haydn. Arr. by J. Goss.

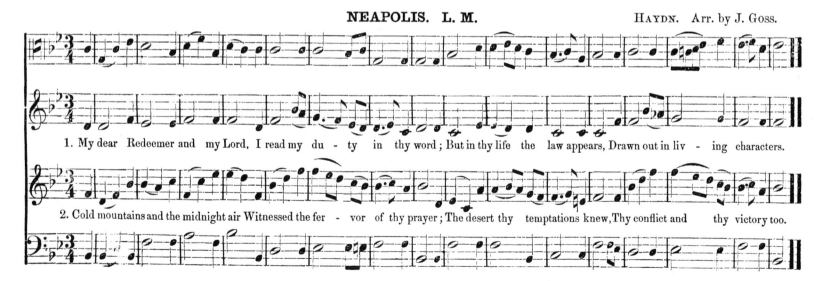

1. My dear Redeemer and my Lord, I read my du - ty in thy word; But in thy life the law appears, Drawn out in liv - ing characters.

2. Cold mountains and the midnight air Witnessed the fer - vor of thy prayer; The desert thy temptations knew, Thy conflict and thy victory too.

SCOTIA. L. M.

German.

1. God is our refuge and de-fence, In trouble our un-fail-ing aid; Se-cure in his om-ni-po-tence, What foe can make our souls a-fraid?

2. Yea, tho' the earth's foundations rock, And mountains down the gulf be hurled, His people smile a-mid the shock, They look beyond this transient world.

DUMAH. L. M.

From a German Choral.

1. Be-fore Je-ho-vah's aw-ful throne, Ye nations bow with sa-cred joy; Know that the Lord is God a-lone, He can cre-ate and he destroy.

DUNSTAN. L. M.

Dr. Madan.

1. Je-sus shall reign where'er the sun Does his successive journeys run; His kingdom stretch from shore to shore, Till moons shall wax and wane no more.

ELA. L. M.

1. Come hither, all ye weary souls, Ye heavy-laden sinners come; I'll give you rest from all your toils And raise you to my heav'nly home, And raise you to my heav'nly home.

WILCOX. L. M.

S. P. CHENEY.

Allegretto.

1. Arise, arise, with joy survey The glory of the lat-ter day! Already is the dawn begun, Which marks at hand the rising sun, Which marks at hand the rising sun.

LOUVAN. L. M.

V. C. TAYLOR.   From "The Chime," by per.

Rather quick.

1. There's nothing bright above, below, From flow'rs that bloom to stars that glow, But in its light my soul can see Some feature of the De-i-ty.

2. There's nothing dark a-bove, be-low, But in its gloom I trace his love, And meekly wait that moment when His touch shall make all bright again.

REST. L. M. — S. P. Cheney.

1. In sleep's se-rene obliv - ion laid, I safe - ly pass'd the si - lent night; Again I see the breaking shade, And drink again the morning light.

2. New-born I bless the waking hour, Once more with awe rejoice to be; My conscious soul resumes her power, And springs, my guardian God, to thee.

MASON. L. M. — S. P. Cheney.

1. Jesus! and shall it ev - er be, A mor-tal man ashamed of thee? Ashamed of thee, whom angels praise, Whose glories shine thro' endless days?

Slow.

RIGGS. L. M. — J. V. Cheney..

When the soft dews of kindly sleep My weary eyelids gently steep, Be my last thought how sweet to rest, Forev - er on my Savior's breast.

Congregational Tunes.

OLD HUNDRED. L. M.

German Choral.

1. Be thou, O God! ex-alt-ed high; And as thy glo-ry fills the sky, So let it be on earth displayed, Till thou art here as there obeyed.

HAMBURG. L. M.

Gregorian.

1. Kingdoms and thrones to God be-long; Crown him, ye nations, in your song; His wondrous name and pow'r rehearse; His honors shall enrich your verse.

DEVOTION. L. M.

D. READ.

Spirited.

Sweet is the day of sacred rest, No mortal care shall seize my breast;

O may my heart in tune be found, Like David's harp, Like David's harp of solemn sound.

O may my heart in tune be found, Like David's harp of solemn sound.

O may my heart in tune be found, Like David's harp of solemn sound, Like David's harp of solemn sound.

Sweet is the day of sacred rest, No mortal care shall seize my breast; O may my heart in tune be found, Like David's harp of solemn sound.

PARK STREET. L. M.

VENUA.

Hark! how the choral song of heaven Swells full of peace and joy above; Hark! how they strike their golden harps, And raise the tuneful notes of love, And raise the tuneful notes of love.

TRURO. L. M.

DR. BURNEY.

Now to the Lord a no - ble song: Awake, my soul, a - wake, my tongue; Hosan - na to th'eter - nal name, And all his boundless love proclaim.

SEASONS. L. M.

PLEYEL.

The flowery spring, at God's command Perfumes the air and paints the land; The summer rays with vig - or shine, To raise the corn, and cheer the vine.

CREATION. L. M. Double.

From HAYDN's Oratorio of the "Creation."

1. The spa-cious fir - ma - ment on high, With all the blue e - the - real sky,
And spangled heavens, a shin - ing frame, Their great O - ri - gi - nal pro - claim. Th' unwearied sun, from day to day,

Does his Cre - a - tor's power dis - play, And pub - lish - es to ev - 'ry land, The work of an al - migh-ty hand.

WELLS. L. M.

HOLDRAD.

Life is the time to serve the Lord, The time t' in-sure the great reward ; And while the lamp holds out to burn, Ye sinners, hasten to return.

ALABAMA. L. P. M.

D. READ.

I love the vol - ume of thy word: What light and joy those leaves af - ford To souls be - night - ed and dis - tressed.

Thy pre-cepts guide my doubt-ful way; Thy fear for - bids my feet to stray; Thy prom - ise leads my heart to rest.

WARE. L. M.

GEO. KINGSLEY. By per.

O for a glance of heav'nly day, To take this stubborn heart a - way; And thaw, with beams of love divine, This heart, this frozen heart of mine.

RETREAT. L. M.

T. HASTINGS.

From ev'-ry storm-y wind that blows, From ev'-ry swelling tide of woes, There is a calm, a sure retreat, 'Tis found beneath the mer-cy seat.

DUKE STREET. L. M.

Hatton.

Lord, when thou didst ascend on high, Ten thousand an-gels filled the sky; Those heavenly guards around thee wait, Like chariots that at-tend thy state.

WARD. L. M.

Arr. from a Scotch tune, by L. Mason.

There is a stream, whose gentle flow Supplies the ci-ty of our God; Life, love, and joy still gliding thro', And watering our di-vine a-bode.

GERMANY. L. M.

Beethoven

Lord, at thy feet I prostrate fall, Oppressed with fears, to thee I call; Reveal thy pardoning love to me, And set my cap-tive spir-it free.

ROTHWELL. L. M.

ENGLISH.

Awake the trumpet's lofty sound, To spread your sacred pleasure round; Awake each voice, and strike each string, And to the solemn organ sing, And to the solemn organ sing.

NEWCOURT. L. P. M.

H. BOND.

I love the vol - ume of thy word; What light and joy those leaves af - ford To souls be - night - ed and distress'd!

Thy pre - cepts guide my doubt - ful way; Thy fear for - bids my feet to stray; Thy prom - ise leads my heart to rest.

NATIONAL PSALM. L. M.

Old Ten Commandments' tune, 1562.

All peo - ple that on earth do dwell, Sing to the Lord with cheerful voice; Him serve with mirth, his praise forth tell, Come ye before Him and rejoice.

SAUL. L. M.

1. Un - vail thy bos - om, faith - ful tomb, Take this new treasure to thy trust; And give these sa-cred rel - ics room, To seek a slum - ber
2. Nor pain, nor grief, nor anx-ious fear In-vade thy bounds: no mor-tal woes Can reach the peaceful sleeper here, While an - gels watch the
3. So · Je - sus slept; God's dy - ing Son Passed thro' the grave and blessed the bed; Rest here, blest saint, till from his throne The morning break, and

in the dust. And give these sa - cred rel - ics room, To seek a slumber in the dust.
soft re - pose. Can reach the peace - ful sleep - er here, While an-gels watch the soft re - pose.
pierce the shade. Rest here, blest saint, till from his throne The morning break, and pierce the shade. 4. Break from his throne, illus - trious morn!

At - tend, O earth! his sov - 'reign word; Re - store thy trust, a glo - rious form, Called to as - cend and meet the Lord.

COLUSA. C. M.

S. P. Cheney.

Come, Ho - ly Spir - it, Heav'nly Dove! With all thy quick'ning pow'rs; Kindle a flame of sa-cred love In these cold hearts of ours.

TRIUMPH. C. M.

J. A. Johnson. Aug. 8, 1878.

Oh, for a shout of sa - cred joy To God the Sov' - reign King! Let ev' - ry land their tongues em - ploy,

And hymns of tri - umph sing, And hymns, And hymns of tri - umph sing.

And hymns of tri - umph sing, And hymns of tri - umph sing, And hymns of tri - umph sing.

And hymns of tri - umph sing, And hymns of tri - umph sing. And hymns of tri-umph sing.

HALLOWED PEACE. C. M.

Presented by the author, J. K. Van Slyke, San Francisco.

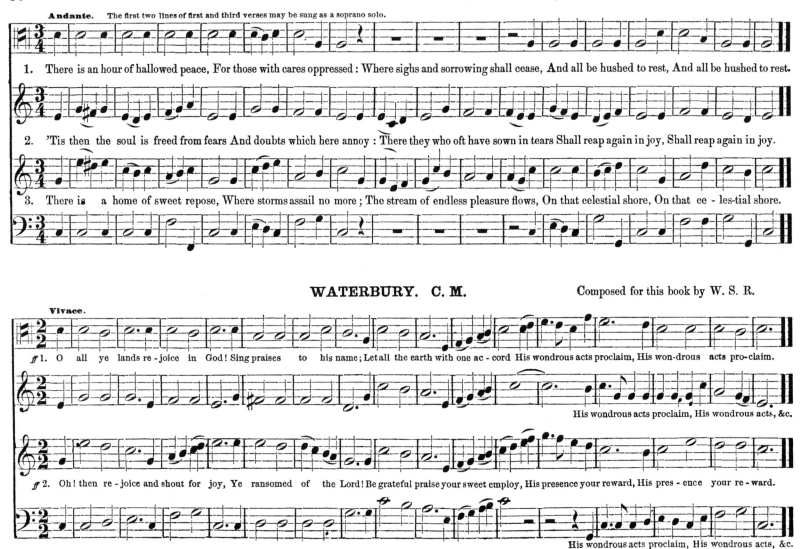

Andante. The first two lines of first and third verses may be sung as a soprano solo.

1. There is an hour of hallowed peace, For those with cares oppressed : Where sighs and sorrowing shall cease, And all be hushed to rest, And all be hushed to rest.

2. 'Tis then the soul is freed from fears And doubts which here annoy : There they who oft have sown in tears Shall reap again in joy, Shall reap again in joy.

3. There is a home of sweet repose, Where storms assail no more ; The stream of endless pleasure flows, On that celestial shore, On that ce - les-tial shore.

WATERBURY. C. M.

Composed for this book by W. S. R.

Vivace.

ff 1. O all ye lands re-joice in God! Sing praises to his name; Let all the earth with one ac - cord His wondrous acts proclaim, His won-drous acts pro-claim.

His wondrous acts proclaim, His wondrous acts, &c.

ff 2. Oh! then re - joice and shout for joy, Ye ransomed of the Lord! Be grateful praise your sweet employ, His presence your reward, His pres - ence your re - ward.

His wondrous acts proclaim, His wondrous acts, &c.

OLIVER. C. M.

Jas. A. Johnson, 1869.

See Israel's gen-tle Shep-herd stand With all en-gag-ing charms; Hark how he calls the ten-der lambs, And folds them in his arms.

HUDSON. C. M.

1. How shall the young secure their hearts, And guard their lives from sin? Thy word the choicest rules im-parts, To keep the conscience clean.

2. 'Tis like the sun, a heavenly light, That guides us all the day; And, thro' the dangers of the night, A lamp to lead our way.

BOYLSTON. C. M.

From Holyoke's Sacred Harmony.

Fa - ther, I sing thy wondrous grace, I bless my Savior's name; He brought sal-va - tion for the poor, And bore the sinner's shame.

VOW. C. M.

E. B. CLEMENT.

Lord, in the morn - ing Thou shalt hear My voice as - cend - ing high; To Thee will I di - rect my prayer, To Thee lift up mine eye.

FURNACE. C. M.

Z. W. VINCENT. From the Union Tune Book.

Now shall my in - ward joys a - rise And burst in - to a song; Al-mighty love inspires my heart, And pleasure tunes my tongue.

JEFFERSON. C. M.

A. B. Cheney.

1. Come, Ho - ly Spir - it, heaven - ly Dove, With all thy quick'ning powers, Kindle a flame of sacred love In these cold hearts of ours.

LENERTON. C. M.

Geo. F. Root.

Moderato.

1. Spirit Di - vine! attend our prayer, And make our hearts thy home : Descend with all thy gracious power : Come, Holy Spir - it, come !

HARBOROUGH. C. M.

From Handel.

The King, O Lord, with songs of praise, Shall in thy strength re-joice, And blest with thy sal - va - tion raise To heaven his cheerful voice.

MENDOTA. C. M.

A. N. Johnson. By per.

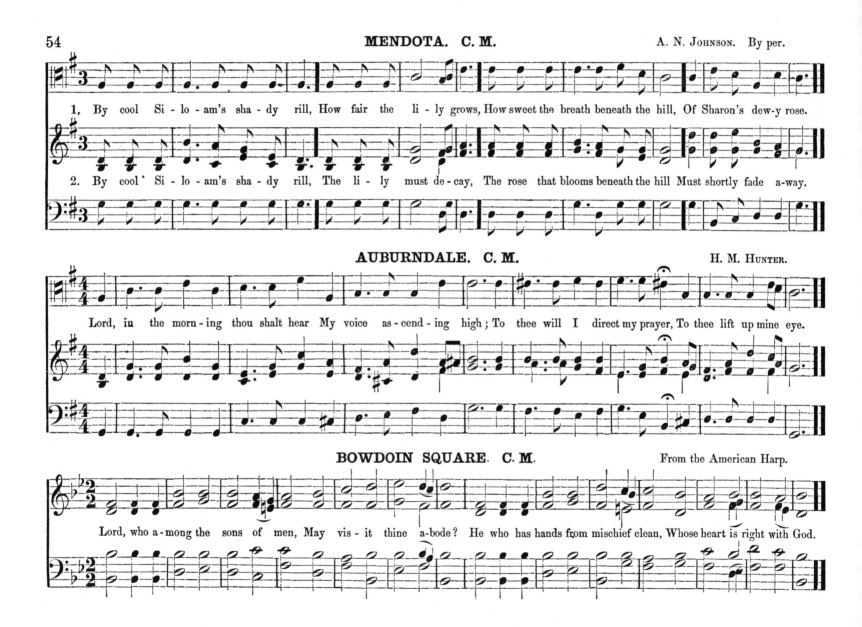

1. By cool Si - lo - am's sha - dy rill, How fair the li - ly grows, How sweet the breath beneath the hill, Of Sharon's dew-y rose.

2. By cool Si - lo - am's sha - dy rill, The li - ly must de - cay, The rose that blooms beneath the hill Must shortly fade a - way.

AUBURNDALE. C. M.

H. M. Hunter.

Lord, in the morn - ing thou shalt hear My voice as - cend - ing high; To thee will I direct my prayer, To thee lift up mine eye.

BOWDOIN SQUARE. C. M.

From the American Harp.

Lord, who a - mong the sons of men, May vis - it thine a - bode? He who has hands from mischief clean, Whose heart is right with God.

LYDIA. C. M.

J. Leach. From the Union Tune Book.

1. Je - sus, I love thy charming name, 'Tis music to my ear; Fain would I sound it out so loud, That heav'n and earth might hear, That heav'n and earth might hear.

2. Yes, thou art precious to my soul, My transport and my trust; Jew-els, to thee are gaudy toys, And gold is sordid dust, And gold is sor - did dust.

VALLEJO. C. M.

Composed for this book by L. Marshall.

ANDANTE.

1. As pants the hart for cool-ing streams, When heated in the chase, So longs my soul, O God for thee And thy re - fresh - ing grace.

SOLI. CRES.

2. For thee, my God, the liv - ing God, My thirst-y soul doth pine; Oh, when shall I be-hold thy face, Thou Maj - es - ty di - vine.

MORNING. C. M.

S. P. CHENEY.

1. Lord, in the morning thou shalt hear My voice as-cend-ing high: To thee will I di-rect my prayer, To thee lift up mine eye.

RENNIE. C. M. Double.

JAS. A. JOHNSON.

1, When I can read my ti-tle clear To mansions in the skies, I'll bid farewell to ev-ery fear, And wipe my weeping eyes.

3. Let cares like a wild deluge come, And storms of sorrow fall; May I but safe-ly reach my home, My God, my heaven, my all,—

2. Should earth against my soul engage, And hell-ish darts be hurled, Then I can smile at Satan's rage, And face a frown-ing world.

4. There shall I bathe my weary soul In seas of heavenly rest, And not a wave of trou-ble roll A-cross my peace-ful breast.

JORDAN. C. M. Double.

S. P. CHENEY.
In part from a Mormon tune.

Allegretto.

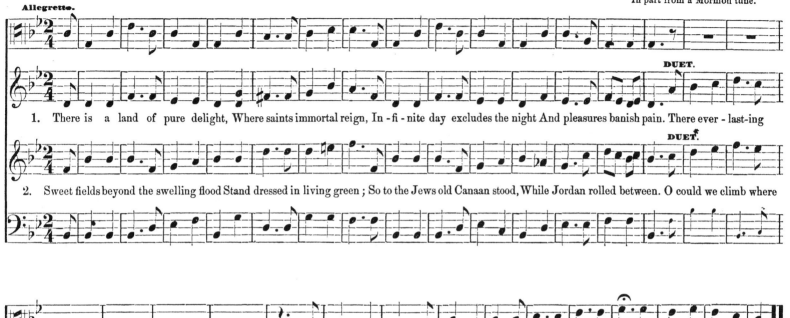

1. There is a land of pure delight, Where saints immortal reign, In-fi-nite day excludes the night And pleasures banish pain. There ever-last-ing

2. Sweet fields beyond the swelling flood Stand dressed in living green; So to the Jews old Canaan stood, While Jordan rolled between. O could we climb where

spring a-bides, And nev-er-fad-ing flowers, Death, like a nar-row sea divides This heav'nly land from ours, This heav'nly land from ours.

Mo-ses stood, And view the land-scape o'er, Not Jordan's stream nor death's cold flood Could fright us from the shore, Could fright us from the shore.

THE SEASONS. C. M.

mf 1. With songs and hon - ors sounding loud, Ad - dress the Lord on high; O - ver the heavens he spreads his clouds,
2. He sends his showers of blessings down To cheer the plains be - low; He makes the grass the mountains crown,

3. His hoar - y frost, his fleec - y snow, De - scend and clothe the ground; The li - quid streams for - bear to flow,
4. The chang - ing wind, the fly - ing cloud, O - bey his migh - ty word: With songs and hon - ors sound - ing loud,

O - ver the heavens he spreads his clouds, And wa - ters vail the sky, And wa - ters vail the sky.
He makes the grass the mountains crown, And corn in val - leys grow, And corn in val - leys grow.

The li - quid streams for - bear to flow, In i - cy fet - ters bound, In i - cy fet - ters bound.
With songs and hon - ors sound - ing loud, Praise ye the sov - 'reign Lord, Praise ye the sov - 'reign Lord!

MENDELSSOHN. C. M.

Andante.

1. In vain I trace cre - a - tion o'er, In search of sol - id rest; The whole cre - a - tion is too poor, To make me tru - ly blest.

2. Let earth and all her charms de - part, Un-wor-thy of the mind; In God a - lone this restless heart En-dur-ing bliss can find.

3. Thy fa - vor, Lord, is all I want, Here would my spirit rest; Oh, seal the rich, the boundless grant, And make me ful-ly blest.

FRAGRANCE. C. M.   Composed for this book by J. A. Johnson.

Lento e Dolce.

1. How sweet the name of Je-sus sounds In a be-liever's ear, It soothes his sorrows, heals his wounds And drives a-way his fear.

2. It makes the wounded spirit whole, And calms the troubled breast; 'Tis man - na to the hungry soul, And to the wea - ry, rest.

MAPLE GROVE. C. M.

S. P. CHENEY.

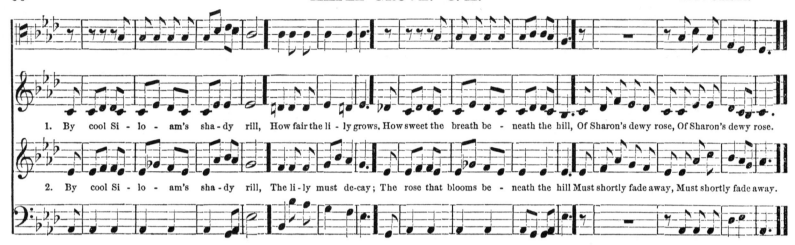

1. By cool Si - lo - am's sha - dy rill, How fair the li - ly grows, How sweet the breath be - neath the hill, Of Sharon's dewy rose, Of Sharon's dewy rose.

2. By cool Si - lo - am's sha - dy rill, The li - ly must de - cay; The rose that blooms be - neath the hill Must shortly fade away, Must shortly fade away.

LIVERPOOL. C. M.

The Choral Book for England.

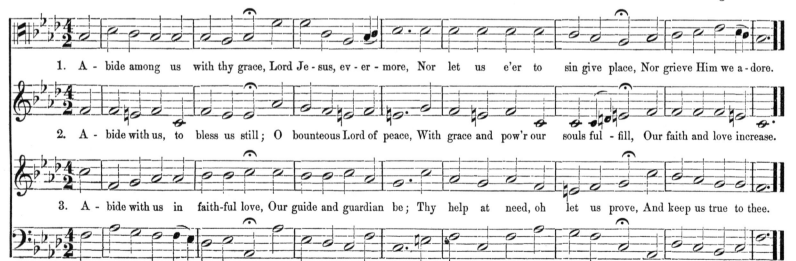

1. A - bide among us with thy grace, Lord Je - sus, ev - er - more, Nor let us e'er to sin give place, Nor grieve Him we a - dore.

2. A - bide with us, to bless us still; O bounteous Lord of peace, With grace and pow'r our souls ful - fill, Our faith and love increase.

3. A - bide with us in faith-ful love, Our guide and guardian be; Thy help at need, oh let us prove, And keep us true to thee.

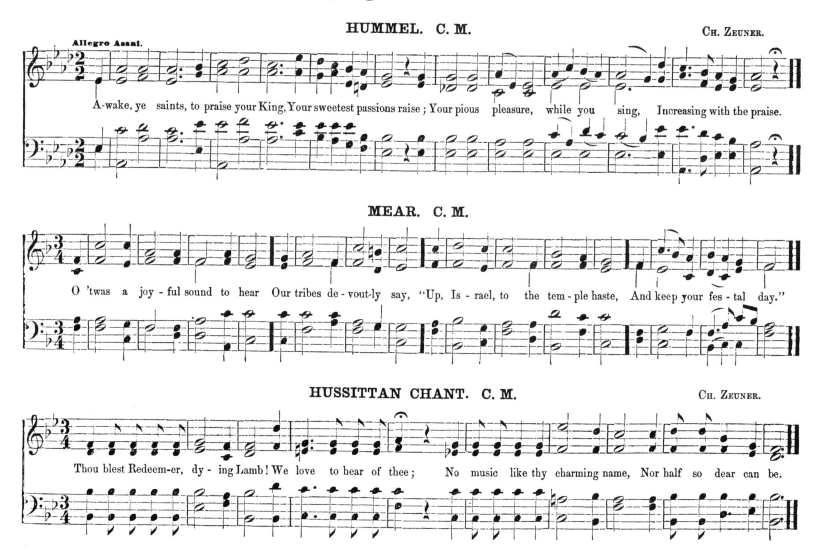

HUMMEL. C. M.

Ch. Zeuner.

Allegro Assai.

A-wake, ye saints, to praise your King, Your sweetest passions raise ; Your pious pleasure, while you sing, Increasing with the praise.

MEAR. C. M.

O 'twas a joy-ful sound to hear Our tribes de-vout-ly say, "Up, Is-rael, to the tem-ple haste, And keep your fes-tal day."

HUSSITTAN CHANT. C. M.

Ch. Zeuner.

Thou blest Redeem-er, dy-ing Lamb! We love to hear of thee ; No music like thy charming name, Nor half so dear can be.

CAMBRIDGE. C. M.

Dr. Randall.

Sing to the Lord a new-made song, Who wondrous things has done; With his right hand and holy arm, The conquest he has won, The conquest he has won, The conquest he has won.

*WINDSOR. C. M. or Dundee.

From the Scotch Psalter of 1615.

Plaintive.

O God, our help in a-ges past, Our hope for years to come; Be thou our guard while troubles last, And our e-ter-nal home.

* Dundee is the old name of this tune. The Scotch claim it as a national tune. Burns has reference to it in the line, " Perhaps Dundee's wild warbling measures rise;" and another poet has said of it, " Could I, when being carried to my grave, wake up just to hear what tune would be sung at it, I should like it to be Dundee; or as we call it, Windsor."

† DUNDEE. C. M. Called also FRENCH.

From the " Scotch Psalter," 1616.

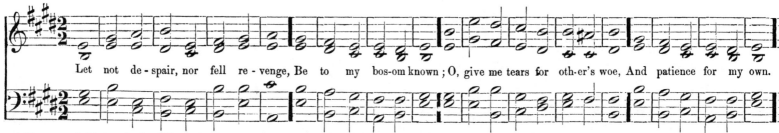

Let not de-spair, nor fell re-venge, Be to my bos-om known ; O, give me tears for oth-er's woe, And patience for my own.

† The name of this tune in the old books is " French." The Dundee of Scotland is the same as the " Windsor " of most of the English and American books of Psalmody.

HERMON. C. M.

By permission.

O, praise the Lord, for he is good, In him we rest ob - tain; His mercy has through a -ges stood, And ev - er shall remain.

PHUVAH. C. M.

MELCHIOR VULPIUS, Cantor in Weimar, 1610.

I love the Lord; he heard my cries, And pit -ied ev - ery groan; Long as I live, when troubles rise, I'll hast- en to his throne

COVENTRY C. M.

ENGLISH.

O, could my thoughts and wish- es fly A - bove these gloomy shades, To those bright worlds beyond the sky, Which sorrow ne'er in - vades.

DEDHAM. C. M.

GARDINER.

Sweet was the time when first I felt The Sav-ior's pard'ning blood, Applied to cleanse my soul from guilt, And bring me home to God.

WARWICK. C. M.

STANLEY.

Lord, in the morn - ing thou shalt hear My voice as - cend-ing high; To thee will I di - rect my prayer, To thee lift up mine eye.

CHRISTMAS. C. M.

HANDEL.

Am I a soldier of the cross, A follower of the Lamb? And shall I fear to own his cause, Or blush to speak his name, Or blush to speak his name.

WOODSTOCK. C. M.

D. DUTTON, JR.

I love to steal a-while a-way, From ev'ry cumbering care, And spend the hours of set-ting day, In humble, grate-ful prayer.

CHINA. C. M.

Andante.

SWAN.

Why do we mourn de-part-ing friends, Or shake at death's a-larms? 'Tis but the voice that Je-sus sends To call them to his arms.

BARTLETT. C. M.

There's not a star whose twinkling light Il-lumes the distant earth, And cheers the solemn hours of night, But goodness gave it birth.

Cres. - - - - - Dim. - - - - Cres. - - - - - - f

BOLTON. S. M.

Composed for this book by W. O. Perkins.

Andante.

1. The Spir-it, in our hearts, Is whis-p'ring, "Sin-ner, come;" The bride, the church of Christ, proclaims To all his children "come."

UTICA. S. M.

Ch. Zeuner.

Oh, where shall rest be found, Rest for the wea-ry soul? 'Twere vain the ocean's depths to sound, Or pierce to ei-ther pole.

ABEND. S. M.

S. P. Cheney.

1. The day is past and gone, The evening shades ap-pear, O! may we all remem-ber well, The night of death draws near.

2. We lay our garments by, Up-on our beds to rest; So death will soon disrobe us all Of what we here possess.

ELM PLACE. S. M.

S. P. CHENEY.

67

And is there, Lord, a place For wea-ry souls designed, Where not a care shall stir the breast, Or sor-row entrance find? Or sor-row entrance find.

SMITHFIELD. S. M.

A. N. JOHNSON. By per.

1. Be-hold the lof-ty sky De-clares its mak-er, God; And all the star-ry works on high Proclaim his power a-broad.

2. The dark-ness and the light Still keep their course the same; While night to day and day to night, Di-vine-ly teach his name.

EVELYN. S. M.

My God, my prayer at-tend; Oh, bow thine ear to me, With-out a hope, with-out a friend, With-out a help but thee.

FRAMINGHAM. S. M.

Composed for this book by L. O. EMERSON.

1. Sweet is the work, O Lord, Thy glorious acts to sing, To praise thy name, and hear thy word, And grate - ful offerings bring.

2. Sweet at the dawning light, Thy boundless love to tell; And, when ap - proach the shades of night, Still on the theme to dwell.

ALTON. S. M.

W. O. PERKINS.

Vigoroso.

1. "The Lord is risen in - deed;" Now is his work per - formed; Now is the mighty cap - tive freed, And death, our foe, disarmed.

2. "The Lord is risen in - deed:" At - tend - ing an - gels, hear; Up to the courts of heaven, with speed, The joy - ful tidings bear.

TOMASCHECK. S. M.

CH. ZEUNER.

Stand up and bless the Lord, Ye peo - ple of his choice; Stand up and bless the Lord your God, With heart and soul and voice.

SANTA ROSA. S. M.

S. P. Cheney.

1. The pi-ty of the Lord, To those who love his name, Is such as ten-der parents feel; He knows our fee-ble frame.

2. Our days are as the grass, Or like the morn-ing flower; If one sharp blast sweep o'er the field, It with-ers in an hour.

MARION. S. M. Double.

E. H. Bailey.

Gently.

1. The Lord my shep-herd is, I shall be well sup-plied; Since he is mine, and I am his, What can I want be-side?

2. If e'er I go a-stray, He doth my soul re-claim; And guides me in his own right way, For his most ho-ly name.

He leads me to the place Where heav'nly pas-ture grows; Where liv-ing wa-ters gent-ly pass, And full sal-va-tion flows.

While he af-fords his aid, I can-not yield to fear; Though I should walk thro' death's dark shade, My shep-herd's with me there.

SUISUN. S. M.

J. P. Cheney.

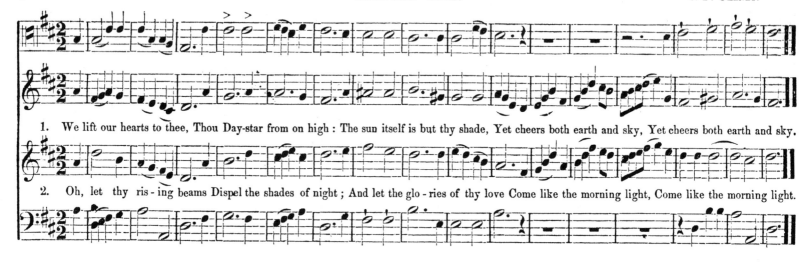

1. We lift our hearts to thee, Thou Day-star from on high: The sun itself is but thy shade, Yet cheers both earth and sky, Yet cheers both earth and sky.

2. Oh, let thy ris-ing beams Dispel the shades of night; And let the glo-ries of thy love Come like the morning light, Come like the morning light.

DORLEY. S. M.

Geo. F. Root. By per

Moderato.

1. If through un-ruf-fled seas Toward heaven we calm-ly sail, With grate-ful hearts, O God, to thee, We'll own the fostering gale.

2. But should the sur-ges rise, And rest de-lay to come, Blest be the sor-row, kind the storm, Which drives us near-er home.

3. Teach us in ev'-ry state To make thy will our own; And when the joys of sense de-part, To live by faith a-lone.

BACCEI. S. M.

L. Marshall.

Allegro Moderato.

1. Come, Ho-ly Spir-it, come; Let thy bright beams a-rise; Dis-pel the sor-row from our minds, The darkness from our eyes.

2. Re-vive our droop-ing faith, Our doubts and fears re-move, And kindle in our breasts the flame Of nev-er-dy-ing love.

3. Come, Ho-ly Spir-it, come; Our minds from bondage free: Then shall we know, and praise, and love The Father, Son and thee.

CAMBRIA. S. M.

Composed for this book by W. O. Perkins.

Religioso.

1. My God, my Life, my Love, To thee, to thee I call; I can-not live if thou re-move, For thou art all in all.

2. Nor earth, nor all the sky, Can one delight afford— No, not a drop of re-al joy—Without thy presence, Lord.

3. Thou art the sea of love, Where all my pleasures roll; The cir-cle where my passions move, And cen-tre of my soul.

VINE LAWN. S. M.

S. P. CHENEY.

Allegretto.

mf 1. Behold the morning sun Be - gins his glorious way! His beams thro' all the na - tions run, And life and light con - vey, And life and light con - vey.

2. But where the Gospel comes, It spreads di - vin - er light; It calls dead sin - ners from their tombs, And gives the blind their sight, And gives the blind their sight.

3. My gracious God, how plain Are thy di - rec-tious given! Oh, may I nev - er read in vain, But find the path to heaven! But find the path to heaven.

SANDOWN. S. M.

S. P. CHENEY.

1. How beauteous are their feet Who stand on Zi - on's hill! Who bring sal - va - tion on their tougues, And words of peace re-veal, And words of peace re-veal.

2. How charming is their voice! How sweet the tid - ings are! "Zi - on, be-hold thy Saviour King! He reigns and tri - umphs here, He reigns and triumphs here."

3. The watchmen join their voice, And tuneful notes em - ploy; Je - ru - sa - lem breaks forth in songs, And des- erts learn the joy, And des - erts learn the joy.

Moderato.

1. Sweet is the friend - ly voice Which speaks of life and peace; Which bids the pen - i - tent re - joice, And sin and sor - row cease.

2. Still mer - ci - ful and kind, Thy mer - cy, Lord, re - veal; The bro - ken heart thy love can bind, The wound - ed spir - it heal.

ORGAN.

STRING TONE.

No balm on earth like this Can cheer the con - trite heart; No flattering dreams of earth - ly bliss, Such pure delight im - part.

Thy pres - ence shall re - store Peace to my anx - ious breast; Lord, let my steps be drawn no more From paths which thou hast blest.

MADONNA. S. M.

Come to the land of peace; From shadows come a - way; Where all the sounds of weep-ing cease, And storms no more have sway.

BARNARD. S. M. No. 2.

E. M. Bowman.

With earnestness and spirit.

Your harps, ye trembling saints, Down from the wil - lows take; Loud to the praise of love di - vine Bid ev'-ry string a - wake.

NIGHT. S. M.

An old melody written from recollection, and harmonized for this book by J. A. Johnson, Aug. 12, 1878.

of death draws near.

The day is past and gone, The evening shades appear; O may we all re - mem-ber well, O may we all remember well, The night of death draws near. Amen.

of death draws near.

COMMOT. S. M.

1. Oh, cease, my wandering soul, On restless wing to roam; All this wide world, to ei - ther pole, Hath not for thee a home.

ORANGE. S. M.

Composed for this book by J. A. J.

Allegretto.

And all the star - - - - - - - ry host, the host on high,

Behold the lofty sky, Declares its maker God! And all the star - ry host on high Proclaim his power abroad.

And all the starry host, the starry host on high,

SONOMA. S. M.

Moderato.

1. Oh, where shall rest be found, Rest for the wea - ry soul? 'Twere vain the ocean's depths to sound, Or pierce to ei - ther pole.

2. Beyond this vale of tears There is a life a - bove, Un-measured by the flight of years, And all that life is love.

SPRAGUE S. M.

A. N. Johnson. By per.

We come with joy - ful song, To hail this hap - py morn; Glad ti - dings from an angel's tongue, This day is Je - sus born.

ST. AUSTIN. S. M.

Owen Davies, North Wales.

The night is wearing fast a - way, The glorious day is dawn - ing; When Christ shall of his grace dis - play The fair Mil - len-nial dawn - ing.

TRUST. S. M.

Moderato.

1. The Lord my shepherd is, I shall be well supplied, Since he is mine and I am his, What can I want beside? What can I want beside?

2. He leads me to the place Where heavenly pasture grows, Where living waters gent-ly pass, And full sal - vation flows, And full salvation flows.

ST. THOMAS. S. M.

A. WILLIAMS.

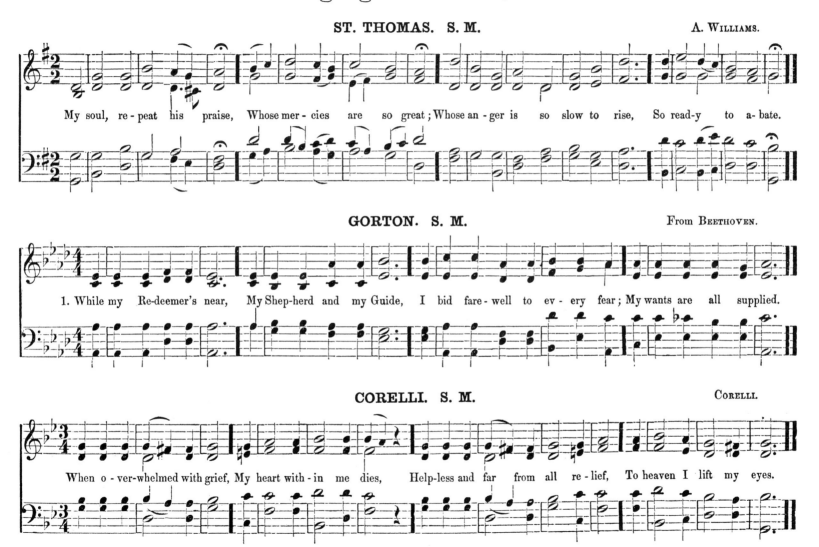

My soul, re-peat his praise, Whose mer - cies are so great; Whose an - ger is so slow to rise, So read-y to a-bate.

GORTON. S. M.

From BEETHOVEN.

1. While my Re-deemer's near, My Shep-herd and my Guide, I bid fare-well to ev - er-y fear; My wants are all supplied.

CORELLI. S. M.

CORELLI.

When o - ver-whelmed with grief, My heart with-in me dies, Help-less and far from all re - lief, To heaven I lift my eyes.

OLMUTZ. S. M.

GREGORIAN.

Your harps, ye trembling saints, Down from the wil-lows take; Loud to the praise of love di-vine, Bid ev'.ry string a-wake.

LISBON. S. M.

READ.

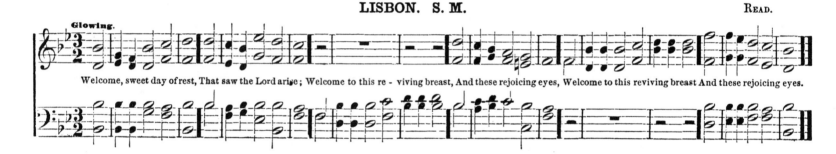

Welcome, sweet day of rest, That saw the Lord arise; Welcome to this re-viving breast, And these rejoicing eyes, Welcome to this reviving breast And these rejoicing eyes.

SHIRLAND. S. M.

STANLEY.

Be-hold! the morn-ing sun Be-gins his glo-rious way; His beams through all the na-tions run, And life and light con-vey.

DENNIS. S. M.

From H. G. NAGELI.

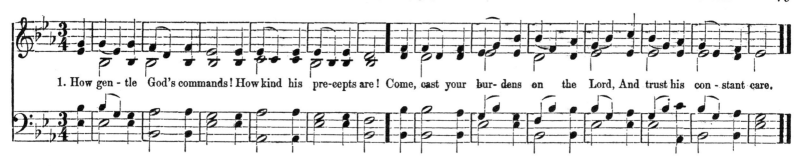

1. How gen - tle God's commands! How kind his pre-cepts are! Come, cast your bur- dens on the Lord, And trust his con - stant care.

SILVER STREET. S. M.

I. SMITH.

Come, sound his praise abroad, And hymns of glo - ry sing; Je - ho - vah is the sov -'reign God, The u - ni - ver - sal King.

MORNINGTON. S. M.

MORNINGTON.

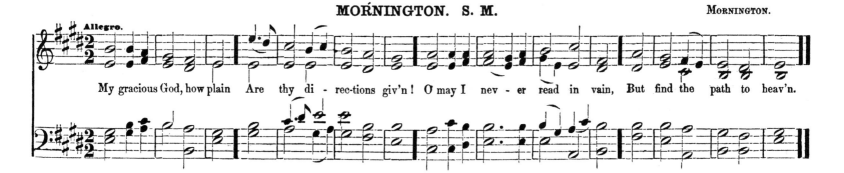

My gracious God, how plain Are thy di - rec-tions giv'n! O may I nev - er read in vain, But find the path to heav'n.

JEEMS. 7s.

S. P. CHENEY.

1. Soft - ly, now, the light of day Fades up - on my sight a - way; Free from care, from la-bor free, Lord, I would com-mune with thee.
2. Soon, for me, the light of day Shall for - ev - er pass a - way; Then from sin and sor-row free, Take me, Lord, to dwell with thee.

CANTERBURY. 7s.

F. J. LEWIS.

Ho - ly Spir - it, Love di - vine! Let thy light with - in me shine; Breathe thyself in - to my breast; Earnest of im - mor - tal rest.

OLYMPUS. 7s.

G. W. BRYANT.

Who, O Lord, when life is o'er, Shall to heav'ns blest man-sion soar? Who, an ev - er wel-come guest, In thy ho - ly place shall rest?

WELLS. 7s.

Composed for this book by Geo. J. Webb.

Ho - ly, ho - ly, ho - ly Lord, In the high - est heav'ns a - dored; Author of all nature's frame, Fa-ther, hallowed be thy name.

THEODORE. 7s.

From "The Beauties of Melody," London. Handel.

1. To thy pastures, fair and large, Heav'nly Shepherd, lead thy charge; And my couch with tend'rest care, 'Midst the springing grass pre - pare.

2. When I faint with summer's heat, Thou shalt guide my wea - ry feet To the streams that, still and slow, Thro' the ver-dant meadows flow.

THE STREAM OF LIFE. 7s.

German.

Gent - ly glides the stream of life, Oft a - long the flowery vale; Or im - pet - uous down the cliff, Rush-ing roars when storms as - sail.

SACRAMENTO. 7s.

Composed for this book by FRANK J. LEWIS.

Praise to God, im-mor-tal praise, For the love that crowns our days! Bounteous source of ev-'ry joy, Let thy praise our tongues employ!

METRE. 7s.

* JOHN MAXIM.

Hark! my soul, it is the Lord! 'Tis my Savior, hear his word; Jesus speaks, and speaks to thee, Sinner, give thine heart to me.

* Brother of Abraham Maxim, (author of "Turner,") teacher, composer, song writer, and contributor to various political and literary periodicals. Born in South Carver, Mass., Jan. 24, 1795, where, in Oct. 1878, he still lived and sang and wrote.

ABA. 7s.

From GOTTSCHALK.

Lord! we come be-fore thee now; At thy feet we humbly bow; Oh, do not our suit dis-dain; Shall we seek thee, Lord! in vain?

ONONDAGA. 7s.

For this book by GEO. GOULD,
Music Printer, 18 P. O. Square, Boston.

83

Andante.

1. Lord, we come be - fore thee now, At thy feet we hum-bly bow; O do not our suit dis - dain, Shall we seek thee, Lord, in vain.

Soli, Alto and Bass. **Tutti.**

2. Com - fort those who weep and mourn, Let the time of joy re-turn; Those who are cast down, lift up, Make them strong in faith and hope.

JESUS, LOVER OF MY SOUL. 7s.

Je - sus, lov - er of my soul, Let me to thy bo-som fly, While the billows near me roll, While the tempest still is high

Hide me, oh my Sa - vior, hide, Till the storm of life be past; Safe in - to the ha - ven guide, Oh, re - ceive my soul at last.

Rit.

84

WARNING. 7s.

Jos. Howard.

Best sung in unison.

Has-ten, sin-ner, now be wise, Stay not for the morrow's sun; Wisdom, if you still de-spise, Harder is it to be won.

LIGHT. 7s.

James A. Johnson. 1876.

Ho-ly Spir-it, light di-vine, Beam up-on this heart of mine; Chase the shades of night a-way, Shine un-to the per-fect day.

mp

MANCHESTER. 7s.

From Schumann, by J. V. C.

Praise to God, im-mor-tal praise, For the love that crowns our days; Bounteous source of ev'-ry joy, Let thy praise our tongues employ.

PEACE. 7s. Double.

S. A. Dow.

Wea-ry, as with closing eye, On my peace-ful bed I lie; Have I thro' the day in aught, Sinned in word, or deed, or thought?
Fa-ther, may thy an-gel keep, Watch around me while I sleep.
Fa-ther, from thy ho-ly throne, Send a sav-ing par-don down.

KENDRICK. 7s. Double.

Bishop Hopkins, by permission.

Who are these in bright ar-ray? This in-nu-mer-a-ble throng, Round the al-tar night and day, Hymning their tri-umphant song.

Worthy is the Lamb once slain, Blessing, hon-or, glo-ry, power, Wisdom, riches to obtain, New do-min-ion ev'-ry hour.

LEONE. 8s & 7s.

Contributed by D. A. FRENCH.

Hark! the notes of an-gels sing-ing Glo-ry, glo-ry to the Lamb; All in heav'n their tribute bringing, Raising high the Savior's name.

OLD JERAULD. 8s & 7s.

CH. ZEUNER.

Where the win-ter's tem-pest low-ers O'er a bleak and cloudy sky, Nature's fading fruits and flowers Hang their drooping heads and die.

THE CHILDREN'S SONG. 8s & 7s

S. P. CHENEY.

1. Little hearts, O Lord, may love thee, Little minds may learn thy ways, Little hands and feet may serve thee, Little voices sing thy praise; Holy Jesus, come and bless us, Bless us, while this song we raise.

2. Small, as now we stand before thee, Larger shall we yearly grow; Help us ever to adore thee, All thro' life thy grace to show; Then, O Jesus, chiefly bless us, Take us home from all below.

BARNARD. 8s & 7s.

MOSES ELA CHENEY.

Love divine, all love ex -cel - ling, Joy of heaven to earth come down !
Fix in us thy humble dwelling; All thy faithful mercies crown :
Vis - it us with thy sal -va - tion ; En - ter ev' - ry longing heart.

Jesus ! thou art all compassion ; Pure, unbounded love thou art:

LOUISE. 8s & 7s. Double.

BISHOP HOPKINS. By per.

Lord, with glowing heart I'd praise thee For the bliss thy love bestows, For the pard'ning grace that saves me, And the peace that from it flows.

Help, O God, my weak endeavor ! This dull soul with rapture raise, Thou must light the flame, or never Can my love be warmed to praise.

ff Tutti.

WALLINGFORD. 8s & 7s.

Composed for this book by L. O. EMERSON.

1. Praise to thee, thou great Cre-a-tor! Praise to thee from ev'-ry tongue; Join, my soul, with ev'ry creature, Join the u-ni-ver-sal song.

2. Fa-ther, source of all compassion, Pure, unbounded grace is thine; Hail the God of our sal-va-tion! Praise him for his love di-vine.

ROLL ON, THOU MIGHTY OCEAN. 7s & 6s. Double.

GERMAN.

Not slow.

1. Roll on, thou might-y o-cean! And, as thy bil-lows flow, Bear mes-sen-gers of mer-cy To ev'-ry vale of woe.

2. O thou e-ter-nal Ru-ler! Who hold-est in thine arm The tem-pest of the o-cean, De-liv-er them from harm.

A-rise, ye gales, and waft them, Safe to their des-tined shore! That men may sit in dark-ness And death's black shade no more.

Thy pres-ence still be with them, Wher-ev-er they may be; Tho' far from those who love them, Let them be nigh to thee.

FRANK. 7s & 8s.

1. He who walks in virtue's ways, Firm and fearless, walketh sure-ly: Dil - i-gent while yet 'tis day, On he speeds and speeds se-cure-ly.

2. Flowers of peace beneath him grow, Suns of pleasure brighten o'er him; Mem' - ry's joys be - hind him go: Hope's sweet an - gels fly be - fore him.

3. Thus he moves from stage to stage, Smiles of earth and heaven attending; Soft - ly sinking down in age, And at last to death de-scend-ing.

TALMADGE or THANKSGIVING. 6s & 4s.

S. P. CHENEY.

1. The God of harvest praise, In loud thanksgiving raise Hand, heart and voice. The valleys smile and sing, Forests and mountains ring, The plains their tribute bring, The streams rejoice.

2. Yea, bless his holy name, And joyous thanks proclaim Thro' all the earth. To glory in your lot, Is comely; but be not God's ben-e- fits forgot, A-mid your mirth.

ROGERS. 7s & 6s. Double.

Arranged by W. S. ROGERS.

1. Rise, my soul, and stretch thy wings, Thy bet - ter por - tion trace, Rise from tran - si - to- ry things Toward heaven, thy native place.

2. Riv - ers to the o - cean run, Nor stay in all their course ; Fire, as - cending, seeks the sun, Both speed them to their source.

Sun and moon and stars de - cay, Time shall soon this earth remove ; Rise, my soul, and haste a - way To seats prepared a - bove.

So a soul that's born of God, Pants to view his glo - rious face ; Upward tends to his a-bode, To rest in his em - brace.

LONGING.

Composed for this book by JAMES A. JOHNSON.

mp *cres.* *f*

1. Nearer, my God, to thee, nearer to thee! E'en tho it be a cross that raiseth me ; Still all my song shall be, nearer, my God, to thee, Nearer my God, to thee, nearer to thee.

2. Tho' like the wanderer, the sun gone down, Darkness be over me, my rest a stone ; Yet in my dreams I'd be nearer, my God, to thee, Nearer, my God, to thee, nearer to thee.

FLIGHT OF TIME. 6s.

S. P. CHENEY.

How still and soft the night Spreads darkness o'er the earth; How still the morning light Reveals each day's new birth. Thus years fly swiftly by, Thus life is worn a- way, And

man is left to sigh, Be-hold its brevi - ty, Behold its brevi - ty.

THOU SWEET GLIDING KEDRON. 11s.

S. P. CHENEY.

1. Thou sweet gliding Kedron, By thy silver stream, The Saviour would linger in
2. How damp were the vapors that fell on his head! How hard was his pil-low, how

moonlight's soft beam; And by thy bright waters would oftentimes stray, And lose in thy murmurs the toils of the day, And lose in thy murmurs the toils of the day.

humble his bed! The angels, astonish'd, grew sad at the sight, And follow'd their Master with solemn delight, And fol-low'd their Mas - ter with solemn delight.

SAVIOR, THY GENTLE VOICE.

E. Tourjee. By per.

1. Sa-vior! thy gen-tle voice glad-ly we hear; Author of all our joys, ever be near; Our souls would cling to thee, Let us thy fullness see, our life to cheer.

Mrs. M. A. W. Cook.

THE LORD WILL PROVIDE. 6s & 5s.

Prof. C. S. Harrington, by per. Dr Tourjee.

1. In some way or oth - er, the Lord will provide; It may not be *my* way, It may not be *thy* way, And yet in his *own* way, The Lord will provide.

2. At some time or oth - er, the Lord will provide; It may not be *my* time, It may not be *thy* time, And yet in his *own* time, The Lord will provide.

ENTREATY. 10s.

J. A. J., Aug. 19, 1878.

Abide with me! fast falls the eventide, The darkness deepens, Lord, with me abide! When other helpers fail, and comforts flee, Help of the helpless, O abide with me.   A-men.

As pants the wearied hart for cooling streams, That sinks exhausted in the summer chase, So longs my soul for thee, great King of kings, So longs to reach thy sacred dwelling-place. Why throb, my

yet an in - mate of   thy breast.

heart; why sinks my saddening soul?   Trust thou in God, in Him secure - ly rest;   Thy years shall yet in blissful circles move,   And joy be yet an in - mate of   thy breast.

yet an inmate of .... thy breast.

JAMES HASKINS.

DORSET. 5s & 8s.

S. P. CHENEY.

Rejoice in the Lord, Be-lieve in his name, Con-fide in his mer-cy and grace, His throne shall endure, His promise is sure, In

Him shall the righteous have peace, In Him shall the righteous have peace.

AILENROC. 10s.

1. A - long the banks where Babel's current flows, Our captive bands in

2. The tuneful harp that once with joy they strung, When praise employed and

deep de - spondence strayed, While Zi - on's fall in sad re - membrance rose, Her friends, her children min - gled with the dead.

mirth in - spired the lay, Was now in si - lence on the willows hung, While growing grief prolongs the tedious day.

Allegretto.

1. Come, let us a-new our jour-ney pur-sue, Roll round with the year, And nev-er stand still Till the Master ap-pear;

2. Our life is a dream; our time as a stream Glides swift-ly a-way, And the fu-gi-tive moment re-fu-ses to stay.

3. Oh, that each, in the day of His com-ing may say, "I have fought my way through, I have finished the work thou didst give me to do.

His a-dor-a-ble will Let us glad-ly ful-fill, And our talents improve, By the patience of hope and the la-bor of love.

The ar-row is flown, The moment is gone; The Mil-len-ni-al year Rushes on to our view, and e-ter-ni-ty's near.

Oh, that each from his Lord May re-ceive the glad word, "Well and faithful-ly done! En-ter in-to my joy and sit down on my throne."

TRANQUIL AND PEACEFUL .11s & 5s.

1. Tranquil and peaceful is the path to heaven, Where now so many, fresh from earth's ripe vintage ; So many happy, high and blessed spirits, Wait to receive us.

2. There life is blissful, shall the spirit tremble ? Bright, heav'nly angels wait to lead us yonder ; There dwell the spirits, purified by suff'ring, Blessing and blessed.

MISSION. 7s & 6s.

Jas. A. Johnson.

1. From Greenland's i - cy mountains, From In - dia's cor - al strand, Where Af - ric's sun - ny fountains Roll down their golden sand ;

2. What though the spi - cy breez - es Blow soft o'er Ceylon's isle, Though ev' - ry pros - pect pleas - es, And on - ly man is vile.

From many an an - cient riv - er, From many a palm - y plain, They call us to de - liv - er Their land from er-ror's chain.

In vain with lav - ish kind - ness The gifts of God are strown ; The hea - then in his blind-ness Bows down to wood and stone.

OH! TRUST IN ME.

Soprano and Alto.

Tenor and Bass.

1. Go and tell Jesus, When the heart is full of keen and bitter ago - - - - ny and woe; When the dear, precious form of one belov'd Is taken from thee,
2. Go and tell Jesus, When thy weak heart fails, In looking through the mists of coming years : Thou think'st of sorrow, pain and loneliness, And the bright world seems

in the grave laid low, Go and tell Je - sus, He will soothe thy grief, To thy poor, sorrowing spir - it bring re - lief.
but a vale of tears: Go and tell Je - sus, He will say to thee, "I thy good Shepherd am, Oh! trust in me."

GENTLE VOICE. 6s & 4s. Double.   F. J. LEWIS.

1. Savior, thy gentle voice, Gladly we hear; Author of all our joys, Ev - er be near. Our souls would cling to thee, Let us thy fullness see, Let us thy fullness see, Our life to cheer.

2. Fountain of life divine! Thee we adore ; We would be wholly thine, Forevermore. Freely forgive our sin, Grant heavenly peace within, Grant heavenly peace within, Thy light restore.

mp   *cres.*   *f*   *dim.*   *m*   *cres.*   *mf*   *f*   *dim.*

BURR. H. M.

S. P. Cheney.

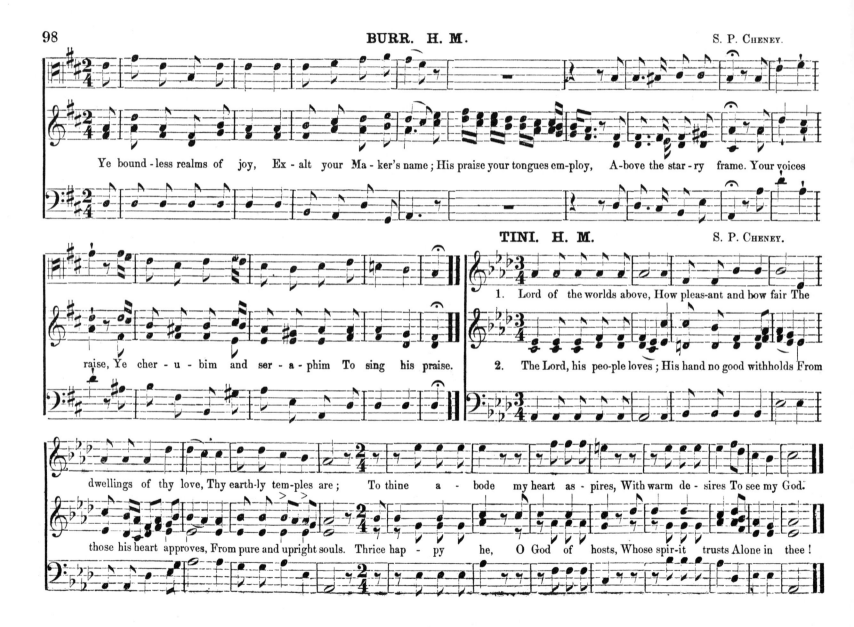

Ye bound-less realms of joy, Ex-alt your Ma-ker's name; His praise your tongues em-ploy, A-bove the star-ry frame. Your voices

raise, Ye cher-u-bim and ser-a-phim To sing his praise.

TINI. H. M.

S. P. Cheney.

1. Lord of the worlds above, How pleas-ant and how fair The

2. The Lord, his peo-ple loves; His hand no good withholds From

dwellings of thy love, Thy earth-ly tem-ples are; To thine a - bode my heart as - pires, With warm de - sires To see my God.

those his heart approves, From pure and upright souls. Thrice hap - py he, O God of hosts, Whose spir-it trusts Alone in thee!

"THE ANGEL OF THE LORD." 7s & 5s.

John Vance Cheney.

1. Onward speed thy conquering flight, An-gel, onward speed! Cast a-broad thy ra-diant light, Bid the shades re-cede;

2. Onward speed thy conquering flight, An-gel, onward fly! Long has been the reign of night; Bring the morn-ing nigh;

Tread the i-dols in the dust, Heathen fanes de-stroy; Spread the gos-pel's love and trust, Spread the gos-pel's joy.

Un-to thee earth's sufferers lift Their im-plor-ing wail; Bear them heav-en's ho-ly gift, Ere their courage fail.

BELVIDERE. 8s, 7s & 4s.

A. N. Johnson. By per.

1. Christian! see the orient morning Breaks along the heathen sky; Lo, th' expected day is dawning, Glorious day-spring from on high : Hallelujah ! Hail the day-spring from on high.

2. Heathen at the sight are singing, Morning wakes the tuneful lay ; Precious offerings they are bringing, First fruits of more perfect praise : Hallelujah ! Hail the dayspring from on high.

John Henry Newman. 1833.

LEAD, KINDLY LIGHT.

Rev. J. B. Dykes, Mus. Doc.

1. Lead, kindly Light, amid the circling gloom, Lead Thou me on; The night is dark, and I am far from home, Lead Thou me on. Keep Thou my feet; I

2. I was not ever thus, nor prayed that thou Shouldst lead me on; I loved to choose and see my path; but now, Lead Thou me on. I loved the ga - rish

do not ask to see The distant scene; one step enough for me.

day, and, spite of fears, Pride ruled my will; remember not past years. A - men.

HOLY, HOLY, HOLY!

Rev. Dr. Dykes.

1. Ho - ly, ho - ly, ho - ly! Lord God Al - might - y! Ear - ly in the

2. Ho - ly, ho - ly, ho - ly! All the saints adore Thee, Casting down their

morning, our song shall rise to Thee; Ho-ly, Ho-ly, Ho - ly! Merci - ful and might- y; God in Three Persons, Blessed Trini - ty!

golden crowns around the glassy sea; Cheru- bim and Sera- phim falling down before Thee, Which wert and art and ev - ermore shalt be. Amen.

THE SACRED MAN. 6s. 8 lines.

S. P. Cheney.

1. Thou child of Bethlehem, Born in a man-ger there, Worshipped by hosts from heaven, By wise men sought with care:

2. Thou taught us how to pray To Him who is in heaven, How to for-give each day, That we may be forgiven.

3. Our heads in grief we bow, And thus we come to thee, Kiss-ing the ground so low. In deep hu-mil-i-ty.

Thou wast the sin-ner's friend, While dwelling here be-low, And will be to the end, Feel-ing for oth-ers' woe.

Thou saidst, "come un-to me," All ye who are oppressed; Come ye and learn of me, And I will give you rest.

Thou sa-cred Man of God, Come with thy quick-'ning power: Oh, lift this chast'ning rod, And heal me from this hour.

ZION. S. P. M.

1. How pleased and blest was I To hear the people cry, "Come, let us seek our God to-day! Yes, with a cheerful zeal We haste to Zion's hill, And there our vows and honors pay.

Zion, thrice happy place, Adorned with wondrous grace, And walls of strength embrace thee round! In thee our tribes appear To pray and praise and hear The sacred gospel's joyful sound.

3. May peace attend thy gate, And joy within thee wait To bless the soul of every guest: The man who seeks thy peace, And wishes thine increase, A thousand blessings on him rest!

NEUMARCK'S HYMN. P. M.

WEIMAR.

1. If thou but suf-fer God to guide thee, And hope in him thro' all thy ways, }
He'll give thee strength, whate'er betide thee, And bear thee thro' the e-vil days; } Who trusts in God's unchanging love Builds on the rock that naught can [move.

2. What can these anxious cares a-vail thee? These never-ceasing moans and sighs? }
What can it help if thou bewail thee O'er each dark moment as it flies? } Our cross and trials do but press The heavier for our bitterness.

3. God knows full well the hour when gladness Shall be the needful thing for thee. }
When he has tried thy soul with sadness, And from all guile has found thee free. } He comes to thee all un-aware, And makes thee own his loving care.

HOLMES. 6s & 5s.

Through thy pro- tect-ing care, Kept till the dawn-ing, Taught to draw near in prayer, Heed we the warn-ing; O thou great One in three, Gladly our

souls would be Evermore praising thee, God of the morning.

MALCOM. C. P. M. Composed for this book by L. MARSHALL.
Allegro Moderato.

Begin, my soul, th' exalted lay, Let each enraptured tho't obey, And praise th'Al-

mighty's name. Lo! heav'n and earth and seas and skies, In one me-lo-dious concert rise, To swell th'in-spir - ing theme, To swell th'inspir-ing theme.

cres. _ _ _ _ f

MISS JANE SLOMAN of New York, previous to 1850, published " The Melodist, or gems from celebrated composers," among which are quite a number of her own compositions. The book is a long quarto of 112 pages, and is dedicated by the compiler, to her father; and as evidence that the work was one of merit, it may be mentioned that several editions were printed by William Hall and Son, New York. From the edition of 1850 we copy the accompanying tune, "Holmes." MOORE'S NEW ENCYCLOPEDIA OF MUSIC.
* This beautiful tune is slightly altered from the original, and a bass added, to make it more useful for choirs. S. P. C.

HATFIELD. P. M.

1. Hal - le - lu - jah! praise the Lord, In the heights of glo - ry; Hosts of heav'n! with one ac-cord, Shout the joy-ful sto - ry;
2. Praise him with the trum-pet's tongue, Far and wide re - sound-ing; Praise him with the harp well-strung, While your hearts are bounding.
3. Praise him with the vi - ol's strings, Wak--ing joy-ous feel - ing; While the vault of glo-ry rings With the or-gan's pealing:

Praise him for his might - y deeds, Praise ye him, whose grace ex - ceeds All that heav'n in songs concedes, Worlds of bliss! his praise record.
Praise him with the sweet-toned lyre; Let his praise the lute in - spire; Praise him in a mighty choir; Let his praise be loudly sung.
Let the cym - bals ring his praise, Wake the clar - ion's grandest lays, Praise the Lord thro' endless days: Lo! his praise cre-a - tion sings.

PRAYER FOR PEACE. P. M.

1. God, the all-terrible! thou who ordainest Thunder thy clarion, and lightning thy sword; Show forth thy pity on high where thou reignest, Give to us peace in our time, O Lord.
2. God, the all-mer - ci-ful! earth hath forsa-ken Thy ways all ho-ly, and slighted thy word; Let not thy wrath in its terror a -waken, Give to us par-don and peace, O Lord.

1. I was a wandering sheep, I did not love the fold, I did not love my Shepherd's voice, I would not be con-trolled.

2. The Shepherd sought his sheep, The Father sought his child; They followed me o'er vale and hill, O'er des-erts waste and wild.

3. Je-sus my Shepherd is, 'Twas he that loved my soul, 'Twas he that washed me in his blood, 'Twas he that made me whole.

I was a wayward child, I did not love my home, I did not love my Father's voice, I loved a-far to roam.

They found me nigh to death, Famished, and faint, and lone; They bound me with the bands of love; They saved the wandering one.

'Twas he that sought me lost, That found the wandering sheep, 'Twas he that brought me to the fold, 'Tis he that still doth keep.

MISSIONARY HYMN. 7s & 6s.

Dr. Lowell Mason.

1. From Greenland's icy mountains, From India's coral strand, Where Afric's sunny fountains Roll down their golden sand, From many an ancient river, From

2. What tho' the spi - cy breez - es Blow soft o'er Ceylon's isle ; Tho' ev' - ry pros-pect pleas-es, And on - ly man is vile ? In vain with lavish kindness The

GOODWIN. 7s & 6s.

Geo. James Webb.

Vivace.

many a palm-y plain, They call us to de - liv - er Their land from error's chain.

gifts of God are strown ; The heathen, in his blindness, Bows down to wood and stone.

1. The morning light is breaking, The darkness disappears ; The

2. Rich dews of grace come o'er us, In many a gentle shower, And

sons of earth are waking To pen - i - tential tears : Each breeze that sweeps the ocean Brings tidings from afar, Of nations in com-mo-tion, Prepared for Zion's war.

brighter scenes before us Are opening ev' - ry hour; Each cry to heav-en go - ing, Abundant answers brings, And heav'nly gales are blowing, With peace upon their wings.

NUREMBURG. 7s.

GERMAN.

Praise to God, im-mor-tal praise, For the love that crowns our days: Bounteous Source of ev-ery joy, Let thy praise our tongues employ.

MOZART. 7s.

MOZART.

Lord, we come be-fore thee now, At thy feet we humbly bow; O, do not our suit disdain; Shall we seek thee, Lord, in vain?

HADDAM. H. M.

ENGLISH.

{ The Lord Jehovah reigns; His throne is built on high; }
{ The garments he assumes (OMIT - - - - - - - -) } { Are light and ma-jes-ty; His glo-ries shine with beams so bright, No mortal eye can bear the sight.

AMERICA. 6s & 4s.

1. My coun-try, 'tis of thee, Sweet land of lib-er-ty, Of thee I sing: Land where my fathers died, Land of the pilgrims' pride, From ev'ry mountain side Let freedom ring.

2. My na-tive country, thee, Land of the noble free, Thy name I love: I love thy rocks and rills, Thy woods and templed hills; My heart with rapture thrills Like that above.

Let music swell the breeze, And ring from all the trees Sweet freedom's song! Let mortal tongues awake; Let all that breathe partake; Let rocks their silence break, The sound prolong.

4. Our father's God! to thee, Author of lib-er-ty, To thee we sing: Long may our land be bright With freedom's holy light; Protect us by thy might, Great God, our King.

LYONS. 10s & 11s.

HAYDN.

Allegro.

O praise ye the Lord, prepare a new song, And let all his saints in full cho-rus join; With voices u - ni-ted, the anthem prolong, And show forth his praises in music divine.

ITALIAN HYMN. 6s & 4s.

GIARDINI.

Bold.

Come, thou al-mighty King, Help us thy name to sing; Help us to praise! { Fa-ther all glo-ri-ous, } { O'er all vic-to-ri-ous, } Come, and reign over us, Ancient of days.

SICILIAN HYMN. 8s, 7s & 4s.

Lord, dis-miss us with thy bless-ing, Fill our hearts with joy and peace; { Let us, each thy love pos-sessing, Tri-umph in re-deeming grace; {
{ O, re-fresh us, O re-fresh us, Travelers thro' this wil-der-ness. }

GREENVILLE. 8s & 7s. Double.

J. J. ROUSSEAU.

1. { Far from mor-tal cares re-treat-ing, Sor-did hopes and vain de-sires, }
{ Here our will-ing foot-steps meeting, Ev-ery heart to heaven as-pires. } 2. From the fount of glo-ry beam-ing, Light ce-les-tial cheers our eyes;
D.C. Mer-cy from a-bove pro-claiming, Peace and par-don from the skies.

DALSTON. S. P. M.

A. WILLIAMS. 1760.

The Lord Jehovah reigns, And royal state maintains, His head with awful glories crowned; Arrayed in robes of light, Begirt with sovereign might, And rays of majesty around.

O, PRAY FOR THE PEACE OF JERUSALEM. Sentence, No. 1.

J. A. JOHNSON.

O, pray for the peace, the peace of Je - ru - sa - lem; They shall pros-per that love   thee. Peace be with-in thy walls, with-in   thy walls, and

plenteous - ness, and plenteous - ness with-in   thy pal - a - ces, and plenteousness with-in thy pal - a - ces.   Peace,   Peace.

"FROM THE RISING OF THE SUN." Sentence No. 2.

Jas. A. Johnson. 1858.

ENTER NOT INTO JUDGMENT. Sentence No. 3.

James A. Johnson.

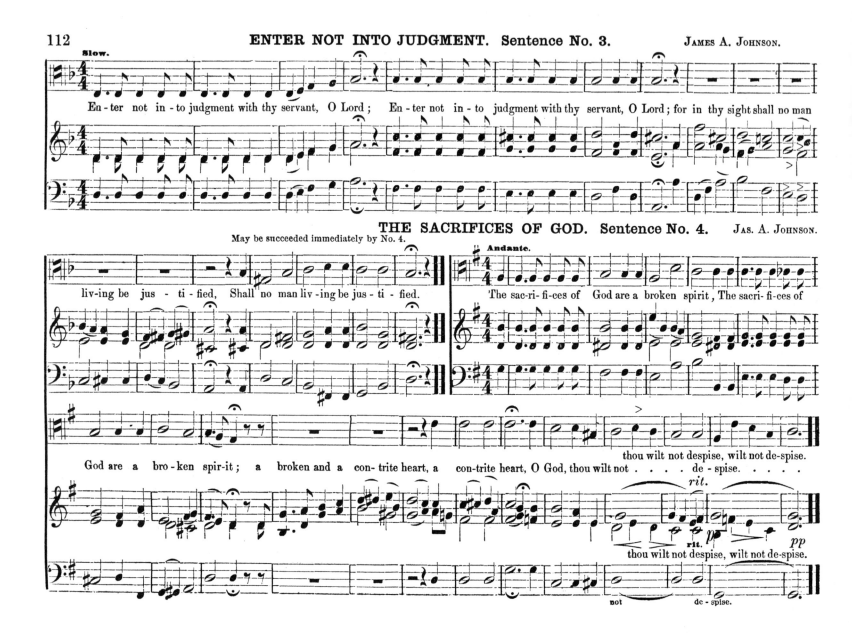

Slow.

En-ter not in-to judgment with thy servant, O Lord; En-ter not in-to judgment with thy servant, O Lord; for in thy sight shall no man

THE SACRIFICES OF GOD. Sentence No. 4.

Jas. A. Johnson.

May be succeeded immediately by No. 4.

Andante.

liv-ing be jus-ti-fied, Shall no man liv-ing be jus-ti-fied.

The sac-ri-fi-ces of God are a broken spirit, The sacri-fi-ces of

God are a bro-ken spir-it; a broken and a con-trite heart, a con-trite heart, O God, thou wilt not . . . . . de-spise. . . . .

thou wilt not despise, wilt not de-spise.

rit.

thou wilt not despise, wilt not de-spise.

pp

not de-spise.

* HE THAT HATH PITY. Sentence, No. 5. From "Offertory Sentences," by J. A. JOHNSON.

He that hath pi - ty, hath pi - ty on the poor, lend - eth un - to the Lord.

DUET.

And look! what he layeth out,

And look! what he lay - eth out.

Look! what he lay - eth out, it shall be paid un - to him a - gain; it shall be

And look! what he layeth out,

paid unto him a - gain. He that hath pi - ty on the poor, lendeth un - to the Lord.

Slow and soft.

* Johnson's Offertory Sentences are published by S. T. Gordon, 14th street, New York.

THE SABBATH.

S. P. Cheney.

When, as returns this sol - emn day, Man comes to meet his God, What rites, what hon - ors shall he pay? How spread his

praise a - broad, How spread his praise a - broad? From mar-ble domes and gild-ed spires Shall clouds of in - cense rise, And

Rit. and dim.   *f*   *p*   *m*

gems,   and gold,   and gar- lands deck the cost-ly sac - ri - fice! Vain, sin - ful man! vain, sin - ful man! Cre - a - tion's Lord, cre-

Rit. and dim.   *f a tempo.*   *p*   *m*

f   dim.   *pp*

a - tion's Lord, Thy offerings well may spare ; But give   thy   heart, But give   thy heart,   and thou shalt find Thy God will hear thy prayer.

f   dim,   *pp*

COME, THOU FOUNT.

Suggested by a Theme of D. A. French's.

Accomp. by J. A. Johnson.

Come, thou Fount of ev'-ry bless-ing, Tune my heart to sing thy grace; Streams of mer-cy nev-er ceas-ing, Call for

Teach me some me-lo - dious meas-ure, Sung by rap-tured hosts a-bove; Fill my soul with

songs of loud-est praise.

sa - cred pleas-ure, While I sing redeem - ing love; While I sing, While I sing re - deem-ing love. Teach me some me - lo - dious

Teach me some me - lo-dious

Teach me some me - lo-dious

measure, Sung by raptured hosts a - bove, Fill my soul with heav'nly pleasure, While I sing re-deem-ing love, While I sing re - deem-ing love.

AS PANTS THE HART. C. M.

Yarndley, of San Francisco. By per.

As pants the hart for cool-ing streams, When heated in the chase, So longs my soul, O God, for thee, And thy re-freshing grace.

For thee, my God, the liv-ing God, My thirsty soul doth pine: O when shall I be-hold thy face, Thou Ma-jes-ty di-vine?

Why restless, why cast down, my soul? Trust God, who will em-ploy His aid for thee, and change these sighs To thankful songs of joy.

THE LORD IS GREAT.

1. The Lord is great! The Lord is great! Ye hosts of heav'n a-dore Him, And ye who tread this earth-ly ball, In ho-ly songs re-

2. The Lord is great! The Lord is great! His maj-es-ty, how glo-rious! Resound his praise from shore to shore; O'er sin and death and

3. The Lord is great! The Lord is great! His mer-cy how abound-ing! Ye an-gels, strike your gold-en chords! O, praise our God with

For the last verse.

joice a-loud be-fore Him, And shout His praise, and shout His praise, and shout His praise who made you all. and Lord of lords.

hell now made vic-to-rious, He rules and reigns, He rules and reigns, He rules and reigns for-ev-er-more, and Lord of lords.

harp and voice re-sound-ing, The King of kings, the King of kings, the King of kings and Lord of lords. . . . .

UNTO THEE, O LORD.*

TRIO AND QUARTET.

Composed for this book by W. A. BRIGGS, Organist, Montpelier, Vt.

TRIO. *Andante religioso.*

Unto thee, O Lord, unto thee do I lift my voice. O hear my prayer, Teach me thy paths, and lead me in thy truths. O hear my

prayer as I cry to thee, O Lord, un- to thee. Un - to thee, O Lord, unto thee do I lift up my voice as I cry to thee. A - men.

* To be sung without accompaniment.

Words by JAMES HASKINS.

OUR GOD IS OUR HELPER.

S. P. CHENEY.

Allegretto.

1. Our God is our help - er and shield, We fear not the bat - tle, the foe; The sword of the Spir-it we'll wield, *f* And

2. Sin, sin and his pes - ti - lent train Have kept us in thraldom too long; We shrink not from per - il, from pain, *f* In the

smite till the ty - rant lies low. The ty - rant whose en - mi - ty cast Wide space 'tween our souls and their God, Our warfare a - gainst him shall

cres.

help of the Lord we are strong. Like sol-diers in - ured to the war, The heat of the bat - tle we'll brave, And car - ry our conquest a-

OUR GOD IS OUR HELPER. Concluded.

last, Our war-fare a-gainst him shall last, Till down in the dust he be trod, Till down - - - - - in the dust he be trod.

Till down - - - - - in the dust he be trod.

Till down - - - - - -

far, And car-ry our con-quest a-far, Thro' Him who is might-y to save, Thro' Him - - - - - - - who is might-y to save.

Till down in the dust he be trod.
Through Him who is might-y to save.

COME UNTO ME.

S. P. CHENEY.

All ye that labor,

Come unto me, Come un-to me, Come un-to me, All ye that labor, Come, all ye that labor and are heavy - laden, and I will give you

All ye that labor,

THE LORD IS IN HIS HOLY TEMPLE.

F. J. Lewis.

The Lord is in His ho - ly temple, The Lord is in His ho - ly temple; Let all the earth keep silence be -

fore Him, Let all the earth keep si - lence be - fore Him, keep si - lence be - fore Him, keep si - lence be - fore Him.

Rit. and dim.

HYMN OF THE LAST SUPPER.

Mrs. Richmond.

D.C.1. The winds are hush'd, the peaceful moon Looks down on Zion's hill; The city sleeps, 'tis night's cold noon, And all the streets are still. How soft, how ho - ly

2. Affection's smile, devotion's prayer Are in that ho - ly strain : And hope and love and trust are there, And friendship won by pain. 'Tis Je -sus and his

is the light, And hark! a sweet, low song, As gently as the breeze of night, Floats on the air along, Floats on the air a-long.

faithful   few, That soul-deep hymn who pour, Like seraphs on their wings of light, Those strains of music soar, (OMIT...... ....) Those strains of music soar........

D.C. TO FIRST STANZA.

BENEDICTUS.

James A. Johnson. 1860.

Allegretto.

ff
and hath rais-ed up,   rais-ed up, hath raised up   a mighty sal-

he hath vis-it-ed and re-deem-ed his peo-ple;   and hath raised up   a mighty sal-

Piu moto.

and hath rais-ed up, hath raised up

ff   *ff*
and hath rais-ed up, hath rais-ed up, - - - - - hath raised up a mighty sal-

p QUARTET.   *cres.*   > *p*   > TRIO. *p*

va-tion for us in the house of his servant Da - vid, in the house of his servant Da - vid; as he spake by the mouth of his ho-ly

QUARTET.   *cres.*   > *p*   *p*
p

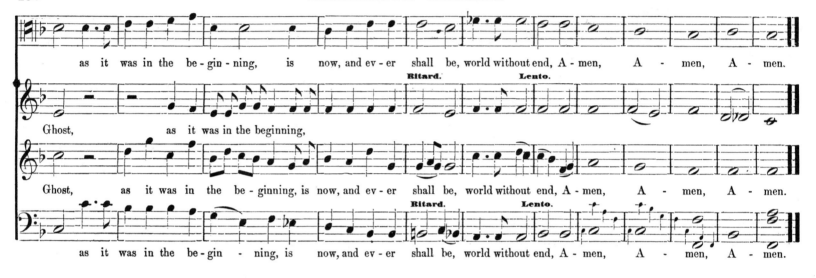

as it was in the be - gin - ning, is now, and ev - er shall be, world without end, A - men, A - men, A - men.

Ghost, as it was in the beginning,

Ghost, as it was in the be - ginning, is now, and ev - er shall be, world without end, A - men, A - men, A - men.

as it was in the be - gin - ning, is now, and ev - er shall be, world without end, A - men, A - men, A - men.

SENTENCE.   **If ye love me, keep my commandments.**   Contributed by L. O. EMERSON.

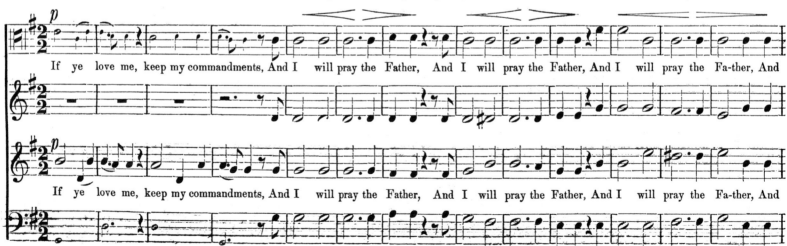

If ye love me, keep my commandments, And I will pray the Father, And I will pray the Father, And I will pray the Fa-ther, And

If ye love me, keep my commandments, And I will pray the Father, And I will pray the Father, And I will pray the Fa-ther, And

THE LORD IS MY SHEPHERD.

S. P. Cheney.

The Lord is my Shepherd, I shall not want, The Lord is my Shepherd, I shall not want. He maketh me to lie down in green pastures, He

leadeth me beside the still waters, be-side the still waters. The Lord is my Shepherd, I shall not want, He maketh me to lie down in

green pastures, He lead-eth me be-side the still waters, He re-storeth my soul. Yea, tho' I walk thro' the val-ley of the

He leadeth me beside the still wa-ters,

shadow of death, I will fear no e-vil; for thou art with me, Thy rod and thy staff, they comfort me, Thy rod and staff, they comfort me, they

Thy rod and staff,

comfort me.   Surely, goodness and mercy shall follow me all the days of my life : good - ness and mercy shall follow me all the days of my

life, and I will dwell, will dwell in the house of the Lord forev - er, will dwell in the house, the house of the Lord forever, for - ev - er, A - men.

* A native of Vermont, commenced music at ten years of age. In 1866 was a pupil of William Mason and J. P. Morgan of New York, and was elected Organist at Trinity Church. In 1872 went to Europe, and in Berlin studied the Piano with Franz Bendel, Musical theory with C. F. Weitzman, and the Organ with August Haupt. Twice visited Liszt, received favorable criticisms on his playing, and the artistic benediction of the great Pianist on leaving for America. Prof. B. is an organist and teacher in St. Louis, Mo., and 30 years of age.

THE DAY IS PAST AND OVER.

Jas. A. Johnson.

1. The day is past and o-ver, All thanks, O Lord, to thee: I pray thee now that sin-less, The

2. The joys of day are o-ver; I lift my heart to thee, And ask thee that of-fence-less, The

3. Be thou my soul's pre-serv-er, Oh! God, for thou dost know How ma-ny are the per-ils 'Through

hours of dark may be. O Fa-ther, keep me in thy sight, And save me through the com-ing night.

hours of dark may be. Oh! Je-sus, make their dark-ness light, And keep me through the com-ing night.

which I have to go. Lov-er of men, oh, hear my call, And guard and save me from them all. A-men.

CAROL FOR CHRISTMAS.

Arranged from Billings' "Boston,"
and the 2d and 3d stanzas added by JAS. A. JOHNSON.

1. Methinks I see a heav'n-ly host Of an - gels on the wing, Methinks I hear their cheer-ful notes, So mer - ri - ly they sing.

2. In Beth'lem's ci - ty in Ju - dea, A heav'n-ly babe you'll find; "Im-man - u - el" shall be his name; The friend of all mankind.

3. His gov - ern - ment shall have no end, But last for aye, se - cure; To him shall thrones and kingdoms bend, While sun and moon endure.

CHORUS.

Let all your fears be banished hence; Glad tid - ings we pro-claim, For there's a Sa-vior born to - day, And Je - sus is his name.

The Won - der - ful, the Counsel - lor, The might - y God and Lord; "The Prince of peace," the King of kings By earth and heav'n a-dored.

Glo - ry to God and peace on earth, Glad tid - ings we pro-claim, For there's a Sa-vior born to - day, And Je - sus is his name.

* WHEN ALL THY MERCIES. C. M.

From GUIGLIELMO.

When all thy mer - cies, O my God, My ris - ing soul sur- veys,...... Transport - ed with the view I'm lost In won - der, love, and praise, Transport - ed with the view I'm lost In wonder, love, and praise....

O how can words with e - qual warmth The grat - i -tude de - clare,......

* Given to this book from JAS. A. JOHNSON'S work, "The Church Quartette," in press and shortly to appear.

*LORD, TO THEE FOR REFUGE FLYING.

Mendelssohn. Parts added by J. Howard.

Lord, to thee for ref - uge fly - ing, When oppress'd with care and grief; Where but on thy bosom ly - ing, Can a wounded spir - it

Where......

Where can a wound-ed spir - it

Where but on thy bo - som ly - ing,

fast.......... for aid and find re - lief.

rit. p tem. dolce.

sigh - ing, Cling fast for aid and find re - lief, Cling fast for aid, find re - lief.

re - lief, Cling fast, Cling fast for aid, find re - lief, find re - lief.

p tempo dolce.

REJOICE IN THE LORD.

re - joice in the Lord, re - joice in the Lord, re - joice, re - joice, re - joice,.......... praise the

Rejoice, re-joice, re-joice,

re - joice, re - joice, re - joice re - joice in the Lord....... rejoice, rejoice, rejoice, praise the

rejoice in the Lord, praise the

Lord, praise the Lord, praise the Lord, praise the Lord with harp, sing unto Him with the psaltery, with an instrument of ten strings.

REJOICE IN THE LORD. Continued.

Sing un - to Him a new song, Praise the Lord with harp, sing unto Him with the psaltery, with an in - strument of ten strings, sing unto Him a

Praise the Lord with harp, praise the Lord with harp, praise the Lord with harp,

new song,

With an in - stru - ment of ten strings, with an in - stru - ment of ten strings, with an

sing un - to Him with the psaltery, sing unto Him with the psaltery, sing un - to Him with the psaltery, sing........

sing un - to Him a new song, sing unto Him a new song, sing unto Him a new................

praise the Lord with harp,   with harp,   with harp,   *cres......*   *ff*

in - stru - ment of ten strings,   of ten strings,   ten strings,   play skillful - ly, play skillful - ly with a   loud   noise.

...... unto Him with psaltery,   with psaltery,   with psaltery   *cres......*   *ff*

.... song,   a new   song.

Andante.

Solo.

For the word of the Lord   is   right,   and   all   his   works   are   done   in

Instrument.

Cast thy bur - den on the Lord, Lean thou on - ly on his word; Ev - er will he

Lean thou on - ly on his word;

Lean thou on - ly on his word; Ev - er will he

be thy stay, Though the heav'ns shall melt a - way: Ev - er in the rag - ing storm, Thou shalt see his

Though the heav'ns shall melt a - way: Ev - er in.........

cres.

cres.

cheer - ing face, Hear his pledge of com - ing aid, ... "It is I; be not a - fraid.....

Hear his pledge............

WORLDS UNBORN SHALL SING HIS GLORY.

BEETHOVEN.

f Praise the

Praise the Lord, ye ev - er - last - ing choir, in ho - ly songs of

Praise the Lord, ye ev - er - last - ing choir, in ho - ly songs of joy! in ho - ly songs of joy! in ho - ly songs of

.... the Lord, the Lord! Praise .... the Lord in songs of joy, in songs of joy!

Praise .... the Lord in songs, in songs of joy!

Praise .... the Lord in songs, in songs of joy!

.... the Lord, the Lord! Praise .... the Lord in songs of joy, in songs of joy!

Worlds un - born shall sing his glo - ry,   the ex-

Worlds un-born shall sing his glo - ry,

Worlds un-born shall sing his glo- ry,

Worlds un - born shall sing his glo - ry,   the ex - alt - ed,   the ex - alt - ed,   the ex-

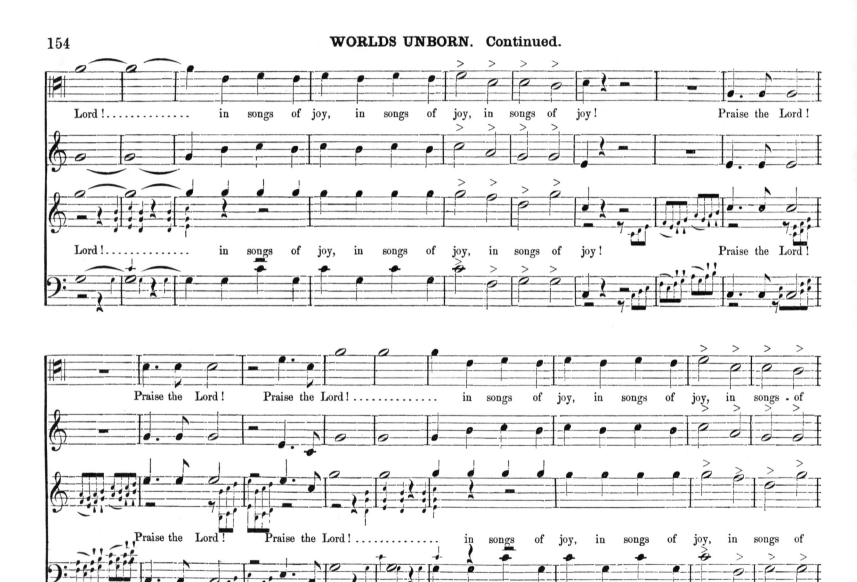

joy! Praise the Lord in ho - ly songs, in ho - ly songs! Praise the Lord in songs of joy!

joy! Praise the Lord in ho - ly songs, in ho - ly songs! Praise the Lord in songs of joy!

Praise the Lord! Praise the Lord! in ho - ly songs of joy, in ho - ly songs of joy!

Praise the Lord! Praise the Lord! in ho - ly songs of joy, in ho - ly songs of joy!

Allegro non Troppo.

Hal-le-lu-jah, hal-le-lu-jah, hal-le-lu-jah, hal-le-lu-jah, hal-le-lu-jah, hal-le-lu-jah, hal-le-lu-jah, hal-le-lu-jah, hal-le-lu-jah, hal-

Hal-le-lu-jah, hal-le-lu-jah, hal-le-lu-jah, hal-le-lu-jah, hal-le-lu-jah, hal-le-lu-jah, hal-le-lu-jah, hal-le-lu-jah, hal-le-lu-jah, hal-

Hal-le-lu-jah, hal-le-lu-jah, hal-le-lu-jah, hal-le-lu-jah, hal-le-lu-jah, hal-le-lu-jah, hal-le-lu-jah, hal-le-lu-jah, hal-le-lu-jah, hal-

le - - lu-jah,   For the Lord God omnip - o-tent reigneth.   Hal-le - lu-jah, hal-le-lu-jah,   For the Lord God omnip - o-tent reign-eth.   Halle-

le - - lu-jah,   For the Lord God omnip - o-tent reigneth.   Hal-le - lu-jah,   hal-le-lu-jah,   For the Lord God omnip - o-tent reign-eth.   Halle-

le - lu - jah,   For the Lord God omnip - o-tent reigneth.   Hal-le - lu-jah, hal-le-lu-jah,   For the Lord God omnip - o-tent reign-eth.   Halle-

Unison.....................................   Unison.....................................

lords,.......................... And he shall reign forever, forev-er and ev - er, King of kings, and Lord of lords, King of kings, and Lord of lords, And he shall reign for

lords, Halle - lu - jah, hal-le - lu - jah, And he shall reign for-ev-er and ev - er, King of kings, and Lord of lords, King of kings, and Lord of lords, And he shall reign for

Hal-le-lu - lu - jah, hal-le - lu - jah, And he shall reign forever, forever and ev - er, King of kings, and Lord of lords, King of kings, and Lord of lords, And he shall reign for

lords, And he shall reign forever, for

ev - er and ev - er, for-ev-er and ev - er, for-ev-er and ev - er, Hal-le - lu-jah, hal-le - lu-jah, hal-le-lu - jah, hal-le - lu - jah, halle - lu-jah.

ev - er and ev - er, for-ev-er and ev - er, for-ev-er, and ev-er, Hal-le - lu-jah, hal-le - lu - jah, hal-le-lu - jah, hal-le - lu - jah, halle - lu-jah.

ev - er and ev - er, King of kings, and Lord of lords, Hal-le - lu-jah, hal-le - lu - jah, hal-le-lu - jah, hal-le - lu - jah, halle - lu jah.
ev - er and ev - er, for-ev-er and ev - er, for-ev-er, and ev - er,

VENITE EXULTEMUS DOMINO.

C. C. Hard. 1873.

O come, let us sing un-to the Lord; let us heart-i-ly re-joice in the strength of our sal-va-tion. Let us come be-fore his pres-ence

with thanksgiv-ing, and show ourselves glad in Him with psalms. For the Lord is a great God; and a great King a-bove all gods.

In his hand are all the cor-ners of the earth; and the strength of the hills is his al-so. The sea is his, and he

made it; and his hands pre-par-ed the dry land. O come, let us worship and fall down, and kneel be-fore the Lord our Maker.

For he is the Lord our God; and we are the peo-ple of his pas-ture, and the sheep, the sheep of his hand. O wor-ship the

Lord in the beau-ty of ho-li-ness; let the whole earth stand in awe of him. For he com-eth to judge the earth; and with righteous-

ness to judge the world, and the peo-ple with his truth. Glo-ry be to the Fa-ther, and to the Son, and to the Ho-ly

Ghost, As it was in the be-ginning, As it was in the be-gin-ning, is now and ev-er shall be, world without end. A-men, A-men.

Anthem. "GLORY TO GOD."

HAYDN.

Glo-ry to God in the high-est, glo-ry, Glo-ry to God! Sing praises! Glo-ry to God! sing praises! Glory be to God on high.

Glo-ry to God in the high-est, glo-ry, Glo-ry to God! Sing praises! Glo-ry to God! sing praises! Glory be to God on high.

Glo-ry, Glo-ry to God! Sing prais-es! Glo-ry be to God on high.

Glo-ry, Glo-ry to God! Sing prais-es! Glo-ry be to God on high.

Peace on earth, good will, Peace, good will to men, Peace on earth, good will to men, on earth good

Peace on earth, good will, Peace, good will to men, Peace on earth, good will to men, on earth good

Peace on earth, good will to men, good

will to men, Peace on earth, good will to men, on earth good will to

will to men, Peace on earth, good will to men, on earth good will to

will to men, Peace on earth, good will to men, good will to

BIOGRAPHICAL DEPARTMENT.

Here are given biographies of the leading teachers, composers and bookmakers of sacred music in America, now deceased, with a characteristic tune of each, from William Billings, born in 1746, the first man who published music on this continent, to I. B. Woodbury, born in 1819; also sketches of three living men, whose special labors for many years make this their proper place of record. And here can be found an account of The Star Spangled Banner, and the very best programme for an Old Folks' Concert.

MAJESTY. C. M.

BILLINGS.

The Lord de - scend - ed from a - bove, And bow'd the heav'ns most high; And un - der - neath his feet he cast The dark - ness of the sky.

On cherub and on cherubim, Full royally he rode, And on the wings of mighty winds, Came flying all abroad, And on the wings of mighty winds Came flying all abroad.

WM. BILLINGS. From "Appleton's Cyclopedia" we glean the following: "Wm. Billings was a tanner by trade, and born in Boston Oct. 7, 1746, and died there Sept. 26, 1800. He published at least six collections of tunes, mostly his own composition. His style was after the Englishmen, Tansur, Williams, Arnold, &c. He was a firm patriot, and an intimate friend of Samuel Adams, who frequently sat with him at church in the singing choir. Many of his tunes composed during the war of independence, breathe the true spirit of patriotism, and were sung and played wherever the New England troops were stationed. Billings may fairly claim the title of the first American composer, for before his time there is no record of any musical composition by any native of this country. The "Singing Master's Assistant," published in '78 was commonly known as 'Billings' best'."

Next, we copy from a genealogical book the following: "Peggy Dawes Billings was the daughter of Wm. Billings, who was distinguished in his time for singing and composition of music, musical teaching, &c. It is said of him that he was the first author of music published in this country, and that none have ever come after him who excelled him in musical genius. He was a son of Wm. Billings of Dorchester and Stoughton; grandson of Wm. Billings of Milton, and great grandson of Roger Billings of Dorchester. Wm. Billings (the author) married first, Mary Leonard of Stoughton, and second, Lucy Swan of Stoughton."

We will next copy from "Hood's History of Music in New England." "The New England Psalm Singer was published by Billings in 1770, and the music composed by him. It contains 22 pages of elementary instruction. It has also a preface and an essay on the nature and properties of musical sound, which occupy ten pages. In the body of the work are 108 pages, containing 120 tunes and several anthems. 2d, 'The Singing Master's Assistant', published in '78, 104 pages. 3d, 'Music in Miniature,' 32 pp. 4th, 'The Psalm Sing-er's Amusement,' containing a number of fuguing pieces and anthems, by Wm. Billings; printed and sold by the author at his house near the White Horse, Boston, 1781, 104 pp. 5th, 'The Suffolk Harmony,' consisting of Psalm tunes, Fugues, and Anthems, engraved and printed by J. Norman for the author, Boston, 1786, 56 pp. 6th, 'The Continental Harmony' by Wm. Billings, Boston, 1794, 199 pp."

Billings' Revolutionary Hymn, commencing "Let tyrants shake their iron rod," both words and tune composed by him in war time, and published in '78, was the result of patriotic courage as well as of genius. In the same book with the hymn are two anthems in which the author indulged most freely in daring sentiment, condemning the king, and fearlessly hitting off all opponents right and left. His promptness in patriotism gave him the lead over all the music men of his day; but aside from his patriotic ardor, no Yankee from his time to the present has surpassed him in quality of productions.

His "Anthem for Easter" is still used in the cities and country. Many of his tunes, like Jordan and Majesty, continue popular. In the fugue style, Daniel Read of Conn. equals him in "Sherburne", and so does Maxim of the District of Maine, in "Turner". Edson of N. Y. gave us Lenox, and Kimball gave us "Invitation". Holden's "Coronation", and Holyoke's "Arnheim" are splendid, "Worcester" by Wood and "Ode on Science" by Sumner are excellent, "Sutton New" by Goff, and Corinth by Blanchard are admirable, but Wm. Billings must stand chief among American composers until some one sends forth a production superior to his "Anthem for Easter". M.E.C.

MONTGOMERY. C. M.

MORGAN.

Ear- ly, my God, with-out de-lay, I haste to seek thy face, My thirst-y spir-it faints a-way, With -

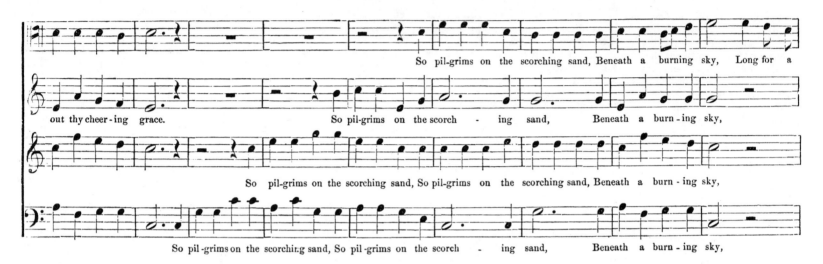

So pil-grims on the scorching sand, Beneath a burning sky, Long for a

out thy cheer-ing grace.   So pil-grims on the scorch - ing sand, Beneath a burn-ing sky,

So pil-grims on the scorching sand, So pil-grims on the scorching sand, Beneath a burn - ing sky,

So pil-grims on the scorching sand, So pil-grims on the scorch - ing sand, Beneath a burn-ing sky,

cooling stream at hand, Long for a cooling, Long for a cooling stream at hand,   Long for a cooling stream at hand, And they must drink or die.

Long for a cooling stream at hand, Long for a cooling stream at hand,

Long for a cooling stream .... at hand,   Long for a cooling stream at hand, And they must drink or die.

Long for a cooling stream at hand,

JUSTIN MORGAN was born in West Springfield, Mass. on the banks of the Connecticut, in 1747. He was a farmer's son, but took to learning and became a school-master, and was also a writing-master and a singing-master. He had two daughters of considerable attainments, whose biographies were written and published by the author of "Nutting's Grammar," of Randolph, Vt. His son Justin, who died some years since in Stockbridge, Vt., was a gentleman of fine parts and titles of honor, a fine penman and an excellent tenor singer; and his family, of which three sons and one daughter are still living, are blessed with literary taste, education and refinement; and, as were their father and grandfather, they are very superior in both music and penmanship. Thus, it appears that the senior Justin Morgan was of a family of high order, and the saying of forty years ago of those who had known him, that "he was an old school gentleman," we are prepared to believe. He moved his family from Springfield to Randolph, Vt., in 1788, when 41 years of age, and died in 1798. He was town clerk of Randolph three years. During his ten years' service as teacher in Vermont, his instructions were highly appreciated in the three departments above mentioned. He was the author of much church music, mostly of the fugue stamp, and some anthems, of which the "Judgment Anthem" is the most remarkable. Such was Mr. Morgan's musical fame that in a singing-book compiled with much taste by Andrew Adgate, President of "Uranian Academy" Philadelphia, six of his tunes were inserted, to wit: Montgomery, Huntington, Amanda, Pleasant Valley, Despair and Wethersfield. If we test his music by public opinion, Montgomery is his best tune, and one of the few tunes of this world's music having the vitality for long life.

His grave is in Randolph Centre burying ground; and as he was the man who gave name to Vermont's most famous breed of horses, "The State Agricultural Association," and the musicians of Vermont should unite in placing a monument to his memory. The late Mahlon Cottrill, formerly of the "Pavilion House," Montpelier, Vt., has said that he used to meet Mr. Morgan on "The Morgan Horse," going to his singing schools, as he (Mr. Cottrill), was driving stage from Royalton to Montpelier. A manuscript book containing much of Mr. Morgan's music by his own hand, is preserved by his descendants.

M. E. C.

LENOX. H. M.

EDSON.

Ye tribes of Adam join, With heav'n and earth and seas, And offer notes divine To your Creator's praise.

Ye holy throng of angels bright, In worlds of light Begin the song.

Ye holy throng of angels bright, In worlds of light Begin &c.

Ye holy throng of angels bright, Ye holy throng of angels bright, In worlds of light, Begin &c.

Ye holy throng of angels bright, Ye holy throng of angels bright, In worlds of light, Begin &c.

LEWIS EDSON was born in Bridgewater, Mass. Jan. 22, 1748. He was famous as a teacher, singer and composer. He was called "The great singer." Was married in 1770, and moved to New York in 1776. He was one of a large family, and resided in New York city as late as 1812. Some of his early compositions were first published in "The Chorister's Companion," a collection made by Simeon Jocelyn, in 1782. He composed a number of excellent tunes which remained popular; among them, Bridgewater and Lenox, tunes which will last as long as any of the old American compositions. They have been published in very many of the collections which have flooded the country since his day.

In regard to the time of the death of Edson we applied to an old gentleman whom we thought might know about it, and he replied as follows: "Dr Pierce of Brookline, Mass. was a man of remarkable memory, and was often consulted with respect to persons and things of the past, and especially as to the dates of births and deaths. I once applied to him concerning the birth and death of a person of whom I could nowhere obtain information, and he told me *he did not know.*

Later, the friend to whom I applied for the same dates, advised me to go to Dr Pierce, and when I told him that I had already done so, without success, he in astonishment exclaimed, ' Dr. Pierce does not know! Well, then you may be sure the man was never born anywhere, and of course never died.'" — *Moore's New Encyclopedia of Music.*

SHERBURNE. C. M.

READ.

DANIEL READ was born at Rehoboth, Conn., Nov. 2, 1757. At the age of twenty-one he removed to New Stratford, Conn., and subsequently to New Haven, where he resided till his death, Dec. 4, 1836.

He began the composition of music when only about seventeen years old, and continued the work, though a business man, as pastime or duty, to the end of life. In New Haven he was intimately associated with such men as Prof. Fitch, and the lamented Fisher. Lisbon and Windham have embalmed the memory of the good man for generations to come. GEO. HOOD.

White Lake, Sull. Co. N. Y. June 25, 1878.

P. S. Daniel Read was quite an industrious book maker; began to publish in 1785 and continued it to 1806. One of his books, "Columbian Harmonist," published in Litchfield, Conn., went through 4 editions. He was a "Singing Master" and a comb maker, and composed a good deal, and some of the *very best* of "the old Fugues" are his. There is doubt about his being the author of Windham. Zeuner says he took it from "Luther's Choral," and if you will examine *that tune* in *this book* you may agree with him. S. P. C.

CHINA. C. M.

SWAN.

1. Why do we mourn de-part-ing friends, Or shake at death's a-larms? 'Tis but the voice that Je-sus sends To call them to his arms.

2. Are we not tend-ing up-ward, too, As fast as time can move? Nor would we wish the hours more slow, To keep us from our love.

TIMOTHY SWAN, the author of "The New England Harmony," published in 1801 in Northampton, was born in Worcester, Mass., July 23, 1758. His musical talent manifested itself very early. At the age of 16 he went to Groton, Mass. where he attended singing school three weeks, which was the only instruction he ever had from any person as a teacher. Soon after this he composed several airs, when as yet he had never seen a singing book. In the same year he joined the army at Cambridge, and a British fifer showed him how to play his fife. When 17, he went to Northfield to learn the hatter's trade. Here he found an article on the science of music in an encyclopedia, which was all the work he ever read on music before publishing his books. His mode of composing was to write down on a board his strains as they came to his mind while at work. His first tune in four parts was Montague, and sung everywhere so long as minor

fugues were fashionable; and Poland, his best tune, except China, made its appearance before the author was 18. His tunes were first sung from manuscripts, and were much admired by select circles which he met for practice. Here he heard of Billings, and had such a desire to see him that he was strongly tempted to run away for the purpose. In after years he met him in Boston and had much conversation on the subject of music, so interesting to them both. His apprenticeship completed, he went into business in Suffield, Conn., and there found that his tunes had preceded him. There for 28 years he taught singing schools and composed most of his music. At the age of 25, he married Mary Gay, daughter of Rev. Ebenezer Gay, of Suffield. Herself a fine singer, their ten children, some of whom are still (1878) living, all inherited extraordinary musical gifts.

While Mr. Swan was yet a young man, Mr. Oliver Brownson, who had published a book of his own compositions, hearing of Mr. Swan, came a long distance to see him. He was surprised to find him a *young* man, and said to him, "From your reputation as a composer I supposed you to be a man well stricken in years, with a wig and cocked hat." A gentleman in N. Y., an acquaintance of Swan's, on hearing Poland sung, was delighted, and on being told the author, said at once, and with emphasis, "It was never composed by that boy." He could not understand, he said, how such music as Poland could be made by a person so young. His rule in composition was to make the air and throw as much melody into it as he was able; then, in adapting the other parts, he endeavored to give each of them a good share of melody; melody was ever a great object with him. His music of his own preference, lies in the tunes, China, Poland, Flanders, Quincy, London, Spring, Granby, Appleton and Vernon. As a singer he had great celebrity. His voice could carry any part, but was best for bass. Swan and Ely published at Suffield a small collection of songs, called the "Songster's Assistant." He lost money in his publications, but his spirits in later life were kept good by faith in his own genius and merits. In 1807 he removed to Northfield, Mass., where he resided until his death, on his birthday, July 23, 1842, aged 84 years. As a teacher in singing schools, Mr. Swan was very particular to have attention, and to give thorough instruction. The scholars had to beat time and to read the notes before singing the words. He seldom joined his own voice, but would sing alone to correct mistakes, or to improve their style, and let them try again and again. Thus he patiently labored until his school sang to suit him, and the consequence was, that on exhibition days his schools made a fine appearance. His biographer states that "his songs were sung with much applause, and the 'Shepherd's Complaint' gained much celebrity; after that, his 'Seasons', 'Solomon's Songs', &c., were much admired. * * * His fuguing music was not written in accordance with his own taste, but to adapt himself to the spirit of the times. Mr. Swan was much absorbed in literary pursuits; read much of old literature, was fond of the ancient and the distant. He was an admirer of Burns and the sweet simplicity of the Scottish dialect; the only poetry he was known to have written, was a few fugitive pieces in that language. * * * It may finally be said of him, that he was truly a man of sterling moral worth; pleasing and affable in his manners, possessing a gifted mind, well stored with the treasures of knowledge. * * * Mr. Swan was rather large personally, and well proportioned; had light hair and a complexion unusually delicate. In his latter years he had the habit of reading till a very late hour of the night, and not to rise till approaching noon. He passed his last night in this manner, and died in his bed." We would add that his China was sung at funerals for fifty years, more than any other tune in America, and that superior professors of music now living, have admired the form of its melody.

M. E. C.

SOLITUDE-NEW. C. M.

WEST.

Fly like a tim'rous, trembling dove, Fly like a tim'rous, trembling dove.............

My ref-uge is the God of love, My foes in-sult and cry,

Fly like a tim'rous, trembling dove, Fly like a

Fly like a tim'rous, trembling dove, Fly like a

Fly like a tim'rous, trembling dove................. ...... Fly like a

ELISHA WEST came from "below" to Woodstock, Vt., in 1791. He called himself a "housewright," and he farmed it to some extent; but it soon became known that he was altogether a greater musician than mechanic or farmer, and he at once by common consent and desire, became the all-controlling music-man in the vicinity; and being a thorough teacher as well as a superior singer and a man of intelligence, he commanded universal patronage; for in those days singing schools were considered indispensable to well-regulated communities.

Dec. 17, 1794, a subscription of $21.50 was raised for Mr. West's school at Woodstock, sustained by such honorable men as Charles

Marsh, Benj. Swan and Jesse Williams; which gives an idea of the expense of singing tuition at the best schools in the most aristocratic towns of Vermont in ancient times.

Mr. West made it a point to have at his bidding a sufficient number of well-trained singers to supply music for great occasions; and like other singing masters, at the close of a winter's work he had great pride in calling his schools together for a grand exhibition. Then, before it was time to work on his land, he would employ himself at his whetstone ledge at the bottom of a ditch eight or ten feet deep. One day some person happened along just in time to look down and see him straighten up and hear him say to himself, "Quite a change in my livelihood! One week ago this very hour all eyes of a vast assembly were turned on me as I stood at the head of five schools, singing like an *angel! Now*, here I am in this dismal, wet hole, *alone*, digging *whetstones* like the *devil!*" Mr. West was a composer of much music that arose into popular use throughout New England. His Mount Paron was a dignified anthem, much in vogue for many years; and many of his tunes were household airs in the early years of the present century.

About 1801, Elisha West and Benj. Billings Jr., published a collection of tunes and anthems containing many original pieces. Printed by Andrew Wright, Northampton, Mass. In Jan. 1809, the Windsor bookstore advertised for sale "*The Musical Concert*, containing the rudiments of music and a great variety of psalm tunes, together with a number of anthems suitable for churches and singing societies, many of which were never before published. By Elisha West, Philo Musico."

Mr. West's fame rests upon his first dozen years in Windsor County, soon after which his property diminished, his domestic troubles increased, and his great popularity waned, all owing to his fondness for strong drink. Another warning to musicians.

Previous to his coming to Woodstock, we know nothing of Elisha West save that on the first of Dec. 1776, he was joined in marriage to Abigail Delano of North Yarmouth, in the Province of Maine.

M. E. C.

The above facts are mostly from Henry Swan Dana, as published in the "Vermont Standard," Mar. 20, 1870.

INVITATION. C. M.

KIMBALL.

Come, my be-lov-ed, haste away, Cut short the huors of thy de-lay, Fly like a youthful hart or roe, O-ver the hills where spices grow.

Fly like a

Fly like a youthful hart or

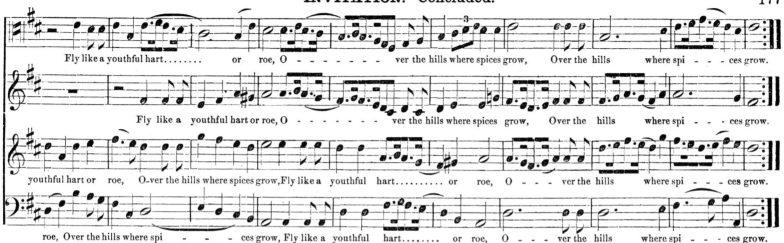

Fly like a youthful hart........ or roe, O - - - - ver the hills where spices grow, Over the hills where spi - - - ces grow.

Fly like a youthful hart or roe, O - - - - - - ver the hills where spices grow, Over the hills where spi - - - ces grow.

youthful hart or roe, O-ver the hills where spices grow, Fly like a youthful hart.......... or roe, O - - - ver the hills where spi - - - ces grow.

roe, Over the hills where spi - - - ces grow, Fly like a youthful hart........ or roe, O - - - ver the hills where spi - - - ces grow.

JACOB KIMBALL was born in Topsfield, Mass., Feb. 1761. His father, Jacob Kimball, and Moses Perkins, according to the "Topsfield Records," were, by the brethren of the church in that town, chosen in March 1764, to set the Psalms, they being appointed to sit in the Elder's seat; so it seems the father was a leading singer. Young Jacob was a graduate at Harvard College, in 1780; he studied law with Judge Wetmore, of Salem, and was admitted to the bar in Strafford County, N. H. in 1795; he was in practice at the Court of Common Pleas, at Rindge, as early as 1797, and was there in 1800: was a man of superior talents, and for many years a celebrated teacher and composer of music. He taught in many of the towns of New England with success; having a fine genius and some talent at writing poetry, as appears by his verses of the 65th Psalm, inserted in Dr. Belknap's collection. He was very popular as a school teacher, but did not remain long in New Hampshire. Among his psalm-tunes, one known as Plainfield, named for a town where he had a school, is yet sung at Old Folks' Concerts. He died in Topsfield, Mass., July 24, 1826, in the 66th year of his age. He published "The Rural Harmony," at Boston, in 1793, consisting mainly of original music. *Moore's New Encyclopedia of Music.*

JEREMIAH INGALLS was born in Andover, Mass., Mar. 1st. 1764. He lived in N. H. several years, and in 1795 moved to Newbury, Vt., where his wife's father resided as a physician. In the year 1800 he built a two story house opposite "Ingalls' Eddy," in which he "kept tavern" ten years. He was so great a devotee to music as to stop his team and sing for hours with some friend he might meet on the way, while his mechanics would be waiting for his load of lumber; and he said that oftentimes when wandering in the fields in the evening, "tunes would sing themselves into his head." He had a high voice, was expert on the "bass viol," and a ready reader of music. He was a member of the Congregational church, as well as always leader of the choir, and his Newbury singers had the honor of introducing into the sanctuary his two very best tunes, New Jerusalem and Northfield. sung from manuscript copies, though it is believed that Northfield was composed at an inn in Northfield, N. H., while the author was waiting and hungering an unusually long time for a dinner. He frequently composed both words and music for special occasions: of this sort we find in his book three pieces, to wit: "Election Hymn," "Election Ode," and "An Acrostic on Judith Brock," a funeral piece. This book of 200 pp. is entitled "The Christian Harmony," printed for the compiler by Henry Ranlet, Exeter, N. H., 1805. In his advertisement he says, "Some of the tunes are wholly, and some in part, the original compositions of the author, and others are selected from various authors, which are credited when known." It seems that not many were known, for "The True Penitent" by Billings is the only tune in his book accredited to anybody. Very likely Ingalls composed more than half of the music and much of the poetry of his book, as it contains very little to be found in previous works. Much of the old-fashioned conference meeting music is in it, and attributed to his authorship by later compilers, making him the author of many of the tunes sang forty, fifty, sixty and seventy years ago to the sweet old "Penny Royal Hymns" of those times. His "Livonia" and "Pennsylvania" were for years very popular.

Publishing his book and building his house and his continued passion for music made it necessary for him to sell out, which he did in 1810, and removed to Hancock, Vt. Here and in neighboring towns he continued teaching singing schools till he was called from earth in 1838. Notwithstanding he lived to the age of only 64, the rising aspirants for choristership were disposed to rank above him in his latter days, towards whom he showed no resentment, but modestly gave up his place; and at the dedication of Rochester meeting-house was content to play his "bass viol" in the rear.

His children were musical, and his sons could play clarinet, bassoon, flute and violin; and they would often practice for hours, the old gentleman leading the band with his bass viol. One Sunday they were having an excellent time performing anthems, and after a while the youngsters started a secular piece, the father with composure joining in; from that they went on until they found themselves furiously engaged in a boisterous march, in the midst of which the old gentleman stopped short, exclaiming, "Boys, this wont do! Put *away* these corrupt things and take your Bibles." Jeremiah Ingalls was short in stature, and corpulent. M. E. C.

NORTHFIELD. C. M.

INGALLS.

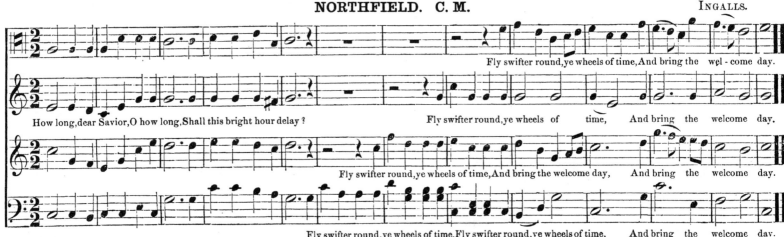

OLIVER HOLDEN of Charlestown, Mass., was born in Shirley, Mass. Sept. 18, 1765; was a carpenter and joiner by trade, who from his youth was passionately fond of music; and though in the latter years of his life he ceased to instruct and compose, he retained his love of the art; and when he ceased publishing music, there had been no American whose productions had been received with more regard or any more generally admired. His "Coronation" will live for many generations yet to sing and admire, as will his "Paradise," and many other tunes. He published "The American Harmony" in 1793, and also the "Union Harmony;" and in 1795 he was associated with Hans Gram and Samuel Holyoke, in the production of several music-books; in 1797 he was engaged by Isaiah Thomas, of Worcester, Mass., to edit and compile the "Worcester Collection," and he superintended the production of three editions of that work. He died Sept. 4, 1844.

At one time Mr. Holden opened a store in Charlestown for the sale of music and other books, having a carpenter's shop in another part of the same building. A short time before his death he wrote a beautiful hymn, and set the words to music, which was published by the family in sheet music form. *Moore's New Encyclopedia of Music.*

CORONATION. C. M.

O. HOLDEN.

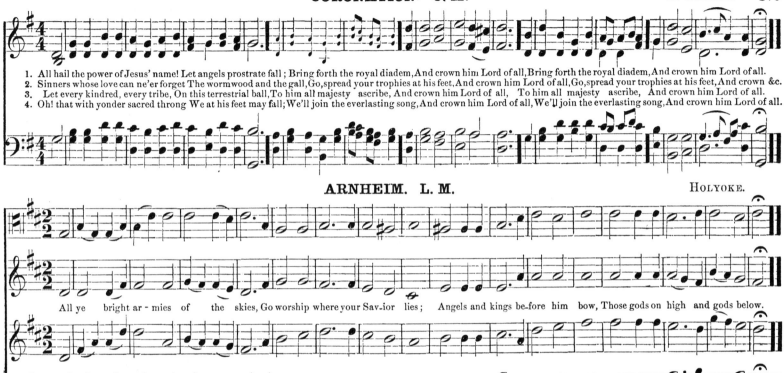

1. All hail the power of Jesus' name! Let angels prostrate fall ; Bring forth the royal diadem, And crown him Lord of all, Bring forth the royal diadem, And crown him Lord of all.
2. Sinners whose love can ne'er forget The wormwood and the gall, Go, spread your trophies at his feet, And crown him Lord of all, Go, spread your trophies at his feet, And crown &c.
3. Let every kindred, every tribe, On this terrestrial ball, To him all majesty ascribe, And crown him Lord of all, To him all majesty ascribe, And crown him Lord of all.
4. Oh! that with yonder sacred throng We at his feet may fall; We'll join the everlasting song, And crown him Lord of all, We'll join the everlasting song, And crown him Lord of all.

ARNHEIM. L. M.

HOLYOKE.

All ye bright ar - mies of the skies, Go worship where your Sav-ior lies ; Angels and kings be-fore him bow, Those gods on high and gods below.

SAMUEL HOLYOKE, A. M., son of the venerable Dr. Holyoke of Salem, Mass., was born at Boxford in 1771, soon after which, his father and family moved to Salem. In 1790, at the age of 19, living in Salem, he prepared for the press his "Harmonia Americana," a collection of sacred music in three and four parts, which made its appearance in Jan. 1791, typographically printed by Isaiah Thomas and Ebenezer T. Andrews, at Boston; 250 copies subscribed for in advance. In 1806 he published Vol. 1st., and in 1807, Vol. 2nd of his "Instrumental Assistant," quarto, 80 pp. and 104 pp. respectively. These volumes contain "Rules for learning music," and complete scales for all instruments in use, and 200 pieces for practice, arranged in parts from two to eight. Printed at Exeter, N. H. In 1809 he issued his "Columbian Repository of Sacred Harmony," the most extensive collection of sacred music ever published in this country. It is a third wider and considerably longer than ordinary singing-books, contains 495 pp. and 750 pieces of music, from 115 sources, and 320 of its tunes were never before published. This mammoth repository has a tune set to every one of Dr. Watts' psalms and hymns, each psalm or hymn printed on the page with its tune. The book also includes a "Supplement" of tunes adapted to the metres in "Tate and Brady's," and Dr. Belknap's "Psalms and Hymns." Published by subscription ; price per copy, $3.00. Printed by Henry

Ranlet, Exeter, N. H. Mr. Holyoke was concerned in the publication of the "Massachusetts Compiler," with Mr. Oliver Holden of Charlestown, Mass., and at the time of his death was preparing a third collection of instrumental music.

Samuel Holyoke possessed superlative gifts. It was a rare boy, who, at the age of fourteen, from the inspiration of the hymn "All ye bright armies of the skies," originated the tune "Arnheim," a majestic melody worthy of any author in his best days, of any nation, at any period of the world. His genius and learning commanded universal admiration; and had he reasonably spiced his books with the class of tunes which took the popular ear of his time, instead of rejecting and ridiculing them, he might not have died poor. Even as early as 1791, in the preface of his first book, speaking of fugues by other compilers, he says, in closing his criticism, "the parts falling in one after another, each conveying a different idea, confound the sense, and render the performance a mere jargon of words." Mr. Holyoke undoubtedly surpassed his American contemporaries in depth of science and breadth of practice. He composed and taught in various departments of vocal and instrumental music. He was author of marches and leader of bands. As a teacher of church music he was of the best. His voice for many years was remarkably good; and when it became defective, he used the clarinet in his vocal classes. His "Columbian Repository of Sacred Harmony" would pass now for a magnificent "Hymn and Tune Book;" and if it was financially a failure, the principal cause of its being so, made it of great use in the long run, by way of advancing musical taste, and as a *literal repository* to help supply subsequent compilations. In the spring of 1816, soon after the close of his winter's teaching in Concord, N. H., there was a social gathering of Mr. Holyoke's musical friends at the house of Jacob B. Moore, Esq. At the close of the musical exercises, he requested the choir present to sing "Arnheim," remarking that perhaps he would never meet with a choir on earth so well qualified to do justice to his first composition. It was twice sung, and Mr. Holyoke was affected to tears. He never sang again. Five days from that evening he died of lung fever at Lang's Tavern, East Concord, aged 45. M. E. C.

Mostly from Moore's Encyclopedia of Music.

TILDEN. L. M.

BARTHOLOMEW BROWN. A. B. 1802.

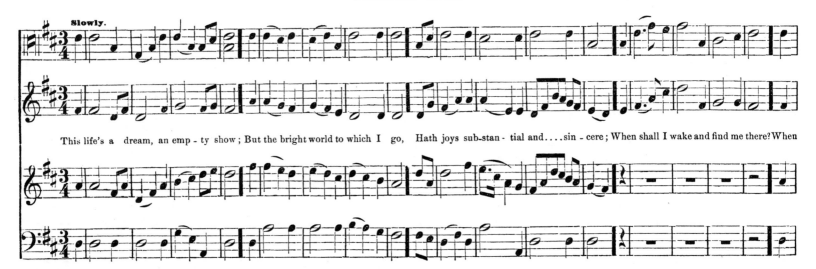

This life's a dream, an emp - ty show; But the bright world to which I go, Hath joys sub-stan - tial and....sin - cere; When shall I wake and find me there? When

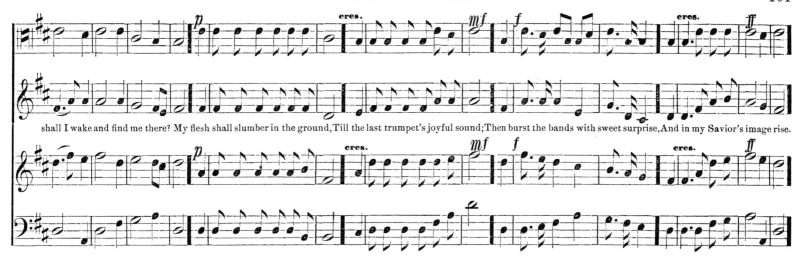

shall I wake and find me there? My flesh shall slumber in the ground, Till the last trumpet's joyful sound; Then burst the bands with sweet surprise, And in my Savior's image rise.

BARTHOLOMEW BROWN, A. B., was born in Sterling, Mass., Sept. 8, 1772, and in 1813 resided in Abington, where he was a teacher of music of great and growing reputation; so great was his skill in the art that he was employed by Judge Nahum Mitchell to assist in the compilation of the "Bridgewater Collection" of church music, in which appeared many pieces of his composition. This collection of music was highly esteemed and very much used in all New England for more than twenty years, passing through many editions. Mr. Brown became a very prominent teacher and composer, and for some years resided in Boston, and died there, April 14, 1854, aged 82. *Moore's New Encyclopedia of Music.*

GROTON. L. M.

SANGER.

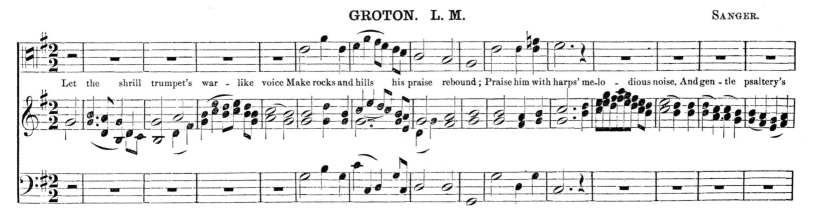

Let the shrill trumpet's war - like voice Make rocks and hills his praise rebound; Praise him with harps' me-lo - dious noise, And gen - tle psaltery's

silver sound ; Let virgin troops soft tim - brels bring, And sons with grace - ful motions dance ; Let instruments with various strings, With organs joined, his praise advance.

ZEDEKIAH SANGER was born in 1771, and resided in Boston, Mass., where he was known as a singer, teacher and composer. In 1808, he published a collection of music under the title of "The Meridian Harmony ;" it was printed by H. Mann, at Dedham, Mass., for the author, and contained 112 pages. Janes, Belknap, Ellis and Jenks contributed original music; and several of the tunes contained in the book were by the compiler himself. The music shows about the same amount of musical proficiency as is noticeable in the compositions of his contemporaries. The fugue style predominates, although there are several tunes in the book of a graver character, and not without considerable merit. Mr. Sanger died in August, 1821, aged 50.

Moore's New Encyclopedia of Music.

DETROIT. P. M.

JENKS. 1800.

Come, thou Fount of ev - ery blessing, Tune my heart to sing thy grace ; Streams of mer - cy ne - ver ceas-ing, Call for songs of loud - est praise. praise.

STEPHEN JENKS was born in Ellington, Tolland County, Conn., in 1772, and was one of the most prolific writers, publishers and teach-ers of his time. In 1800 he published his first work, the " New England Harmony," at Ridgefield, Conn. In 1805, he published the " Delights of Harmony, or The Norfolk Compiler." In 1808, ap-peared "The Hartford Collection," published at Northampton, Mass ; and his last book, " The Harmony of Zion," was published at Ded-ham, Mass., in 1818. He loved his profession, and did all he could to advance its interests. A great many anecdotes might be related in regard to Jenks. We give one: at the time he was about publishing his " Norfolk Compiler," he went about among his scholars and ac-quaintances, soliciting subscribers. One day he applied to a rich and miserly old farmer by the name of *Selleck*, desiring him to subscribe. The old fellow, not having anything like as much music in his soul as cash in his pocket, promptly refused to contribute a cent, and at the same time made some crushing remarks that chilled, for the time, the musician's ardor in his enterprise. Jenks at once left in disgust, and went home to his room, where he composed music to the words:

" Some walk in honor's gaudy show,
Some dig for golden ore ;
They build *for heirs, they know not who,*
And straight are seen no more."

The tune he named *Selleck* and whenever he saw the old farmer at church, or at a social gathering. he would have it sung. Finally the tune made such an impression on the mind of the farmer. that he contributed handsomely towards the book, and ever after, was more liberal on all occasions. Stephen Jenks was twice married. By his first wife he had two sons. Her maiden name was Hannah Dauchy. She died at Ridgefield, Conn., August 11, 1800, aged 28 years. He married his second wife in Providence, R. I. By her he had two sons and four daughters, and moved with them, in 1829, to Thompson, Geauga County, Ohio, where he died, June 5, 1856, aged 84 years.

TURNER. C. M.

MAXIM.

ABRAHAM MAXIM. From a recent letter from Mr. John Maxim of South Carver, Mass., the youngest brother to the subject of this biography, and an old letter of his brother's which he sent with his own, dated "Turner, Dec. 20, 1815," I gather the following facts and conclusions : Abraham Maxim was born in Carver, Mass., Jan. 3, 1773. From early youth he was noted for love of singing, and uncommon attachment to music. "His heart and mind were so absorbed in it that he was of little use on the farm." He began his composing early, and when thus engaged knew nothing else, and "would be as likely to take a basket to bring water from the well, as a pail."

Maxim had a bright, active mind, and at music parties would "interest the company by singing, playing the bass viol, doing a sum in the rule of three, and telling what the company was talking about, all at the same time." "He studied music a while with William Billings, in Boston." Turner, Buckfield and other good tunes he composed in Carver. After he became of age he removed to Turner, Maine, where he married "and raised a large family of singing children." There and all about there he taught "reading schools and singing schools," and compiled books. He published his "Northern Harmony" in 1803, which went through several editions. From Turner he removed to Palmyra, Me., Dec. 1827, where he lived several years, farming and teaching, and where he died suddenly of apoplexy one evening "just after leaving his singing school, at the age of fifty-six." Mr. Maxim appears to have been a very cheerful, happy man, with a natural taste for literature, and if he had left us *only* "Old Turner," his pleasing name-must pass along from generation to generation as the name of a man of rare musical thought. S. P. C. 1878.

SOUNDING TRUMPET. L. M.

JOEL HARMON, JR.

Let the seventh an - gel sound on high ; Let shouts be heard through all the sky; Kings of the earth with glad accord, Give up your king - doms to the Lord.

JOEL HARMON, JR. was born at Suffield, Conn., May 17, 1773; was a teacher of music all his life. He settled at Pawlet, Vt., in 1808, and published in Mass. a collection of music that year, which was sold only in Vermont and New York, for his schools, at 75 cents a copy. The music was mostly original. Later, while residing at Geneva, N.Y., he published other editions of this work. In 1809, he published at Northampton, Mass., "The Columbian Sacred Minstrel," 80 pages with 53 tunes and anthems, all original; and this was the earliest publication by any one then living in Vt. It was published for subscribers. Mr. Harmon held the office of Major in the war of 1812. He published one collection of music at Harrisburg, Penn., and was preparing another book when he died at York, Penn., March 17, 1833, aged 60 years. When in Pawlet he was one of the earliest merchants of the town, and married his wife in that place. He was accounted a good musician, and it is reported that in his schools he used his own compositions exclusively. *Moore's New Encyclopedia of Music.*

1. A-way, my un-be-liev-ing fear! Fear shall in me no more have place; My Sa - vior doth not yet ap-pear, He hides.......... the brightness of his face;

2. Although the vine its fruit de - ny, Although the olive yield no oil, The with - 'ring fig-trees droop and die, The fields.......... e - lude the til - ler's toil, —

But shall I therefore let him go, And basely to the tempter yield? No, in the strength of Je - sus, no, I never will give up my shield, I never will give up my shield.

The empty stall no herd afford, And perish all the bleating race, Yet will I tri - umph in the Lord, The God of my salvation praise, The God of my sal - va - tion praise.

WALTER JANES was born at Ashford, Conn., Feb. 27, 1779, and became well known as a teacher and composer of music, and also as a poet, though he was a mason by trade. In 1807, he published at Dedham, Mass., the "Harmonic Minstrelsy," a collection of sacred music in three and four parts, 104 pages. He taught many singing schools, and was the leader of the music at the ceremony of laying the corner-stone of the famous Bunker Hill monument, in Charlestown, Mass., in 1825; this being about his last appearance as a conductor of music. He died July 24, 1827, aged 48.

Moore's New Encyclopedia of Music.

GENEVA. C. M.

JOHN COLE.

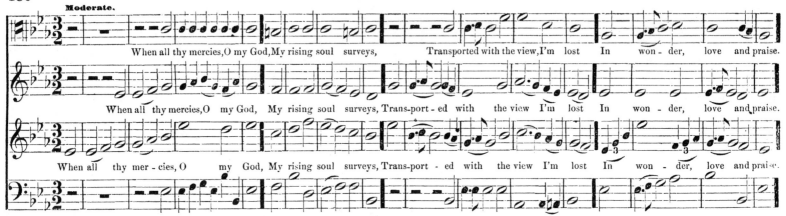

When all thy mercies, O my God, My rising soul surveys,   Transported with the view, I'm lost   In   won - der,   love   and praise.

When all thy mercies, O my God, My rising soul surveys, Trans-port-ed with   the view   I'm   lost   In   won - der,   love   and praise.

When all   thy mer - cies, O   my God, My rising soul surveys, Trans-port - ed   with   the view I'm lost   In   won - der,   love   and praise.

When all thy mercies, O my God, My rising soul surveys,   Transported with the view, I'm lost   In   won - der,   love   and praise.

JOHN COLE of Baltimore, Maryland, was a compiler, teacher, bandmaster and composer of music; his band was, in the war of 1812, one of much popularity; and in that year he published a collection of celebrated songs, set to music, entitled "The Minstrel;" it was a 12mo. of 316 pages, and contained a great variety of English, Scotch and Irish airs. He also published in 1827, "The Seraph," containing 230 pieces of music: and very soon afterwards the "Beauties of Psalmo-dy," containing ninety pieces of music. Of this last work he issued as many as three editions; and a new edition of the Seraph was published in 1846. *Moore's New Encyclopedia of Music.*

P. S. John Cole was born in Tewksbury, Eng., about 1774; came to America in 1785. "Was a voluminous writer, and published nine or ten books of psalmody and anthems," and died in Baltimore on the 17th of August, 1855. So writes H. P. Main, Esq.   S. P. C.

EXHORTATION. L. M.

DOOLITTLE.

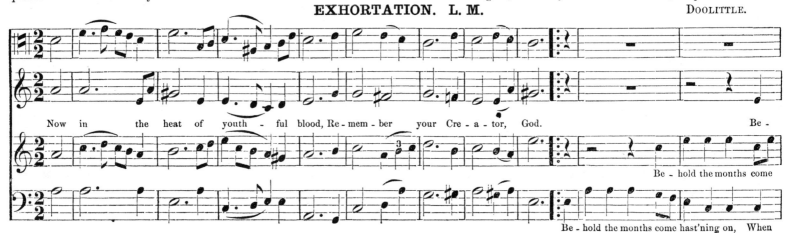

Now   in   the   heat   of   youth - ful   blood, Re - mem - ber   your Cre - a - tor,   God.   Be -

Be - hold the months come

Be - hold the months come hast'ning on,   When

Be - hold the months come hast'ning on, When you shall say, my joys are gone,........ When you shall say, my joys are gone.

- hold the months come hast'ning on, When you shall say, my joys are gone,............... When you shall say, my joys are gone.

hast'ning on, When you shall say, my joys are gone, Be - hold the months come hast'ning on, When you shall say, my joys are gone.

you shall say, my joys are gone, Be - hold the months come hast 'ning on,

ELIAKIM DOOLITTLE was born in Cheshire, New Haven Co. Conn., on the 28th of August, 1780, so his children now living believe. His father was a farmer, and had a large family. This son never worked on the farm much, as he was altogether for books. He was a hard student in his boyhood, and was not more than 20 or 21 when he graduated at Yale College. He was there with John C. Calhoun; and his daughter, Mrs. Martha Smith of Poultney, Vt., who often heard her father refer to the circumstance, thinks he was a *class-mate*. So she informed me in July, 1878. After graduating, he commenced teaching in his native state. He taught both common schools and singing schools, and excelled in both. He removed from Conn. to Hampton, N. Y., a state-border town, opposite to Poultney, Vt., in 1802, possibly a year or two later. There, in Hampton and Poultney, and in the surrounding towns all about, on either side of "the line," he taught day and singing schools. He was very popular, and is still remembered by the old people as the most remarkable singer and leader of his time. He left the *general impression* that he was a man, not only of wonderful musical capacities, but that he was *a genius*. He made music a special study in New Haven; where, in 1806, he had published his "Psalm Singers' Companion," 49 pages, containing 41 tunes and an anthem, all of which he composed. In a few years after this he began to be insane, but continued his teaching for some years. He never recovered, however, but led a wandering, visiting life, round through the old towns where he had taught, the rest of his days, " nearly 40 years."

In 1811, he was married to Miss Fuller of Hampton, and they had six children, one son and five daughters. The son and three daughters still survive him, and *none* of them have ever been insane. Various causes have been assigned for Mr. Doolittle's insanity. He may have inherited a tendency to it, though I have learned of none of his ancestors who were insane; but his twin brothers *died insane*, and, "strange to relate," as nearly as could be ascertained, at precisely the same hour, one being in Hampton, N. Y., and the other in Connecticut. From all the evidence I can gather, it seems plain that the insanity was the direct result of a continued over-taxing of the mind. Even in childhood he was a hard student, and he never ceased to be so. Before he left Connecticut he had insane attacks. He was teaching day and night, composing and publishing a book, and wherever he was, it was always his habit to read and study after other people were asleep, and often far *into the morning hours*.

Mr. Doolittle was a religious man, a member of the Congregational church, and in those midnight studies the Bible was oftener his text-book, than any other. He had a very severe illness, which seemed to hasten his calamity. Among the first indications of Mr. Doolittle's insanity in Hampton, was the manner in which he closed his school one afternoon. The last exercise was the spelling by a large class, at the close of which, he formed them into a circle, and then said, "You are now all at the head, and you may so inform your parents when you go home. That is the way with the world; we are all moving in a circle, and each one may consider himself at the head."

His "Psalm Singers' Companion" was a popular singing book in its day, and his tune, Exhortation, L. M., which accompanies this biography, is among the still popular "old fugues," and the words are wonderfully prophetic of his own case. It was *his favorite*. In his "General Directions for Learners," may be found the following: "The bass must be grave and solemn, the tenor harmonious and sedate; the counter soft and sublime, the treble brilliant and seraphic; thus proceeding, the voices will unite and blend in every part, (like the beautiful colors in the rainbow,) and make complete harmony."

Mr. Doolittle was something of a poet. He wrote and composed songs and sung them. In "The Poultney Journal" of May, 1874, I find among other things concerning the subject of this biography, the following: "In 1835 he wrote a poem upon the death of Joseph Marshall, which appeared in the history of the Marshall family, in our first number. It is in the old style of penmanship, but we never saw the penmanship excelled." During all the long years of his insanity, he would, at times, join with others in singing, with delight, and he would converse for hours at a time, especially upon the subject of religion, in a most interesting and rational manner. It was common for him to steal into church and listen attentively to the preaching and singing; but if the latter was discordant, he would rush out, uttering furious words of condemnation. He liked to attend interesting courts and watch the testimony; after which he would give his decisions and make his sarcastic remarks, which were not surpassed for justice and keenness by judges or lawyers. His *wit* never failed him, no matter what the emergency. A rude girl once threw from a chamber window, a bucket of cold water upon him. He made a tremendous bound, and then looked up to the window with a terrifying countenance and exclaimed with a loud voice, "Baptised from above, without *faith*, *works* or *repentance*; where in h—ll did you get your authority?" There was a certain miller whom "Uncle Kim," as Mr. Doolittle was generally called by every body after he became insane, very well knew, and knew, too, that he was said to "take too much toll." Uncle Kim was not very well treated by the miller, which caused him to paraphrase the familiar psalm of Dr. Watts, beginning with,—

> "Teach me the measure of my days,
> Thou Maker of my frame,"

in such a manner as to fit the miller's case rather closely. One day at the mill, the miller, in a very rough and disagreeable manner, ordered Uncle Kim to "leave." Uncle Kim "stood his ground," and in a very deliberate manner, repeated to the miller his new form of the psalm, as follows:—

> Teach me the measure of my *grist*,
>   Thou maker of my meal;
> I would survey what I have **missed**,
>   And learn how millers deal.
>
> See the vile miller lift the pole;
>   The mill begins to crawl;
> He keeps the grist, sends home the toll,
>   And tells the boy, "*that's all!*"
>
> What can I look or wait for, then,
>   From millers, meal and dust,
> Who take *my* portion of the grain,
>   And disappoint my trust?
>
> Such millers now I will forsake,
>   My empty bags recall,
> And give my custom to such men
>   As send me home *my all*.

(Read the Psalm and you will "see the points.")

On one occasion he called at a house where he was well known, and a company of ladies was visiting. Uncle Kim's strange appearance disturbed them. The woman of the house assured them he was perfectly harmless, was never known to commit any improper act, and in an undertone remarked, "poor man, he has lost his senses;" but Uncle Kim heard it and replied in a very pitiful manner, "ladies, this poor woman has not lost *her* senses; she never had any to lose."

A young man was talking with him one day about studying law, and said to him, "Uncle Kim, do you think I could get a living without hoeing corn?" "Well, I don't know," said Uncle Kim, "you have some brains, but you are not *made up just right*; I guess you better keep your hoe."

In 1848, when the R. & W. R. R. was being surveyed up through Poultney, Uncle Kim in his wanderings came upon a surveyor who was just then using a transit, an instrument through which one can look equally well in opposite directions. Uncle Kim watched the man and saw him squint north and then south without moving the instrument, and passed on without a word. Soon he came upon Deacon Joseph Joslin, an acquaintance, who was also surveying; he asked Uncle Kim if he saw the other surveyors as he came along. "Your surveyors," said he, "I saw some chaps back here looking through the devil's spectacles, trying to find the way to heaven. Good Lord! Your name is Joseph!"—and on he went.

But at last, in April, 1852, the "wanderings," both of the mind and body of this man of sorrows came to a close in the "county house" at Argyle, N. Y., and he went home, "where the wicked cease from troubling and the weary are at rest." There he "changed worlds" without one soul to care for his, except the blessed who were waiting for him "*there*," "on the other shore," thank God, without a kind hand to press his aching, shattered but noble head, this great and good man, this Christian, this great singer and teacher, this composer and poet, this genius, who had done so much for so many, *died of neglect!* May God forgive every-body, for I can't.

For the foregoing facts I am indebted to the Hon. James R. Doolittle, U. S. Ex-Senator from Wisconsin, for a very interesting letter about the subject of this biography, who was great uncle to the sen-

ator; to Silas Doolittle, son of Eliakim, for another, and to Mrs. Smith, daughter of Eliakim, already referred to, and *her* daughter, Mrs. Ann E. Morris, for a most interesting hour's conversation concerning their father and grandfather, of whose great and good heart they spoke with glowing zeal, and for whose memory they manifested a most tender and affectionate regard. God bless them and every one who gave Eliakim Doolittle "bread," or "a cup of cold water."

S. P. C. Aug. 1878

ORTONVILLE. C. M.
DR. THOMAS HASTINGS.

Ma-jes-tic sweetness sits enthron'd Up-on the Savior's brow; His head with radiant glories crown'd, His lips with grace o'er-flow.

THOMAS HASTINGS, Mus. Doc., was born in Washington, Litchfield Co., Conn., Oct. 15, 1784. His father was Dr. Seth Hastings, a farmer and physician. His mother was "a woman of *uncommon ability* and piety." In 1796 the family removed to Clinton, N. Y., in the winter, "upon sleighs and ox-sleds." The country was new, "and the Indian still lingered in the neighborhood." There young Thomas began a new life, and had the experiences incident to making a home in a new country. But he had a love for book knowledge, and a special love for music, and "early commenced the study of music with a sixpenny gamut of four diminutive pages." The schools were of little worth, and for two winters he attended the Academy, which made him a walk of six miles each day. "In the winter of 1806—7, he began what was to be his life work, at Bridgewater in Oneida, and Brookfield in Herkimer." There he taught his first *singing schools;* but he managed his father's farm four years after that.

In 1816 he commenced the work of compiling music for a county musical society. "This was the origin of that famous old collection, the "Musica Sacra," which consisted at first of two numbers of pamphlet size, afterwards enlarged to a considerable volume, subsequently united with the *Springfield* Collection, edited by Col. Warriner, which passed through many editions." His business of teaching increased, and his fame went abroad. In the winter of 1817—18, he had "nine schools," and at about the time of their closing, he was "very unex-

pectedly" invited to Troy. He went, and "in his first lecture won the confidence of the people." He was soon a successful teacher and leader there. From Troy he went to Albany, and was chorister for Dr. Chester. There, in 1822, he published "A Dissertation on Musical Taste," and took the ground that "Religion has substantially the same claim in song as in speech. Praise and prayer, therefore, though circumstantially different, are the same in spirituality. Neither the one nor the other admit of representative worship. *Personated* devotion is appropriate only in the drama. Even there, as in concerts and musical conventions, it is continually exposed to abuse."

In 1823, Mr. Hastings removed to Utica, to become the editor of a new religious paper, the first number of which was issued in Jan. 1824. Before he went to Utica, he was married in Buffalo, N. Y., Sept. 15, 1822, to Miss Mary Seymour. "His editorial labors extended to the ninth volume of the *Recorder,* and during them all he never lost sight of the interests of religious music. His articles were widely copied, and he was invited to lecture on the subject in Brooklyn, and before the students in the Theological Seminary at Princeton." He also addressed the General Assembly of the Presbyterian church in Philadelphia, and with marked effect in each instance. Thus Mr. Hastings, when a young man, broke new ground, and proved himself to be a strong, original thinking and acting man,—*a Pioneer.*

In 1832, Mr. Hastings received an urgent invitation to take up his abode in New York city, where "twelve churches" were ready to sustain him in a work of reform in the music of their churches. *That was a loud call,* and he answered it. He went to the great city, looked the ground over, conferred with the clergy, talked and lectured. One Sunday evening, Broome St. church, Dr. Patton, pastor, was thronged to hear him. He spoke with power, as one having authority, of the prevailing abuses in psalmody; of the necessity of a radical reform in the manner of its performance. He himself said of his lecture, "I could but feel at the time that I was divinely assisted, and spoke with ease and comfort; and as I turned to resume my seat, Dr. Patton whispered, *" You have got to come here ; the case is decided."*

Mr. Hastings disposed of his interest in the "Recorder," at Utica, and in November went to live in New York. He went from church to church, attending their meetings and studying their wants. He taught them that "music as an *art* might be pursued in the parlor, but music which was to set forth with energy and pathos the solemn utterances of praise, required specific Christian training. If Christians sought the gratification of *taste merely*, they had ready access to the *concert* and *oratorio ;* but applying music to the language of their devotions was an entirely different matter, requiring personal exertions and sacrifices. Psalmody, therefore, was to be placed on the same basis with other religious enterprises." New choirs were formed and drilled. "Two or three churches were combined in each evening's labors." Afternoons, at one central place, were devoted to instruction in the rudiments of notation. These were open to all, and thousands attended. The plan seemed successful. The meetings afternoon and evening were well attended." Mr. Hastings found the poetry of the churches needed reform as well as the music; and in 1836 compiled and published a hymn book, the "Christian Psalmist." In the following year he published a singing book, the "Manhattan Collection." Meanwhile his work of instruction went on in private and in public classes. In 1840, he published The Sacred Lyre. In 1844, Mr. Wm. B. Bradbury joined him in publishing the Psalmodist; in 1847, The Choralist ; in 1849, The Mendelssohn Collection ; and in 1851, The Psalmista. He also edited a new edition of his Dissertation on Musical Taste, and published his History of Forty Choirs, and a Sunday School Hymn and Tune Book. In 1856, he published "Selah," which he regarded as his best collection of the kind. In 1858, in connection with his son, the Rev. Dr. Hastings, he brought out the Church Melodies. Mr. Hastings published various other minor works: Indian Melodies, Sacred Songs, Songs of Zion, Presbyterian Psalmodist, Juvenile Psalmodist, Spiritual Songs, Nursery Songs, A Collection of Hymns for Mothers' Meetings. A volume of Original Hymns, and a

little volume of Essays on Prayer. His contributions to the newspaper and periodical press through all these years were almost without intermission ; and among his papers was found an unfinished article for The Evangelist, upon which he was engaged a few days before his death, which occurred May 15, 1872.

This brief biography is taken from a pamphlet prepared for private distribution by Anson D. F. Randolph, and sent me by Rev. Dr. Hastings of New York. From this authority I make the closing quotation. "Childlike as he was in spirit, there was, nevertheless, in and about him, a personal force, a depth of feeling, a clearness of conviction, a rigidity of purpose, a manly piety, and all so united, so tempered and refined, that few could resist his influence. No one unfamiliar with his manner of life, could form a conception of his *industry and steadfast application.* With his imperfect eyesight, it seems a marvel that he accomplished so much with eye and hand. There lies before me now a clean, clear MS., a part of the revised, completed copy of his 600 original hymns, with his name and the date inscribed on the cover, Thomas Hastings, May 2, 1872, thirteen days before his death. To the last he retained the free use of his faculties, his habits of study and of work, and a lively interest in the public affairs of the church and the world. A few days of illness, in which he suffered little bodily pain, closed his long and well-spent life, in the 88th year of his age. He was not, for God took him." S. P. C.

NATHANIEL DUREN GOULD, teacher, composer and publisher, was born in Chelmsford, Mass., 1789. [Hitchcock says 1781; and H. P. Main of New York, says his name was Nathaniel Dater.] His elder brother, Elnathan Duren, was born in Chelmsford, 1784, and was well known, after 1812, as a vocalist and teacher in New England ; he excelled as a vocalist, and was one of the fathers of church music among us ; he died at Bangor, Maine, 1859, aged 75. Nathaniel Duren had his name changed to GOULD, (Nathaniel D. Gould,) to secure the estate of an uncle, in 1806 ; the property being willed to him, provided he adopted the name GOULD, which he lawfully did. Deacon Gould, as he was generally called, though he was a teacher of "Gould's System of Penmanship," was, later in life, more known as a teacher of music. He resided in Boston, but taught in all New England ; and in his "Church Music in America," he says: "It may savor somewhat of egotism, but will be gratifying to those who have been members of my schools, numbering not less than *fifty thousand*, to furnish a list of them ;" which he does, from 1799 down to 1843. Deacon Gould also states that he "has presided over *nineteen* regularly organized singing societies. In addition to his duties as a teacher, he published in 1823,

"The Social Harmony," in 1832, the "National Church Harmony," in 1840, the "Sacred Minstrel," in 1844, the "Companion for the Psalmist," in 1853, "Church Music in America," and some other works. He died in Boston in 1864, aged 75 ; or, if Hitchcock is correct as to his birth, aged 83. *Moore's New Encyclopedia of Music.*

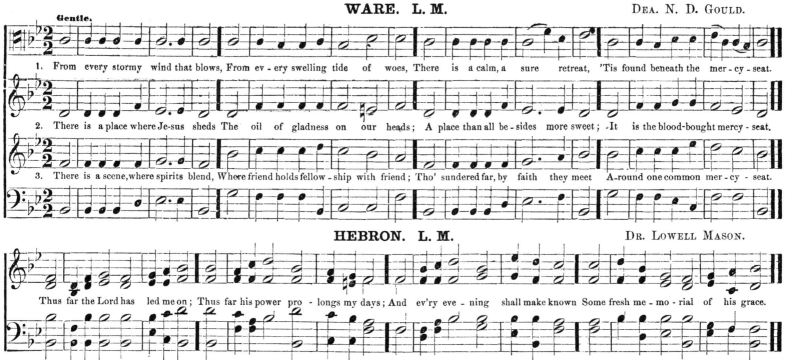

WARE. L. M. — DEA. N. D. GOULD.

Gentle.

1. From every stormy wind that blows, From ev-ery swelling tide of woes, There is a calm, a sure retreat, 'Tis found beneath the mer-cy-seat.

2. There is a place where Je-sus sheds The oil of gladness on our heads; A place than all be-sides more sweet; It is the blood-bought mercy-seat.

3. There is a scene, where spirits blend, Where friend holds fellow-ship with friend; Tho' sundered far, by faith they meet A-round one common mer-cy-seat.

HEBRON. L. M. — DR. LOWELL MASON.

Thus far the Lord has led me on; Thus far his power pro-longs my days; And ev'ry eve-ning shall make known Some fresh me-mo-rial of his grace.

DR. LOWELL MASON was born in Medford, Mass., Jan. 8, 1792. He never attended any school but the common school. In boyhood he began his work in music, which lasted almost to the day of his death, which was the Sabbath day of Aug. 11, 1872. When but a boy he taught and "led the choir." His first composition was an anthem "for the dedication of a church in a neighboring town," when he was 16 or 17 years old. "About this time he taught a class for musical instruments in Athol." When he was "21" he went to live in Savannah, Georgia. There he taught singing and led the choir in "the most important church in that city." There he found a *good teacher in harmony*, and there composed the "Missionary Hymn," and compiled his first singing-book, which was published by the Handel and Haydn Society of Boston. The book was compiled "from the best masters" and was the beginning of a long series of books, edited and published in the same way, which wrought a great change in the psalm singing of New England, by which Mr. Mason made some money, and established his reputation as the leading man in the sacred music of this country.

It is not to be overlooked, however, that Holyoke and others had preceded Mr. Mason in the reformation, and Mr. Hastings was doing a grand work in the State of New York a few years in advance of him. Mr. Mason was teller in a bank in Savannah eight years, and five years in a bank in Boston, after his return. These thirteen years in banks may have given him important hints on the power and uses of money, which he so well understood.

In 1827, when he was 35 years old, he finally removed to Boston to make it his home on the invitation of a large committee consisting of different denominations of Christians, to take a general charge of music in the churches there. How similar to Mr. Hastings' invitation to New York by "twelve churches."

Mr. Mason entered at once upon the great work assigned him. He taught singing-classes and built up choirs and led them six months each; beginning with Dr. Beecher's on Hanover street, then at Essex street, and next at Park street church. But this did not suit him, though it was the plan of "the committee," and he located with Dr. Beecher's new church on Bowdoin street, where he had a wonderful choir for many years. At an early day Mr. Mason, through great difficulties, introduced singing into the public schools of Boston, a *grand achievement.*

In 1830, George James Webb, a well-educated musician and highly cultured English gentleman, came to Boston to make it his home. Mr. Mason soon found him out, and a business union was the result. "Mason and Webb" did *great service* to the cause of vocal music in America. Mr. Webb was first in musical knowledge, while Mr. Mason knew more of the wants of the country, and how to supply them. Through the influence of these men the Boston Academy of Music came into being. Mr. Mason having resigned the office of President of the Handel and Haydn Society, "Mason and Webb" were the professors of the new institution. In 1834, eleven gentlemen and one lady (Edna Lunt) assembled at the rooms of the Boston Academy of Music, in the old Federal street Theatre, which had been leased by that institution for a term of years, in accordance with a call by the professors for a course of lectures on the Pestalozzian method of teaching singing. This was the beginning of the famous "teachers' class" or National Musical Convention, which met annually from that time (1837 excepted, when Mr. Mason was in Europe) with increased interest and members to 1849, when there were *one thousand members.* There "Mason and Webb" did good and lasting work as teachers and counsellors. They shone as great lights to us country teachers. Those were *great days* and *great choruses,* and it is no wonder that "father Mason" in his last years, in his quiet "Silver Spring" home in New Jersey, could close his dimmed eyes and "hear them over again, often," as he wrote he did.

In December 1851 he went a second time to Europe, and was absent sixteen months. On his return he went to New York city; but in two years from that time he was settled for the remainder of his life in Orange, N. J., where he died "with his children and his children's children around him."

Mr. Mason edited sixty or more different books, and millions of them have been spread over his own country and foreign lands. Wherever a Christian missionary has been, there his tunes have been sung. They have been much criticised as not being *original.* But *pure originality* in any thing is very rarely met with; especially so is it with music and poetry. In Solomon's day there was "nothing new." It is certain that "Missionary Hymn," "Ariel," "Naomi," "Hebron," "Mt. Vernon" would never have been, and *many other excellent tunes,* had not Lowell Mason lived.

He was not known as a singer; but at a musical convention in Salem, N. Y., when he called their attention to the page on which was "Comin' through the Rye," he said "now we must all turn right into little Scotch girls," and *walked* and *sang* a verse of that song in a more natural and pleasing manner than I had then ever before or have ever since heard it sung.

And he was a good accompanist for his classes and choirs. At a convention in Lebanon, N. H., being requested to do so, he gave such information as he could of the author of each tune as he turned to it. It was there he related Mr. Zeuner's account of the origin of his "Missionary Chant" (See Zeuner's biography). When Mr. Mason turned to one of his own tunes he looked very sober and said, "this is an old-fashioned man, now away behind the times." After a pause he added in a touching manner, "he lives in New Jersey, but his *home* is in Boston."

He was a good leader and a great *elementary teacher.* He had no equal before "the black-board," and he thought teaching a great profession. I find these words in one of his letters, "You can do more good in elementary teaching than in any other way. So can I." Horace Mann said he never saw a man who could give as much instruction in an hour as Lowell Mason. He was ever a student as well as a teacher. In 1865 Mr. Mason wrote as follows: "I positively think I have learned as much since I was 46 as all I knew before." He was a shrewd business man, systematic and well prepared for whatever he undertook. A man of sound sense and strong will, he generally "carried his points." Mr. Mason was a man of remarkable looks. While travelling in Europe in 1837 it was often said he resembled Beethoven. He was a short and erect man, and slightly corpulent. Mr. Mason loved children and young people. He was orthodox in theory, and decidedly a religious man. Nearly a score of his letters are before me, and there is scarcely one which does not contain religious sentiments and exhortation to Christian life. He was for several years and up to the time of his death, deacon in the church at Orange. Mr. Mason was made Doctor of Music in 1855. by the University of New York. Dr. Ferris, president, in conferring the degree, wrote as follows: "So far as I know, this is the first honor of this kind, conferred in this country, and I know no one on whom it could be conferred more worthily." Dr. Mason was married to Miss Abigail Gregory, in Westboro', Mass., in 1817. His wife and three sons survive him. The Doctor left a Ms. book on harmony, which is soon to be published, and cannot fail of being a book of great interest to many people.

I close the biography of this very remarkable man with a portion of one of his letters, which gives a good idea of the kind of man he was, his style of writing, and his views upon several interesting topics.

"Orange, N. J., Jan. 12, 1865.

"SIMEON P. CHENEY, Esq.

"My dear Sir:—Many thanks for your good long letter from Geneseo, of 8th inst., my birth-day, having on that day completed my 73d year. Jan'y 8th, 1792, as I have been always told, was my birth-day. You begin your letter by thanking me for what I have done. The Lord be praised if I have been enabled to do any thing by which my fellow-men have been in any way benefitted. To me, my life seems to be filled with the *crooked* and the *rough* places, needing to be made *straight* and *smooth*. I can see an abundance of evils, so many *wrongs* indeed, that I can find but few *rights*. I must cry for mercy as my only hope, and yet I do praise God for enabling me to do any thing for the good of others. Blessed be his name forever. Thank you, my kind and faithful friend, for giving me cheer now that I am old and gray-headed. Your next topic is autobiography. Dear friend, excuse me in this. My life has been so unimportant I cannot suppose a written memoir of it would be to any considerable extent useful. You refer to your father. I can never forget him. When I saw him at Windsor, Vt.,—when I heard him speak, his form went in through my eyes and his voice through my ears, impelling tears. Blessed be his memory! To his sons his biography must have great interest; mine might have a similar interest, but this is not sufficient to warrant a book. I do not say *I will not*, I will give it thought, and the Lord will direct."

"I am very doubtful, dear sir, whether I shall ever make another church-music book. I laid out all my strength on the *Asaph*, my last book of the kind. This work contains very much music drawn from the very best sources, and is as good a book as I could now make were I to spend my whole working-hours for two years on another. And yet there are not many who seem to appreciate or to know the difference between such music as comes from the higher regions of science and taste, and that which is made off-hand here by those who have never had the advantages of musical education or association with anything really tasteful or excellent. Look at the many trashy (as they appear to me) books which are constantly being issued; look especially at the wretched Sunday-school books, as numerous and hateful to good taste and to a nice, moral perception as the plagues of Egypt. But enough."

"I wish you success in whatever you do, provided that it be right,—and I have not the least doubt that you intend nothing but what is so.

As ever, your friend &c.,

LOWELL MASON."

THE DAY IS PAST AND GONE. S. M.

BISHOP HOPKINS.

The day is past and gone, The evening shades ap-pear; O, may we all re-mem-ber well, The night of death draws near.

This tune was often sung in the Bishop's family, and is now published for the first time.

194

RT. REV. JOHN HENRY HOPKINS, D. D., was born in Dublin, Jan. 30, 1792, and died at Rock Point, Vt., Jan. 9, 1868. He was Bishop of the Protestant Episcopal Church for the Diocese of Vermont, and for several of his last years, *Presiding* Bishop of the denomination in the United States. He came to America with his parents when he was eight years old. Was educated for a lawyer and admitted to the bar in Pittsburg, Penn., but in 1823, a few years after, he left the bar for the ministry. Bishop Hopkins was a very intellectual man, and he applied himself to the work of life in various and useful ways. He was one year in a counting-room in Philadelphia. He assisted Wilson, the ornithologist, in the preparation of his plates for the first four volumes of his work, and when he was 19 years old, engaged in the manufacture of iron in Pennsylvania. He was a lawyer, a preacher, a teacher, an architect, an artist, a musician, a fair player upon the organ and violoncello, the author of "many volumes" on different subjects; and last but not least, a very accomplished gentleman. Not long before his death he visited Europe, and while in England presented Queen Victoria with a volume of sacred music of his composing, for which he received from Her Highness a very complimentary letter. He also had conferred upon him the degree of D. C. L., by the University of Oxford. Several of the Bishop's sons are distinguished as editors, clergymen and musicians. The Rev. John Henry Hopkins, D. D., is a good composer of sacred music, and Charles Jerome Hopkins has a wide and favorable reputation as the author of several works of a high order, of both vocal and instrumental music,

and as the editor of a musical periodical; also as the institutor and sustainer of a system of *free* singing schools for several years past, in the city of New York and vicinity, by which he has not only proved himself benevolent and philanthropic, but has accomplished much good, and brought that city under great obligations to him. The beautiful tune of his father's, accompanying this biography, is furnished by him. Caspar T. Hopkins, a very active business man in San Francisco, is the author of the "Manual of American Idioms," an interesting and a meritorious book. One of the Bishop's daughters, Mrs. Camp, was a good pianist more than thirty years since, as the writer of this well remembers; he also remembers hearing the Bishop preach in Burlington, in Nov. 1835,—his text, his earnest, engaging manner, and his clear and distinct articulation; at this time "Cashier Cole" was his chorister, and "Kate Kendall" his first soprano. Here for the first time I heard an *organ*. *A memorable Sabbath.*

It will be seen by the foregoing that the Bishop did not devote his life to music; but that he was a man of very uncommon love and admiration for music, there can be no doubt, and his tunes show he was no novice in musical knowledge. He took great pains in the education of his large family in music, and in his Seminary he raised up an orchestra that Jenny Lind highly complimented. But he was mainly interested in sacred music, and composed a good deal. The information upon which this brief account of this most industrious and esteemed man is based, has been mostly gathered from "The American Encyclopedia," and directly or indirectly from the Bishop's sons. S. P. C.

MISSIONARY CHANT. L. M.

CH. ZEUNER.

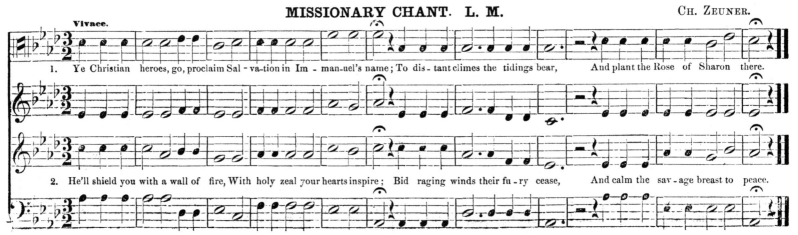

1. Ye Christian heroes, go, proclaim Sal-va-tion in Im-man-uel's name; To dis-tant climes the tidings bear, And plant the Rose of Sharon there.

2. He'll shield you with a wall of fire, With holy zeal your hearts inspire; Bid raging winds their fu-ry cease, And calm the sav-age breast to peace.

"CHARLES ZEUNER, a distinguished organist and composer, was born in Eisleben, near Gotha, Saxony, Sept. 20, 1795." In early life he was a court musician, and evinced decided military qualities, for which he received high tokens of approbation from distinguished generals of Napoleon's army. With musical honors he came to Boston in 1824, and "was considered one of the best educated musicians in this country." He was organist in different churches, and several years for the Handel and Haydn Society. He published various books, and one oratorio, "Feast of Tabernacles." In 1839 he published "The American Harp," with 400 pages, all his own compositions except five tunes. These books were very popular with the *best choirs*.

In 1854, he went to live in Philadelphia, where he continued his profession. For years he was subject to spells of most serious depression of mind, during which he had a singular aversion to music, and felt that he was not appreciated. Several years before his death, Mr. Zeuner said to a friend, I shall eventually die in some solitary spot, suddenly, by my own hand." The sad prediction was fulfilled in every particular, on Saturday, Nov. 7, 1857. He was a bachelor, and without relatives in this country. Mr. Zeuner was a plump, good looking man, with a florid, bright face, and a quick, nervous temperament; an accomplished man, and his habits of life were temperate and regular. In religion he was a Lutheran, and ever kept the Protestant fire alive.

On meeting Mr. Zeuner on Boston Common one morning, Mr. Lowell Mason said to him, "Mr. Zeuner, what makes your Missionary Chant so popular? I hear it *everywhere*." Mr. Zeuner replied, "I was sitting on one of these seats, on a most beautiful moonlight evening, all alone, with all the world moving about me, and suddenly Missionary Chant was *given me*, and I ran home as fast as ever I could and put it on paper before I should forget. That is what makes it *pleese*, Mr. Mason." Missionary Chant has been sharply criticised; but no criticism can rob it of its life, its power and excellence.

Mr. Zeuner was a pupil and admirer of the celebrated Hummel. He was a man and a musician of unusual abilities and rare strength of character. *He stood alone.* His popularity was peculiar, among the very best teachers, leaders and singers in the country, and was based on *real, original merit*. This biography is taken mostly from The Western Musical World.　　　　　　　　　　　　　　　S. P. C.

For Hymns, see 157 and 411 Episcopal Coll.

LAUD.

EDWARD HODGES, MUS. DOC.

"*My soul longeth, yea, even fainteth for the courts of the Lord.*"

1. Lord of the worlds a - bove, How pleas - - ant and how fair The dwellings of thy love, Thine earth - ly tem - ples are!
2. The Lord his peo - ple loves; His hand no good with - holds From those his heart ap - proves, From pure and up - right souls.

To thine a - bode My heart........ as - pires, With warm.... de - sires To see my God, To see my God. A - men.
Thrice hap - py he, O God......... of hosts, Whose spir - - - it trusts A - lone in thee, A - lone in thee. A - men.

EDWARD HODGES, Mus. Doc., was born in Bristol, England, in July, 1796; was a graduate of Sidney Sussex College, Cambridge, and came to New York in 1838, to become director of the music of Trinity Parish of that city, comprising three churches, Trinity, St. Paul's and St. John's. The position was a most inviting and important one, the Cathedral School of church music being then unknown in this country, and New York had no large organ. It gave him a grand opportunity for the display of his great acquirements and of doing much good. Doc. Hodges when he came to this country was not only master of organ playing, being familiar with the music of all the great masters for that instrument, but he had studied the mechanism of the organ, and thoroughly understood *organ building.* Several of his inventions for the improvement of the organ are now in use in this country and in Europe. He wrote extensively for different journals on classical music and mechanical science. In 1841, the large organ in St. John's church was erected under his direction. In 1846, the magnificent organ in Trinity church was opened, the whole of it being built from his own specifications; and the organ at Trinity Chapel which was afterwards completed, contained some of his latest improvements. As a performer on the organ, Doc. Hodges had few if any rivals. He possessed the rare gift of extemporizing well; of thoroughly working up a fugue on the impulse of the occasion, requiring great inventive faculties, perfect knowledge of counterpoint, and complete mastery of the instrument. He was a profound harmonist, and his knowledge of the history of music was exhaustive. Without doubt Doc. Hodges laid the foundation for the *highest school* of *church music* in this country. The Doctor was a devout and conscientious Christian, and worked with one absorbing aim in his vocation, regarding his art as something dedicated to the work of the sanctuary, and

himself not as the organist of this parish or that, but as a liturgical minister of the church universal on earth. He ranked highly as a composer of cathedral music, and some of his anthems, chants, services and hymn tunes are regarded as models of composition in the school to which they belong, and are used in many churches in this country and in England. He was a perfect gentleman of the old English type, benevolent in heart, courteous in manner, his countenance beaming with intelligence and humor. In 1859, he was prostrated by sickness, and after a few years of retirement from active duty, he returned to the land of his birth, and there, at Clifton, in September 1867, he departed this life in peace. His burial place is at Stanton-Drew, Somersetshire, in a lovely, quiet, country church-yard.

Of Doc. Hodges' eight children, only four survived him. His eldest son, George Frederick Handel, and his second, Jubal, (neither of whom are now living,) possessed musical talent to a very extraordinary degree; and the latter, like his father, was remarkable for extempore playing. Both were organists of great ability. The third son, John Sebastian Bach, D. D., is a good composer of church music, a good organist and thorough harmonist. The eldest daughter, Faustina Hasse, has long been known in this country and in England, as an organist, pianist and composer, and several of her compositions have been great favorites. Her beautiful song, "Dreams," has long been a standard song. This combination of extraordinary talent and attainments possessed by Doc. Hodges and his family, so well and so long devoted to the cause of sacred music, is most remarkable. *They have,* and *long will continue to have the respect and admiration of all real sacred music lovers in both the " New World " and the " Old."*

JAMES A. JOHNSON, 1878.

Hymn 94, Episcopal Coll.

CHISHOLM. L. M.

W. A. MUHLENBERG, D. D. 1844.

My God, and is thy Ta - ble spread, And doth thy cup with love o'er - flow? Thith - er be all thy chil - dren led, And let them thy sweet mercies know.

REV. WILLIAM AUGUSTUS MUHLENBERG D. D., was the son of a distinguished clergyman of the Lutheran denomination, in Pennsyl- | vania, in which state, and in the town of Lancaster, Dr. Muhlenberg was born Sept. 16, 1796. He was the founder of St. Luke's Hospital, and for many years its superintendent and chaplain ; also founder of "St. John-Land," Long Island. a *Home* for indigent old men ; and for many years he was pastor of "The Church of the Holy Communion," in New York. Dr. Muhlenberg was a man of originality and strength of character, one who, like Gen. Jackson, sometimes "took the responsibility." He was a minister of high position in the Episcopal denomination in New York, and he did not like the office of "the clerk," whose duty it was to make the responses and say the Amens in the services of the church. He saw the institution was not only in reality useless, but *objectionable.* When ordinary means failed to secure its removal, he took an axe and chopped down the desk where the clerk stood, and told his people that all Christians could say their own "Amens," and if they wished their service to be a *live* service, *they* would, and *they did. Brave and good man!*

Dr. Muhlenberg was a musician of no mean attainments. He knew and felt the inspirational power of music upon the hearts of men, and the necessity of it in worship. Hence he worked for it. He was always at the weekly rehearsal of his choir. He was ever first and foremost in the work of improvement in the music and the hymns of his denomination. He was several times one of a committee to revise the hymns and select the music for the Protestant Episcopal church in the United States. And he was a poet. Whether his hymn, commencing, "I would not live alway," deserves so much credit, or not, it is undoubtedly among the most popular modern hymns of America.

When the author wrote the poem of which the hymn referred to is only a part, it was by no means designed for its present use. It was written when he was a young man, and the cause of its being written was undoubtedly the death of a most estimable young lady, who was the dearest friend he had upon earth. Then it was that, like Job, he would not live alway, and so he wrote. The poem was first published in 1824. It is very well understood by those who have known Dr. Muhlenberg in the last part of his life, that he was not altogether satisfied with the spirit of his hymn. In 1868 he wrote a postscript to it, as follows :

I would not live alway, no longer I sing ;
Live alway I shall while Jesus is King ;
United to Him, His righteousness mine,
My life bound in His, no fate shall untwine.

Ne'er till sin enters heaven and death wields his rod,
Defiant, enthroned in the Palace of God ;
Not till heaven's a graveyard and Christ lies there slain ,
Shall I cease in His glory and with Him to reign.

Dr. Muhlenberg wrote a variety of hymns, and was a composer of sacred music. The pleasing tune preceding this biography, and much of the biography itself, is furnished by Prof. James A. Johnson, who personally knew whereof he wrote. This philanthropist, minister, poet and musician, after a long and most useful life, died at St. Luke's Hospital, April 8, 1877, and his body was buried at St. John-Land.

Thus in his death and burial he honored the two grand institutions he had lived for. S. P. C.

HAYTER. 8s, 7s & 7s.

A. U HAYTER.
By per of O. Ditson & Co.

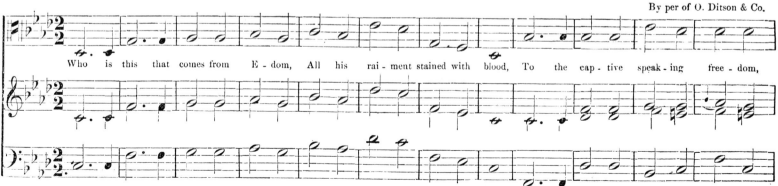

Who is this that comes from E - dom, All his rai - ment stained with blood, To the cap - tive speak - ing free - dom,

Bring - ing and be - stow - ing good; Glo - rious in the garb he wears, Glo - rious in..... the spoil he bears?

A. U. HAYTER was born in Gillingham, England, Dec. 16, 1799; he came to New York in 1835, and removed to Boston, Mass., in 1839, becoming the organist of the Handel and Haydn Society of that city. He was a superior organist and composer of music; and while connected with the Handel and Haydn Society, he brought out many new oratorios, and cleared that association from a standing debt. His father was an organist in England, and his son, George F. Hayter, was his successor, as organist, in Boston. Mr. Hayter died July 28, 1873, aged nearly 74 years. Educated in the thorough English oratorio school, he was a very useful man in his profession, and was much esteemed by his associates, on account of his unassuming character and rare musical talent. *Moore's New Encyclopedia of Music.*

FRENCH. H. M.

E. K. PROUTY.
By per. L. O. EMERSON.

1. Welcome, delightful morn, Thou day of sacred rest! I hail thy kind return; Lord, make these moments blest: From the low train of mortal toys, I soar to reach im-mor-tal joys.

2. Descend, celestial Dove, With all thy quick'ning pow'rs; Disclose a Savior's love, And bless the sacred hours: Then shall my soul new life obtain, Nor Sabbaths be enjoy'd in vain.

"ELIJAH KING PROUTY was born in Charleston, N. H., in 1801. "His father soon removed to Waterford, Vt., and dying when the son was ten years old, the child was fostered in a family of strangers, whom he loved and revered through life." His biographer adds, "His young spirit was pent up with tenderness, and his mother's first visit to father Green's was so great a joy that he marked the chairs on which she sat." From childhood through life he was a devotee to music. Of all his contemporaries in Vermont, no one was so perfectly abandoned to song amid all his vocations. When a peddler, he whiled away more hours rehearsing anthems, than with the more wealthy who might buy his cloths. When a merchant, he seemed more anxious to exhibit a new piece of music than to show his goods. When in Boston after merchandise, it was his chief concern to be with Lowell Mason at every opportunity, in public or in private, in his singing schools, at his rehearsals, or with his Sabbath choir. It was by these means that he became the first Vermont singing master to adopt the Pestalozzian system of instruction, to use the black-board, the syllables do, re, mi, and the modern motions of beating time. Many singers would not submit to the practice of the new syllables, and quit the choir forever; but Prouty increased in friends by it, and we have heard of Mason's saying more than once that E. K. Prouty among Vermont teachers was first in rank. He had taught more or less for years; but at the age of thirty-two or three he gave up mercantile pursuits, and ever after taught public singing schools, or select classes; frequently single pupils; sometimes gave lessons in harmony to small companies or to individuals; and in latter years he became a great convenience in his neighborhood as an expert tuner of pianos. Although a man of prayer, and an exemplary member of the Congregational church, worship in song seemed to possess the highest reverence of his soul. His solitudes were mostly spent in composition of music and in devotional reflections upon his favorite theme. To him, the universe was but an anthem attuned and harmonized by the Great Creator. Such life-long habits told upon his character, and even upon the features of his face, and made him one of the loveliest as well as the most respected of companions. His brethren, Brown, Pennock, Bean, Phillips and the three Cheneys, so long teachers in Windsor, Orange, Caledonia, Orleans, and Lamoille counties, always beheld their senior as an appreciator and friend, as the first to applaud deserts, and to forgive and heal dissensions. In 1837 he stood first as vocal teacher in the leading towns of Burlington, Plattsburg and St. Albans; an enviable position of a master rapidly approaching the zenith of his popularity. We call to mind the singing at the College Commencement under his leadership in those days;

when "Child of Mortality," "Wake the Song of Jubilee" and "Lift up your Stately Heads, Ye Doors," were performed seraphically; Prof. Molt playing the organ, and the renowned James Kendall the trombone; Cashier Cole chief basso, Kate Kendall first soprano, and Harriette Hosford, soloist. At the great whig convention at Burlington, Vt., in 1840, 40,000 present, our professor led the Tippecanoe songs to admiration. He was also director of the "Vermont Musical Convention" held at Newbury in June 1840, and was a member of the committee to annually appoint other like conventions.

Prof. Prouty's life-long passion was so pure and sanctified that no enervation could result from its exercise; up to his last year he held the appearance and reality of prime; his voice was as steady, clear and buoyant as ever, and as formerly, he was in his element on the highest part of male quartets. Who has forgotten Webb's "How blest the sacred tie that binds," with Prouty on the leading part? How his remaining comrades lament that they never more can join their friend in song. How many admirers have sighed that his happy visits could return no more.

Prof. Prouty was twice married; first to Cynthia Loomis, a very estimable lady, a niece of the late Hon. Jeduthan Loomis of Montpelier. She died young, leaving three children, probably yet living. Second, to Miss M. A. Converse, a highly intellectual maiden, young and beautiful, a niece of J. K. Converse, D. D., of Burlington, Vt. She had two lovely and talented daughters; the younger, a great solace to her mother, still survives; but the elder died early, soon after establishing herself in the south as a superior teacher of music: this Providence was severe to her parents almost beyond endurance; and thereafter Prof. Prouty's remaining years were few. His death occurred Sept. 26, 1869, at Newbury, Vt.   M. E. C.

MARCUS. S. M.   COLBURN.

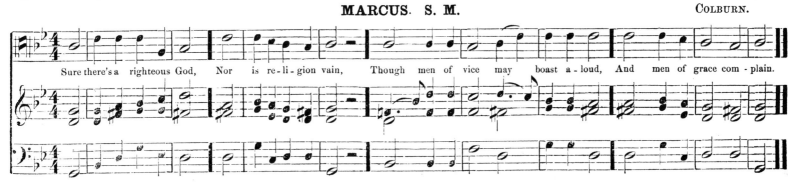

Sure there's a righteous God, Nor is re-li-gion vain, Though men of vice may boast a-loud, And men of grace com-plain.

200

MARCUS COLBURN was at one time the first tenor in Boston and New York; and an oratorio without him as principal tenor was considered almost an impossibility. When the oratorio of "The Messiah" was given, at old Tripler Hall, under the auspices of Miss Jenny Lind, Mr. Colburn sang, for the last time in public, the solo tenor part. Previous to that time comparisons were often made between Mr. Braham (the English tenor) and Mr. Colburn, and in these disputations the preference was often given to Mr. Colburn, over his English contemporary. In the late years of his life Mr. Colburn was engaged as an instructor of vocal music in New York, and in the schools there. He died in that city, after a severe illness, in 1868. *Moore's New Encyclopedia of Music.*

P. S. Marcus Colburn was born in Rindge, N. H., Oct. 16, 1802. He was what is termed a self-made musician, like most of our *leaders*, but in reality, a "natural born," *God-made singer.* He was a real lover of music from first to last. He was a teacher of elocution as well as music. In his last years the study of harmony "was his chief delight." During the war of the rebellion he composed and published a war song. Mr. Colburn was a tall and heavy man, and as yet stands as the *greatest* American tenor. I fear "The last words of Marmion" will long be silent if they wait for an interpreter, the equal of Marcus Colburn. He was admitted a member of the Handel and Haydn Society, Dec. 6, 1825. These facts I received from his daughter, Mrs. Sarah A. Colburn Gans, of Salem, Arkansas. S. P. C., Boston, Nov. 1878.

HENRY. C. M.
HENRY EATON MOORE. 1832.

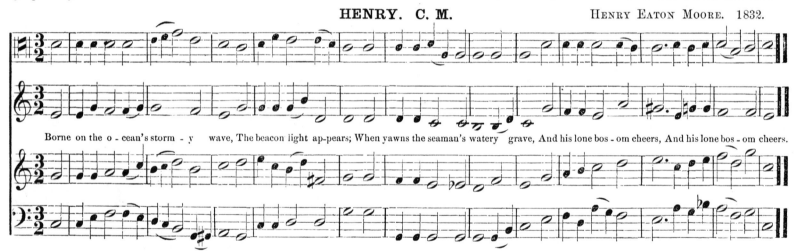

Borne on the ocean's stormy wave, The beacon light appears; When yawns the seaman's watery grave, And his lone bosom cheers, And his lone bosom cheers.

HENRY EATON MOORE was born at Andover, N. H., July 21, 1803. He became known as an organist, teacher, and composer of vocal and instrumental music at Concord, N. H., at the age of 16 years; and his whole life was devoted to the profession of music, excepting the years 1825 and 1826, when he was editing and publishing the "Grafton Journal," at Plymouth, N. H. He was an excellent singer, and a performer upon several wind and stringed instruments. He was very popular as a teacher, much loved among musical people, and ever ready to sustain by his influence and money, all efforts for the advancement and elevation of the art he placed above all other arts. He was the author of the "Musical Catechism," 1829, "New Hamp-

shire Collection of Church Music," 1832, the "Merrimack Collection of Instrumental Music," 1833, "The National Choir," and a "Collection of Anthems and Choruses," 1834, the "Northern Harp," 1837.

Having removed from Concord, N. H., to East Cambridge, Mass., in 1838, he readily became more generally known in that state as a composer and teacher, and many were looking forward to his being a formidable rival of the immensely popular Lowell Mason. A short time before his death he commenced the publication of a weekly musical paper, in Boston, entitled the "Boston Eoliad." Henry E. Moore was a man of wonderful good nature and good cheer. His house was always open to his friends, and his earnings freely distributed among the needy. He lived for others more than for himself; was always cheerful and happy; and for talents, industry and benevolence, it is safe to say, we scarcely meet his equal in a lifetime. He died Oct. 23, 1841, at his home in East Cambridge, aged 38 years and three months, respected and beloved by all who knew him. His widow and son live in Manchester, N. H.; he is editor of the "New Hampshire Journal of Music," a genius and poet.　　　　　　　　　　　M. E. C.

P. S. Having known Henry E. Moore *well*, I cannot forbear my testimony to the truth of the foregoing biography. As a lover of music, a teacher and indefatigable toiler, as a friend, a companion, a good, happy, generous and gentlemanly man, he stands as yet, in my memory, *at the head*.　　　　　　　　　　　S. P. C.

JOHN. 7s.

John W. Moore. 1832.

'Mid the cho-rus of the skies, 'Mid th'an-gel-ic lyres a-bove, Hark! their songs me-lo-dious rise, Songs of praise to Je-sus' love.

John Weeks Moore was born at Andover, N. H., April 11, 1807; he commenced the publication of the "Free Press," a weekly newspaper, at Brunswick, Me., in 1828; commenced the "Gazette," at Bellows Falls, Vt., in 1838, and also the "World of Music;" in 1841 he published the "Vocal and Instrumental Self Instructor," in 1842 "Sacred Minstrel," in 1844 Musician's Lexicon," in 1854 "Complete Encyclopedia of Music:" Elementary, Technical, Historical, Biographical, Vocal and Instrumental, 1004 pages; in 1855, the "American Collection of Instrumental Music," in 1856 the "Star Collection of Instrumental Music;" in 1857, "Comprehensive Music Teacher;" in 1863 he removed to Manchester, N. H., where he was editor of the "Daily News," and of "Moore's Musical Record;" in 1876 he published a "Dictionary of Musical Information," and is now compiling "Songs and Song Writers," and also a volume of "American, Historical, Biographical, Musical and Poetical Sketches." He is likewise the regular correspondent of several musical journals, and an occasional contributor to some of the popular magazines and newspapers; also having employment upon the "New Hampshire Journal of Music." It will be seen that Mr. Moore has been connected with newspapers and other publications since 1828, a period of a full half century, and that after at least 40 years of almost exclusive devotion to works on music, he does not lay his armor down, but is now, (May 1878) laboring on as assiduously as ever, with several irons in the fire.

Although Mr. Moore has wrought so many years *pro bono publico*, in ways peculiar to his taste, he has never cultivated the faculty of boasting his merits before the world; hence the masses know but little of his deserts; but whoever looks after him, will easily come to the conclusion that no other man in America has ever brought into form, tangible to the reader and student, so much valuable information upon music and musicians. We will only add, that lexicographers appeal to his learning for intricate definitions, and often have occasion to thank him for new words to their unabridged dictionaries, and that we believe his portrait, extraordinary for classical features and venerable beauty, should finally hold a conspicuous place in the gallery of choice portraits of the *literati* of the nation.　　M. E. C.

AMITY. 7s. Double.

GEO. HOOD.

Lento cantabile.

Peo-ple of the liv-ing God, I have sought the world a - round; ⎫
Paths of sin and sor-row trod, Peace and com-fort no - where found; ⎬ Now to you my spir-it turns, Turns a fu - gi-tive un-blest;
Brethren, where your al-tar burns, O, re-ceive me in - to rest.

Rev. GEORGE HOOD was born at Topsfield, Mass., Feb. 10, 1807. Early in life he began teaching as a profession, and, in turn, was teacher of a public school, of church music, of a ladies' seminary, and finally became a minister of the Gospel. In 1846, Mr. Hood published "The Southern Church Melodist," a compilation of church music in patent notes, for the southern market. In the autumn of 1846 he published his "History of Music in New England." In 1864 he published his "Musical Manual, a text-book for classes or private pupils." Though he had great facility in the class-room as a writer of exercises on the black-board, both in melody and harmony, he com-posed but few pieces. He was a member of the "Teachers' Class of the Boston Academy of Music," and a member of its "Faculty of Teachers of Vocal Music." But his best work for the cause of sacred music was his "History of Music in New England," already referred to, a work which required a *constant research for ten years*, into which he collected nearly all the available matter extant, opening to others the sources of what has since been written. He is now the pastor of the White Lake Presbyterian church in Sull. Co., N. Y.

S. P. C., Dorset, Vt., June, 1878.

Written by Charles Wesley in 1749.

KNOX. C. P. M.

W. H. SAGE. 1852.

Lo, on a nar-row neck of land 'Twixt two un-cer-tain seas I stand, Yet how in-sen - si-ble;

A point of time, a mo - ment's space, May move me to yon heaven - ly place, Or shut me up in hell.

WM. HARRIS SAGE, born in New York 1809, (son of Harris Sage, leader of the music for many years in the old North Dutch Church, New York,) when a little boy, sang with his father in the North Dutch Church. At the age of seventeen was appointed organist of Broome St. Reformed Dutch Church, N. Y., afterwards in North Dutch Church, until removed to 29th St. and 5th Ave. The organ there was rebuilt under his supervision. He was sometime leader of the Old Euterpian (Instrumental) Society; he also led the New York Sacred Music Society in the absence of Mr. U. C. Hill in Germany, and was one of the original members of the N. Y. Philharmonic Society. He wrote (and left unfinished) much good music, both sa-

cred and secular. He died in 1868, at Orange, N. J. Mr. Sage was of a gentle, sensitive nature, conscientious almost to a fault, and a steadfast friend. It was once remarked by a business friend who knew him well, that "he was just the *honestest* man God ever made," (a rare character in these times.) Besides his proficiency in music, he was exceedingly fond of scientific studies, in some branches of which he was quite proficient. The glee, "May, Sweet May," given in this book, was written by him for a small singing society which he organized and led in Orange, N. J. It is given as one of his shortest and simplest productions. J. A. JOHNSON.

I WOULD NOT LIVE ALWAY. (FREDERICK.) 11s.

GEO. KINGSLEY. By per.

With strong expression.

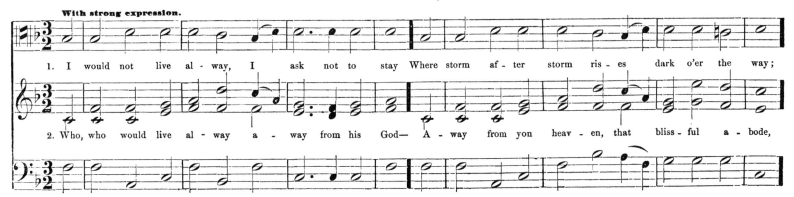

1. I would not live al - way, I ask not to stay Where storm af - ter storm ris - es dark o'er the way;

2. Who, who would live al - way a - way from his God— A - way from yon heav - en, that bliss - ful a - bode,

The few lu-cid morn-ings that dawn on us here, Are fol-lowed by gloom or be-cloud-ed with fear.

Where riv-ers of pleas-ure flow bright o'er the plains, And the noon-tide of glo-ry e-ter-nal-ly reigns.

GEORGE KINGSLEY, teacher, composer, organist and choir-leader, was born in Northampton, Mass., July 7, 1811; and, like many other distinguished American musicians, was a self-educated man, choosing music as a profession because he loved it; he had much native talent as a writer and performer. He became known as an organist at one of the churches in Hartford, Conn., in 1829, when he was eighteen years of age, and afterwards occupied the position of music-teacher, choir-leader and organist, in Boston, Mass., Philadelphia, Penn., New York city, and at Brooklyn and other places. While at Philadelphia, he had the charge of the music in the public schools and at Girard College; and when in Brooklyn, he taught in the Academy there; since which he has resided in his native town, Northampton, Mass., where he has a famous "reputation musical," and where he has been constantly employed as an organist, teacher and composer.

The compositions of Mr. Kingsley have, many of them, been very popular, and his publications have had fair, if not extensive, sales. His "Sunday School Singing Book" was published in Boston, as was his "Harmonist," and three volumes of his "Social Choir," one of the best collections ever made in this country, and containing many pieces which previously were obtainable only in the form of sheet music. Each of the three volumes contained 200 pages, making 600 in all, appearing, vol. 1., in 1835, vol. 2., in 1836, vol. 3., in 1842. His "Sacred Choir" was published in New York, 342 pages, 1838; his "Harp of David" was issued in Philadelphia, 360 pages, 1847; and his "Templi Carmina" was printed at Northampton, his native place, 352 pages, 1853. His "Juvenile Choir" and his "Young Ladies' Harp" were published in New York. The Kingsley family were all musical people, and George, when in his native town, resides in the house formerly owned and occupied by his grandfather. In addition to his many publications, Mr. Kingsley wrote about *thirty* tunes for "The Sabbath," a collection of music edited by C. Everest of Philadelphia; and he has lately supplied about *twenty-five* tunes for a collection of music by the Dutch Reformed Church of Ohio.

Moore's New Encyclopedia of Music.

MATHIAS KELLER, a celebrated German musician, was born at Ulm, Wurtemberg, March 20, 1813. He early displayed a great love for music, and became first violinist at the Royal Chapel, where he remained five years; was afterwards for seven years, band-master to the Third Royal Brigade. He came to America in 1846; became known as a violinist at Philadelphia, Penn., and as a conductor of English opera in New York. He removed to Boston, Mass., where he soon became known as a musician and poet. He was the author of about 250 songs: was uncommonly well-informed, and took rank with the best musicians in this country; but was best known as the author of the "American Hymn." His music was more classical than popular in character; and his lighter productions met with most favor. He died at his residence in Boston, Oct. 12, 1875, aged 62.

The grand American Hymn which Mr. Keller dedicated to his adopted country, and which was performed by the Peace Jubilee chorus of twenty thousand voices and an orchestra of eleven hundred instruments, has made his name and fame ever honorable. *Moore's New Encyclopedia of Music.*

P. S. The patriotic devotion of Mathias Keller to the "Freedom and Independence" of this country, as evinced in his three national compositions, "The American Hymn," "Hymn of the Republic" and "Our Nation's Birthday," will ever be of great interest to the people of this nation; and, though he was of German blood and birth, must forever stamp him as a man of true American heart and feeling.

"Our Nation's Birthday," which accompanies this biography, he wrote and composed for the great Centennial occasion, and was happy in the fond and proud anticipation of joining in the national festivities and listening to his new song as he had formerly listened to "The American Hymn" at the Grand Peace Jubilee. But alas! he had only time to finish it and put it into the hands of the publishers,

ere he was called hence to join the *immortal band*, the grand chorus, the universal orchestra "on The Other Side." It was his last composition and his last manuscript. It was the grand finale to a proud, but honest, earnest, industrious and art-loving life. S. P. C.

OUR NATION'S BIRTHDAY.

Words and music by M. KELLER.

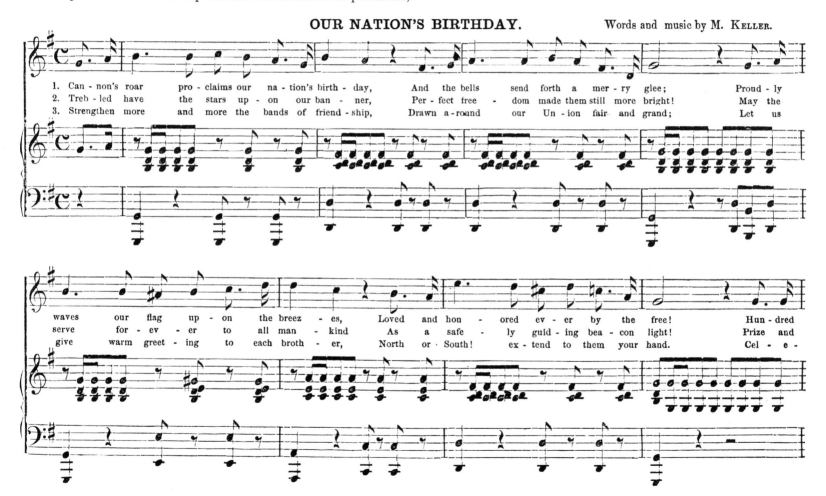

years have passed since our brave fa - ther's Framed and signed that mem - o - ra - ble Deed, Which has
guard that ra - diant con - stel - la - tion; Keep our dear old flag from blem - ish free; Fear - less
brate our glo - rious In - de - pen - dence! Sing with heart and soul the joy - ful song, That is

saved the peo - ple from op - press - ion, Heav - en helped them in the hour of need.
shield its hon - or from all in - sult, As it waves on land or on the sea.
swell - ing now in might - y cho - rus, From a tru - ly grate - ful peo - ple's tongue.

Lib - er - ty! bright Goddess from E - lysium, Stay, oh stay on earth for-ev-er - more! Lead us in those righteous paths once trodden By our gallant, noble sires of yore!

Lib - er - ty! bright Goddess from E - lysium, Stay, oh stay on earth for-ev-er - more! Lead us in those righteous paths once trodden By our gallant, noble sires of yore!

HOLY CROSS. L. M.

Austin Phillips. 1847.

From all that dwell be - low the skies, Let the Cre-a-tor's praise a - rise; Let the Redeemer's name be sung, Thro' ev - ery land, by ev - ery tongue.

Mr. Austin Phillips, organist of Wells Cathedral, England, came to this country in 1837. As a composer and singer of English songs, (as well as a church organist and tasteful accompanist) he had few equals. He was for years the organist of St. Thomas' church, Broadway, New York, when it was the principal up-town church in that city, and celebrated for its music. His songs were for a long time deservedly popular, and some of his set pieces for quartet choirs were models of light church music. He was one of the conductors of the New York Vocal Society, and he organized one of the first male quartets in New York. He died in 1849.   J. A. Johnson.

No change of time shall ev-er shock My firm af-fec-tion, Lord, to thee;

For Thou hast al-ways been my rock, A for-tress and de-fence to me.

GEORGE LODER was born in Bath, England, in 1816. He was a nephew of Edward Loder, the famous composer and conductor. He came to this country in 1838. To him, and a few associates, New York is indebted for the first development of taste for classical music, both vocal and instrumental. Prior to his time the New York Sacred Music Society, under the direction of Mr. Wm. H. Sage and Mr. U. C. Hill, had produced the oratorios of "The Messiah" and "St. Paul" at the old Chatham Chapel; but under Mr. Loder's direction "The American Musical Institute" produced for the first time in New York, "The Seasons" complete, "The Creation," "Paradise and the Peri," by Schumann, "The Mount of Olives," by Beethoven, "The Desert," by Felician David, and several other first class works. The New York Vocal Society commenced under the joint conductorship of George Loder, Henry C. Timm, W. A. Alpers and Austin Phillips, and lasted for three seasons. After the first concert, Mr. Loder was sole conductor. This society, consisting of about fifty carefully selected voices, was the first in New York to perform unaccompanied vocal music, like madrigals, part-songs and light choruses. The first male voice quartet singing in public was done by this society,

under Mr. Loder's direction. They also produced Mendelssohn's "Lobgesang" with orchestra, the score and parts being sent out from England expressly for the society, and several of Mendelssohn's Psalms, and Spohr's "Last Judgment." This society, like other similar societies in New York, finally dissolved through the mutual jealousies of its members.

In conjunction with Messrs. Timm, Hill, Alpers, H. C. Watson and George Bristow, and some others, Mr. Loder was instrumental in founding the present Philharmonic Society of New York. This society met in the "Apollo Rooms," Broadway, near Canal St. The management began by giving away tickets to the rehearsals to such persons as they thought could best appreciate the music. At their first public concert, so low was the taste for classic instrumental music, it was with difficulty they held the audience through *one movement* of Beethoven's C Symphony. Mr. Loder was organist and director of the music in Grace Church, Broadway, for many years. This music was the forerunner of much of the light, quartet choir music of the present day, and became very popular with a certain class of churchgoers. From personal acquaintance, we can say Mr. Loder was one of the most energetic, competent and successful conductors of both vocal and instrumental music ever in this country. He possessed a great amount of that magnetic power which is so necessary to success in teaching and conducting singers, and he certainly could produce better effect with a company of cultivated or uncultivated voices than any man we have ever met with. In 1855 or '56, Mr. Loder was persuaded to visit San Francisco. He afterwards went back to London, thence to Australia, and died at Adelaide, on the 18th of July, 1868. His departure from New York was a real loss to that city, which to-day is greatly indebted to him for the grand and thorough work he did for the advancement of good music there. J. A. J.

P. S. In the fall of 1845 a grand chorus was made up of seceded members of the old Sacred Music Society of New York, which had previously suffered a disruption, and such others as could be selected, with Henry Meiggs, recently known as the South American millionaire railroad builder, as business manager, and George Loder for musical director. There was rivalry between the new and the old associations. Mr. Loder with his company brought out the oratorio of "The Seven Sleepers." It was their first performance, and the first time it was given in this country. Mrs. Edward Loder, a lady of powerful voice and great spirit, was the leading soprano. The old society soon followed the lead, and performed the new oratorio with Miss Julia Northall as first soprano. My sister and myself being invited by Mr. Loder to take solo parts in the oratorio, I was with him considerably at that time, and afterwards still more when we, "The Cheney Family," came under his training. Mr. Loder did not belong exactly to that class of musicians whose works it is my special aim to record, namely, those men whose lives were devoted to sacred music, so called; for he was not only a man of knowledge and good taste in sacred music, but in *all music*. He deserves a place here. It is a great satisfaction, a *relief*, though he is far beyond any need of my praise or thanks, yet, as I believe, not beyond reach, to place on lasting record my appreciation of his great talents and usefulness, and my gratitude for much he did and said for me and for *us*. More than thirty years have gone by, but I see him now as then, in the very prime of life, a graceful, erect, handsome man, with dark hair and eyes, and active and efficient to the last degree. When the trying time came, "*The Debut*," he stood by us, in the old "Society Library Rooms," on Broadway, cheering in the audience, and still better behind the curtain, saying, "It goes well, *that* voice must be subdued a little, we'll have it right the next time," &c. &c. And he was *benevolent*. A very tender feeling presses upon me as I recall the modest and feeling manner in which he refused, at the final moment of separation, any remuneration for all he had done for us, saying, "*Nothing*, Sir, you are welcome to what I have done for you. You will *need all your money*. You have merits and I wish you success. Good bye."

George Loder! All in all the ablest musician I ever knew. The departure of such a man is not only "a real loss" to a *city*, but to the *world*. *George Loder!* May his name pass on to many generations, and with increasing honors. S. P. C.

WATSON. L. M.

HENRY C. WATSON. 1862.

A - wake, my soul, to joy - ful lays, And sing thy great Redeemer's praise; He justly claims a song from thee, His lov - ing kindness, oh, how free.

HENRY C. WATSON, the celebrated musical and art critic, and editor of the New York Art Journal, was born in London, England. He came to this country in 1840, when he was 22 years of age. He was the son of John Watson, director of music at Covent Garden Theatre, London, and the brother of Mrs. Edward Loder, a popular oratorio singer in New York, thirty years since. Mr. Watson received a thorough musical education from his father as his first teacher, after which he studied with Mr. Keans and Mr. Edward Loder, the composer. He commenced his public life as a singer, when he was only 13 years of age, and appeared as "first fairy" in Von Weber's opera of "Oberon," with Von Weber himself as conductor. The Duchess of St. Albans was so pleased with the young singer, she called him to her box to congratulate him. He brought with him to America, letters of introduction to William Cullen Bryant, George P. Morris, Horace Greeley and other literary men of New York.

Mr. Park Benjamin soon installed him as art critic on the "New World" newspaper, and he was afterwards connected with the "Musical Chronicle," "Evening Mirror," "Family Magazine," and other periodicals. In 1844, in connection with C. F. Briggs and Edgar A. Poe, he started the "Broadway Journal." On the death of. Wm. H. Frye, he succeeded him as musical critic of the New York Tribune. He was one of the leading organizers of the present "New York Philharmonic Society." He was also one of the prime movers in the organization of the "New York Vocal Society," in 1843, and the American Musical Fund Association." In 1863 he established the present New York Art Journal, which he continued to edit until his death, which occurred on the 2nd of December in 1875. J. A. J.

ZEPHYR. L. M.

Wm. B. Bradbury.

Soft be the gent-ly breathing notes That sing the Savior's dy - ing love, Soft as the evening zeph-yr floats, And soft as tuneful lyres a - bove.

William Bachelder Bradbury. As I remember the subject of this biography in 1845, he was an active, ardent, sensitive man, of rather slim form, common height and sandy complexion. He inherited his musical talents from his parents, who were both good singers. He was born in York Co., Maine, in 1816, and died at his home in Mont Clair, N. J., Jan. 7, 1868. In 1830 Mr. Bradbury went to live in Boston, where he attended Lowell Mason's singing schools, and studied harmony with Sumner Hill. He made rapid progress, and was soon an organist and choir director. He "achieved his first success in teaching, in Machias, Me." After a year's experience in that place, he returned to Boston and was married. His next move was to St. John, New Brunswick; was unsuccessful, "lost his voice for a whole year," returned again to Boston in "an almost destitute condition." But his "dark days" did not last long. He was soon teaching a class in Marlboro' Chapel, where he was organist for a year, when he was called to Dover, N. H., where he flourished till the Rev. Silas Illsley of Brooklyn induced him to go and become leader of his choir. In about one year he accepted an invitation "to the charge of the organ and choir in the Baptist Tabernacle in New York," and there, "in the year 1841, were held the first free singing classes in that city, which afterwards became so *immensely popular.*"

His special work with the children of New York continued for several years, and was the means of introducing singing into the public schools of that city; and while engaged with the children, he began to compose. He had never dreamed of becoming an author, but the success of a few pieces he introduced to these juvenile classes induced him to try again, and again succeeding, he kept on trying to the end.

His Sabbath school books were numerous and popular. More than three millions are said to have been sold in the United States. The first one was "The Young Choir." Mr. Bradbury was equally successful with his books of church music. The sale of his "Jubilee" up to 1868 amounted to more than 255,000 copies.

Thomas Hastings became the friend of Mr. Bradbury, and in 1844 their names appeared on the lids of "The Psalmista," and for some years they were more or less associated in book making. In 1847 Mr. Bradbury went to Europe. In Leipsic he studied in various departments of music with eminent teachers. On his return he entered largely into the work of holding musical conventions. In 1854 Mr. Bradbury became associated with Dr. Mason, Dr. Hastings and Mr. George F. Root in The Normal Musical Institute, "in which he taught harmony." In the same year he entered upon an extensive business in piano-forte manufacturing. Undoubtedly that was so *much too much.* Still, it is said "he was successful," that is, *he made some money.* Like most musicians, Mr. Bradbury possessed mechanical talents. He had the use of tools in wood work and an *inventive mind.* While in Dover he invented and made a model of a mowing machine, which created no little interest among the thinkers, before mowing machines were in use. Mr. Bradbury learned the art of popular book making well. He used to say, "if I have four or five good, rousing pieces in a book, I will risk the rest of it." In twenty-six years, from 1841 to 1867, he compiled in whole or in part, more than thirty books, the most important of which were "The Mendelssohn Collection," "The Shawm" and "Jubilee." His "Cantata of Esther" has been much sung all over the country. Mr. Bradbury possessed the ability of expressing poetry in music to an uncommon degree. He is said to have composed rapidly at times. Some of his books are among the best of his time; but if he had made *no piano-fortes* and less books, cared less for fame and money, and devoted his peculiar energies to the *solid study of music,* it is easy to think his books would have been more valuable, the music better. and that he might have seen more years.

Mr. Bradbury was a self-reliant and determined man. He was ambitious to the last degree, a brave, heroic worker, and of unsurpassed industry and endurance. Being a nervous man, he was, of course, at times, irritable; but he was really kind and tender-hearted. A few weeks before his death he said to a friend, "I long to be free from this evil body which does so much to drag me down. This busy brain and hasty nature lead me oftentimes to things that are contrary to the real feelings of my heart." Mr. Bradbury was a Christian, and beloved by his brethren. "When it was stated in the church that Mr. Bradbury was failing, the brethren devoted the rest of the evening to prayers for him, and continued it till he was beyond the reach of prayer." The five last days of his life were days of uninterrupted "ecstasy of delight," and he would exclaim, "what have I done that I should have such delightful assurance and comfort?" "How good is my Heavenly Father!" At one time he joined audibly in prayer, and then said, "Brother Smith, may God give me grace to die. I am going to see mother."

Much of the foregoing has been gathered from "The New York Musical Gazette." From the same source I make the following closing quotation. "And what a host of friends he leaves behind; friends among all Christian people, in all lands where the voice of sacred song is heard; friends among the teachers of sacred music throughout this country, who have caught new zeal from his cheerful, animating manner at the scores of musical conventions he conducted in all parts of the land: and more especially, friends among the children, to be counted literally by the million, who have sung and loved to sing his Sunday school music." S. P. C.

ST. CUTHBERT. L. M. H. W. GREATOREX. By per. of O. Ditson.

O all ye peo-ple, clap your hands, And with triumphant voi-ces sing; No force the might-y pow'r withstands Of God, the u - ni-versal King.

HENRY WELLINGTON GREATOREX, well known in this country as the author of several excellent collections of church music, and as an organist, was born at Burton-on-Trent, in 1816. "The Greatorex Collection of Church Music," published in 1851, was one of the best books ever produced in this country. Mr. Greatorex, after coming to America, became a resident of Hartford, Conn.; but died at Charleston, S. C. in 1858, aged 42 years. *Moore's New Encyclopedia of Music.*

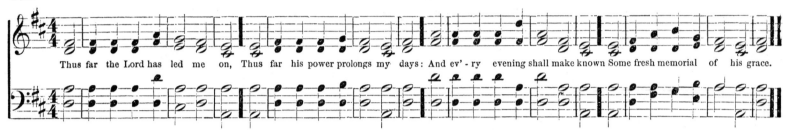

Thus far the Lord has led me on, Thus far his power prolongs my days: And ev'-ry evening shall make known Some fresh memorial of his grace.

ISAAC BAKER WOODBURY. From his family, from papers, and a personal acquaintance are gathered these few reliable statements concerning this interesting man. His middle name has been erroneously given in print, in several instances, as "Beverly" and it is not uncommon to hear him spoken of as "a cousin to B. F. Baker of Boston;" whereas he was not a relation of that gentleman, and his name is as given above. So write his wife and son. Mr. Woodbury was born in North Beverly, Mass., Oct. 23, 1819. His father died of consumption when his son was only eight years old. His education was obtained from the common school. Far enough ahead of common boys, almost in childhood, he seems to have felt and comprehended the stern realities of life, and the necessity of doing something, and doing it well. He made his way to Boston, probably before he was fifteen years old, and soon entered upon the study and practice of music. At a musical convention in North Bennington, Vt., in 1850, he told the writer of this how he went into the country from Boston when he was "seventeen," and *got up* conventions and conducted them "all alone," and laughed at his boyish assurance.

"When eighteen years of age, Lowell Mason employed him to teach music in the public schools of Boston." By constant industry and rigid economy, he saved money enough with "the little his father left him," to take him to Europe when he was twenty years old, and sustain him there one year. This, it seems, had been his grand aim from the start. A brave and noble undertaking for one of his years and circumstances. He spent half of that year in study and practice with Sir Henry Phillips of London, and the other half in Paris with good masters, attending operas, concerts, &c. At the expiration of the year he returned to Boston with a large stock of good music for future use, and established himself in Boston as a teacher and organist, and soon commenced the work of composing. In 1840 he commenced publishing music books, and most industriously continued the work till 1857. During that period he edited no less than 11 church music books, 7 glee books, 4 singing and day school books, 2

Sabbath-school books, 1 anthem collection, 1 oratorio, 1 on thorough bass, 1 on the cultivation of the voice, and 7 volumes of musical papers. Having died when only 39 years old, it is wonderful he accomplished so much. He must have possessed great *business* as well as professional abilities. His books were very popular, and some are still so. It is doubtful if more copies of any singing book in this country have been sold in the same number of years, than of "The Dulcimer" which he published in 1850. His tunes are remarkable for simplicity and sweetness, and will be loved and sung long after *all who knew him here*, have gone to join him with the great choir " on the other shore." Some of his songs, published in sheet form, were immensely popular. "He doeth all things well," and " Be kind to the loved ones" are among his best. Mr. Woodbury had talent for composing music of a higher order, as may be seen by examining the original portions of his oratorio of "Absalom." He saw what the people demanded and supplied them. His New York publisher, F. J. Huntington, who died Feb. 1878, said to me a few days before his sudden and lamented death, "Mr. Woodbury studied the public taste with a keener discernment than any man I ever knew, and knew better what would please." Mr. Woodbury had an excellent voice, and was really an effective and good singer. It is strange that more was not said about it; and he played for himself a good accompaniment. As I remember him in 1850, he was a man a little above the common stature, with dark hair and eyes, easy and graceful manners, and an uncommon smiling face. The ladies called him " fine looking." He conducted musical conventions in *all* parts of the country. I am compelled to believe that he was, like Mr. Bradbury, an over-ambitious and over-worked man. In 1846 Mr. Woodbury married, in Salem, Mass., Miss Mary Abby Putnam, a native of Beverly, and in the same year he united with Dr. Nehemiah Adams' church in Boston. Two years after he removed his connection to the Rutgers St. Presbyterian church in New York city, of which he remained a member till his death. Mr. Woodbury went four times to Europe; two of them for his health. His last winter he spent on "the Nile," but consumption, his inherited disease, could no longer be stayed. He returned home in the summer of 1858, and on the 28th of Oct. following, he died in Charleston, S. C., on his way to Florida. His re-mains were brought home to Norwalk, Conn., where a granite monument marks his grave, with the simple inscription,—"He doeth all things well."

S. P. C.

ANTHEM FOR EASTER.

BILLINGS.

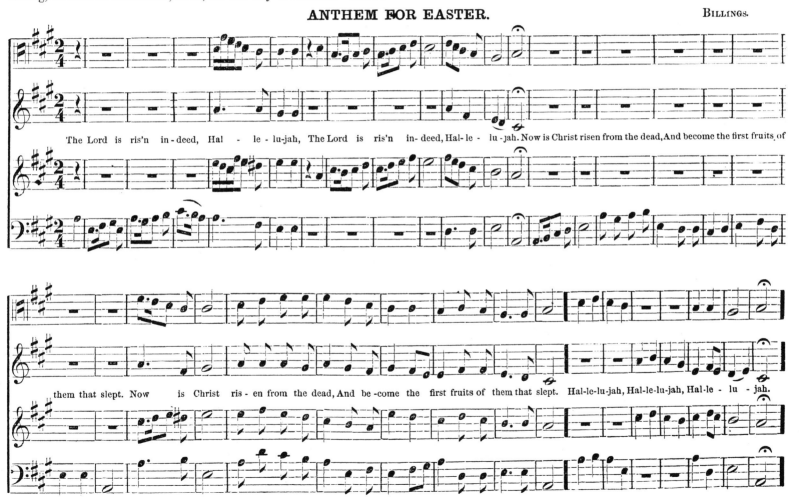

The Lord is ris'n in-deed, Hal - le - lu-jah, The Lord is ris'n in- deed, Hal-le - lu - jah. Now is Christ risen from the dead, And become the first fruits of

them that slept. Now is Christ ris - en from the dead, And be -come the first fruits of them that slept. Hal-le-lu-jah, Hal-le-lu-jah, Hal-le - lu - jah.

And did he rise,   And did he rise,

And did he rise,   And did he rise,   did he rise? Hear, O ye nations, Hear it, O ye dead!   He rose, he rose, he rose, he rose, He

And did he rise,   And did he rise,

And did he rise,   And did he rise, did he   rise....................

burst the bars of death, He burst the bars of death, He burst the bars of death, And triumphed o'er the grave. Then,   then,   then I rose, Then   I rose,

Then I rose. Then first hu - man - i - ty tri - umphant passed the crystal ports of light, And seized e - ter - nal youth. Man, all im -mor-tal, hail!

Rit.

Hail! Heav-en all lav-ish of strange gifts to man, Thine all the glo - ry, man's the boundless bliss, Thine all the glo - ry, man's the boundless bliss.

Rit.

DAVID'S LAMENTATION.

Billings.

QUARTET.
Moderato.

Da- vid the king was griev-ed and mov-ed, he went to his chamber, his chamber, and wept. O my

And as he went, he wept and said, O my

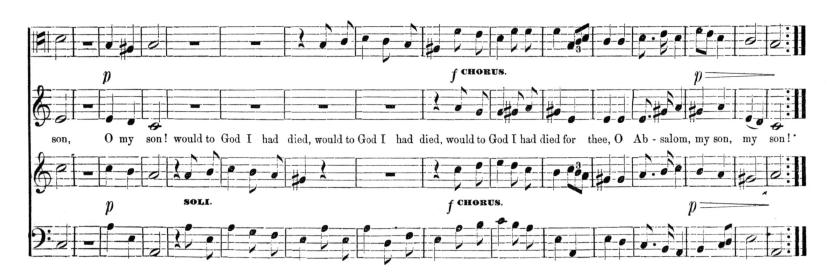

son, O my son! would to God I had died, would to God I had died, would to God I had died for thee, O Ab - salom, my son, my son!

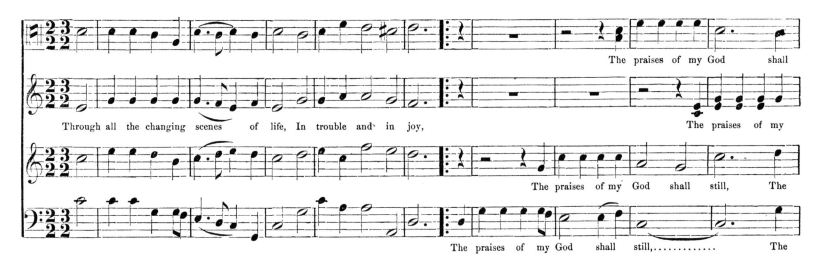

WORCESTER. S. M.

Wood.

Who stand on Zion's Hill, Who bring salvation on their tongues, And words of peace reveal, Who bring sal- va - tion on their

How beauteous are their feet, Who stand on Zi-on's Hill, Who bring sal-va - tion on their tongues, And words of peace reveal ;

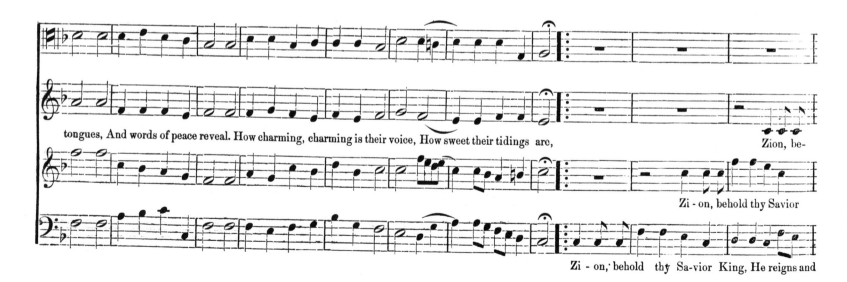

tongues, And words of peace reveal. How charming, charming is their voice, How sweet their tidings are,   Zion, be-

Zi - on, behold thy Savior

Zi - on, behold thy Sa-vior King, He reigns and

Zi - on, behold thy Savior King, He reigns and triumphs here,

hold thy Sa-vior King, He reigns and triumphs here, He reigns and triumphs here; Zion, behold thy Savior King, He reigns and triumphs here.

King, He reigns and triumphs here; Zi - on, behold thy Savior King, He reigns and triumphs here;

triumphs here; Zi - on, behold thy Sa - vior King, ... He reigns and triumphs here;

CHESTER. L. M. (Billings' Patriotic Song.) Words and music by BILLINGS.

1. Let tyrants shake their i - ron rod, And slavery clank her gall - ing chains; We fear them not, we trust in God, New England's God for - ev - er reigns.

2. Howe and Burgoyne and Clin - ton too, With Prescott and Corn - wal - lis joined, To-gether plot our o - ver-throw, In oue in-fer - nal league combined.
3. The foe comes on with haugh - ty stride, Our troops advance with mar - tial noise: Their vet'rans flee be-fore our youth, And Gen'rals yield to beard - less boys.

4. What grateful off - 'ring shall we bring, What shall we ren-der to the Lord? Loud halle-lu - jahs let us sing, And praise his name on ev' - ry chord.

OCEAN. C. M.

Swan's name has been, in some books, over this tune, but if he did anything to it, he arranged it from an old tune.   He did not compose it.

With songs   and honors sounding loud, Address the Lord on high ;   O - ver   the heavens he spreads his clouds, And waters vail the sky. He sends his showers of

He

He sends his showers of

He sends his showers of blessings down To cheer............ the plains be - low,

blessings down To cheer the plains below,He sends his showers of blessings down To cheer the plains below,He makes the grass the mountains crown,And corn in valleys grow.

sends his showers of blessings down To cheer the plains below,

blessings down To cheer the plains be - low...

The new Je - ru - sa-lem comes down, A-

From the third heav'n where God resides, That ho- ly hap - py place, The

The new Je - ru - sa - lem comes down, A-dorned . . . .

The new Je - ru -sa-lem comes down, A- dorned . . . . with

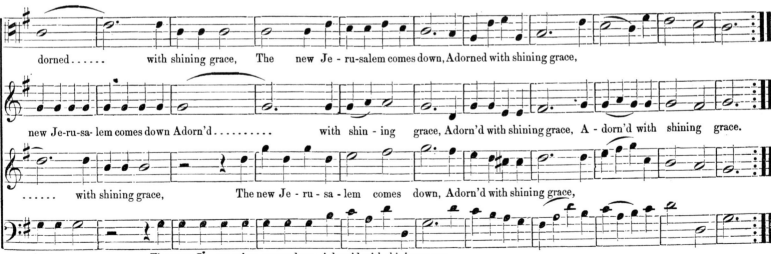

dorned . . . . . . with shining grace, The new Je - ru-salem comes down, Adorned with shining grace,

new Je-ru-sa- lem comes down Adorn'd . . . . with shin - ing grace, Adorn'd with shining grace, A - dorn'd with shining grace.

. . . . . . with shining grace, The new Je - ru - sa - lem comes down, Adorn'd with shining grace,

shining grace, The new Je - ru-salem comes down, Adorn'd with shining grace,

1. Hail! Co-lum-bia, happy land, Hail! ye heroes, heav'n-born band; Who fought and bled in freedom's cause, Who fought and bled in freedom's cause, And when the storm of

2. Immortal patriots, rise once more, Defend your rights, defend your shore; Let no rude foe with impious hands, Let no rude foe with impious hands, Invade the shrine where
3.   Sound, sound the trump of fame, Let Washington's great name Ring thro' the world with loud applause, Ring thro' the world with loud applause, Let ev'ry clime to

4. Behold the chief who now commands, Once more to serve his country stands, The rock on which the storm will beat, The rock on which the storm will beat, But arm'd in virtue

war was gone, Enjoy'd the peace your valor won; Let independence be our boast, Ever mindful what it cost, Ev - er grateful for the prize, Let its al - tar

sacred lies, Of toil and blood the well-earned prize: While offering peace sincere and just, In heaven we place a manly trust, That truth and justice will prevail, And ev'ry scheme of
freedom dear, Listen with a joyful ear: With equal skill, with God-like pow'r, He governs in the fearful hour Of horrid war, or guides with ease The happier times of

firm and true, His hopes are fix'd on heav'n and you! When hope was sinking in dismay, When glooms obscur'd Columbia's day, His steady mind from changes free, Resolv'd on death or

reach the skies. Firm, u – nit – ed let us be, Rallying round our lib – .er – ty, As a band of broth – ers join'd, Peace and safety we shall find.

bondage fail. Firm, u – nit – ed let us be, Rallying round our lib – er – ty, As a band of broth – ers join'd, Peace and safety we shall find.

hon – est peace.

lib – er – ty. Firm, &c.

MARSEILLES HYMN.

FRENCH AIR.

1. Ye sons of Free – dom, wake to glo – ry, Hark! hark! what my – riads bid you rise; Your children, wives, and grand-sires

2. O, lib – er – ty, can man re – sign thee, Once hav – ing felt thy glo – rious flame? Can ty – rants' bolts and bars con –

hoar - y,   Behold their tears, and hear their cries!   Behold their tears and hear their cries!   Shall lawless ty - rants, mis - chief

- fine thee,   And thus thy no - ble spir - it tame?   And thus thy no - ble spir - it tame?   Too long our coun - try wept, be -

breeding,   With hireling host, a ruf - fian band,   Af - fright and des - o - late the land,   While peace and lib - er - ty lie

- wail - ing   The blood-stain'd sword our con-querors wield,   But free - dom is our sword and shield,   And all their arts are un - a -

bleeding.   To arms, to arms, ye brave!   The pa - triot sword unsheath!   March on, march on, all hearts resolved   On lib - er - ty or death!

- vail - ing.   To arms, to arms, ye brave!   The pa - triot sword unsheath!   March on, march on, all hearts resolved   On lib - er - ty or death!

1. Oh say, can you see by the dawn's early light, What so proudly we hailed at the twilight's last gleaming, Whose broad stripes and bright stars thro' the

2. On the shore dim - ly seen thro' the mists of the deep, Where the foe's haughty host in dread silence re - pos-es, What is that which the breeze o'er the
3. And where is the band that so vaunting- ly swore, 'Mid the hav - oc of war and the battle's con - fu - sion, A home and a coun-try they would

4. And thus be it ev - er when freemen shall stand Be - tween their loved homes and the war's desolation; Blest with vict'ry and peace, may the

per - il - ous fight, O'er the ram- parts we watched were so gal-lant - ly streaming; And the rockets' red glare, the bombs bursting in air, Gave

tow - er - ing steep, As it fit - ful - ly blows, half conceals, half dis-clo - ses? Now it catches the gleam of the morning's first beam, Its
leave us no more, Their blood has washed out their foul footsteps pol - lu - tion; No ref-uge could save the hireling and slave From the

heaven-res - cued land Praise the Pow'r that hath made and preserved us a na-tion; Then conquer we must, for our cause it is just, And

proof thro' the night that our flag was still there, Oh say, does the Star-Spangled Banner yet wave O'er the land of the free and the home of the brave.

glo - ry re - flect- ed now shines on the stream. And the Star-Spangled Banner in triumph shall wave O'er the land of the free and the home of the brave.
ter - ror of flight or the gloom of the grave. And the Star-Spangled Banner &c.

this be our mot - to, In God is our trust. And the Star-Spangled Banner in triumph shall wave O'er the land of the free and the home of the brave.

STAR-SPANGLED BANNER. There are few Americans who have not sung, heard sung, or heard played upon instruments, this best of our national songs. It was written by Francis Scott Key, in 1814; and the words were adapted to an old English air, "Anacreon in Heaven," by Ferdinand Durang, of Baltimore, Md. The song was first printed by B. Ides, of Baltimore, and first sung by F. Durang to some soldiers in a house near the Holiday Theatre, Baltimore. The British fleet attempted to take the city of Baltimore, and the bombardment of Fort Mc Henry occurred on the 13th of September, 1814. Mr. Key and one Mr. Skinner were sent in a vessel with a flag of truce, to obtain from the English the release of some prisoners, and were themselves detained lest they might give information of the contemplated attack. The Key vessel was kept under the guns of a frigate in sight of the fort, where they could plainly see the American flag flying from the ramparts. The bombardment commenced in the evening; and Key and Skinner remained on the deck spectators of the terrific cannonading of that night — trembling for the result as they waited and watched through the long hours; and when at daylight they saw that "our flag was still there," Mr. Key took an old letter from his pocket and on the blank portion of it pencilled the Star-Spangled Banner; it originally being entitled "The Defence of Fort Mc Henry." It was at once received with shouts of applause, and never was there a wedding of poetry to music of greater influence; it was soon caught up by the bands and orchestras, and by the people on the streets; and when peace was declared, the soldiers scattering to their homes carried the song to thousands of firesides; and it will live as long as there are American patriots alive to sing it.

The song is pathetic and inspiring; the spirit of truth is in every line; and in every word we find the ardent glow of a patriotic fire which burns as brightly to-day as it did in the breast of Mr. Key when he wrote it. That poet and musician will be indeed immortal whose genius can give us a better song; may our countrymen ever treasure it, and ever be ready to defend it as the stars and stripes flash through the air in protection of a free people. Mr. Key was a native of Maryland, born Aug. 1, 1779; he died in Washington, Jan. 11, 1846.

Moore's New Encyclopedia of Music.

Written by GEN. MORRIS.

YANKEE DOODLE.

1. Once on a time old Johnny Bull Flew in a raging fu - ry, And swore that Jonathan should have No tri-als, sir, by ju - ry: That no e - lec-tions

2. John sent the tea from o'er the sea, With heav-y du -ties ra - ted; But whether Hy-son or Bo- hea, I nev - er heard it sta -ted. Then Jonathan, to

3. A long war then they had in which, John was at last de-feat- ed, And "Yankee Doodle" was the march to which his troops retreated. Cute Jonathan, to

4. I've told you now the or - i - gin, Of this most live -ly dit -ty, Which Johnny Bull dislikes, as "dull And stupid !"what a pi - ty !With Hail Columbia !

should be held, A - cross the bri -ny wa-ters, And now, said he, I'll tax the tea of all his sons and daughters. Then down he sate in burly state and blustered like a

pout be - gan, And laid a strong em-bar-go, I'll drink no tea, by Jove ! said he, Throw overboard the cargo. Then Johnny sent a regiment, Big words and looks to

see them fly, Could not re-strain his laughter : That tune said he suits to a T, I'll sing it ever after. Old Johnny's face to his disgrace, Was flushed with beer and

it is sung, In chorus full and hearty, O'er land and main we sing the strain, John made for this tea-party. No matter how we rhyme the words, The music speaks them

grandee, And in de-ris-ion made a tune call'd "Yankee doodle dan-dy." "Yankee doodle, these are facts, Yankee doodle dandy, My son of wax, your

bandy, Whose martial band, when near the land, Play'd Yankee doodle dandy. Yankee doodle, keep it up! Yankee doodle dandy! I'll poison with a
brandy, E'en while he swore, to sing no more, This Yankee doodle dan-dy. Yankee doodle, ho! ha! he! Yankee doodle dandy, We kept the tune, but

handy, And where's the fair can't sing the air, Of "Yankee doodle dandy."   [*Omit to coda for last verse.*]

[*Coda for last verse.*]

tea I'll tax, Yan-kee doo-dle dan-dy.

tax your cup, Yan-kee doo-dle dan-dy.   Yankee doo-dle firm and true, Yankee doodle dan-dy, Yankee doodle, doodle doo, Yankee doodle dan-dy.
not the tea, Yan-kee doo-dle dan-dy.

1. When Is - rael was in E - gypt's land ; Let my peo - ple go, Oppressed so hard they could not stand,
2. Thus saith the Lord, bold Mo - ses said, Let my peo - ple go, If not I'll smite your first - born dead,
3. The Lord told Mo - ses what to do, Let my peo - ple go ; To lead the chil - dren of Is - rael through,

Let my peo - ple go. Go down, Mo - ses, way down in E - gypt's land, Tell ole Pha - roh, Let my peo - ple go.

4. As Israel stood by the water side,
   Let my people go ;
   At God's command it did divide,
   Let my people go.
   Go down, Moses, etc.

5. When they had reached the other shore,
   Let my people go ;
   They sang their triumph o'er and o'er,
   Let my people go.
   Go down, Moses, etc.

6. Ole Pharoh said he'd go across,
   Let my people go ;
   But Pharoh and his host were lost,
   Let my people go.
   Go down, Moses, etc.

7. I do believe without a doubt,
   Let my people go ;
   That a Christian has a right to shout,
   Let my people go.
   Go down, Moses, etc.

8. This world's a wilderness of woe,
   Let my people go ;
   O, let us on to Canaan go,
   Let my people go.
   Go down, Moses, etc.

9. What a beautiful morning that will be,
   Let my people go ;
   When time breaks up in eternity,
   Let my people go.
   Go down, Moses, etc.

Secular Department.

COLUMBIA.

Arranged for "The Cheney Family" by George Loder.

See gen-tle peace pre-vail - ing. While on the waves that guard thy coast, while on the waves that guard thy coast, Columbia's Navy, freemen's boast,

While on the waves that guard thy coast, the waves that guard thy coast, Columbia's Navy, freemen's boast,

Let my peo-ple go. Go down, Mo-ses, way down in E-gypt's land, Tell ole Pha-roh, Let my peo-ple go.

4. As Israel stood by the water side,
      Let my people go ;
   At God's command it did divide,
      Let my people go.
   Go down, Moses, etc.

5. When they had reached the other shore,
      Let my people go ;
   They sang their triumph o'er and o'er,
      Let my people go.
   Go down, Moses, etc.

6. Ole Pharoh said he'd go across,
      Let my people go ;
   But Pharoh and his host were lost,
      Let my people go.
   Go down, Moses, etc.

7. I do believe without a doubt,
      Let my people go ;
   That a Christian has a right to shout,
      Let my people go.
   Go down, Moses, etc.

8. This world's a wilderness of woe,
      Let my people go ;
   O, let us on to Canaan go,
      Let my people go.
   Go down, Moses, etc.

9. What a beautiful morning that will be,
      Let my people go ;
   When time breaks up in eternity,
      Let my people go.
   Go down, Moses, etc.

Secular Department.

COLUMBIA.

Arranged for "The Cheney Family" by GEORGE LODER.

CHORUS. Soprano.

ff Andante maestoso. *pp*

QUARTET or SEMI-CHORUS.

p Moderato assai.

* Tenor.

* Alto voices may sing the Tenor.

ff Oh! Lib-er-ty, *pp* Oh! Lib-er-ty. *p* Co-lumbia, on thy fer-tile plains, No cru-el war a-round thee reigns. See gentle peace,

Baritone.

Bass. *ff* *pp* *p*

f CHORUS.

f

See gen-tle peace pre-vail - ing. While on the waves that guard thy coast, while on the waves that guard thy coast, Columbia's Navy, freemen's boast,

f CHORUS.

While on the waves that guard thy coast, the waves that guard thy coast, Columbia's Navy, freemen's boast,

freemen's boast, Now is sail - ing; Now is sail - ing, Columbia's Navy, freemen s boast, freemen s

Spite of each foe is sail - ing,

_pp_ QUARTET. _ff_ CHORUS. _pp_ _f_ QUARTET.

Now is sail - ing,

CHORUS
Lively.

spite of each foe is sail-ing, is sail - ing. 1ST TIME P. REPEAT F.

Now is sail - ing, sail - ing.

Long may the yellow harvest glad thy happy land, Long may thy wooden walls repel each hostile band.

spite of each foe is sail-ing, is sail - ing. REPEAT F.

CHORUS.

Now is sail - ing, sail - ing.

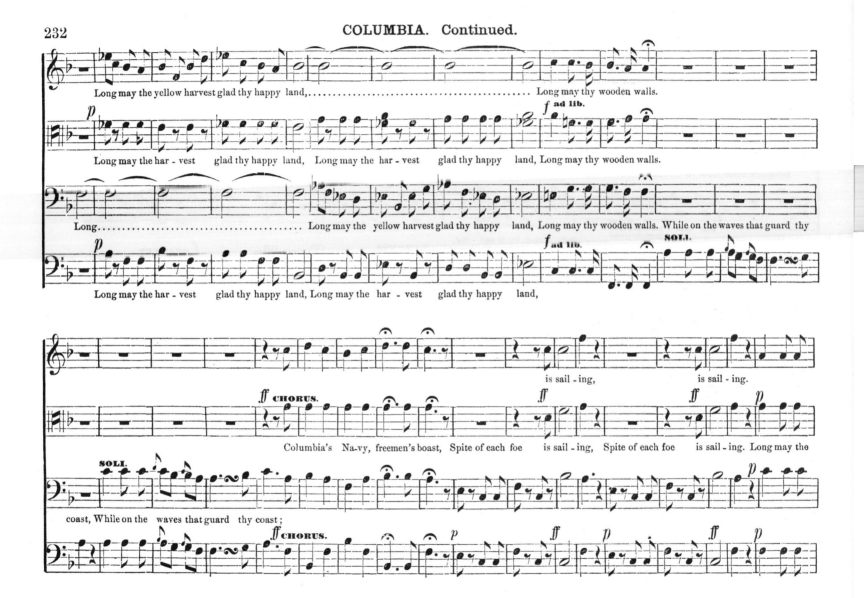

yel - low har - vest glad thy hap - py land, Long may thy wooden walls re - pel each hos-tile band. Long may the

land, Long may thy wood - en walls re - pel each hostile band.   band, Re - pel   each hos - tile band, Re - pel . . . . . . each hos - tile band.

GREEN MOUNTAIN SONG.

Written for " The Cheney Family," by Mary Cutts of Hartland, Vt., 1846.

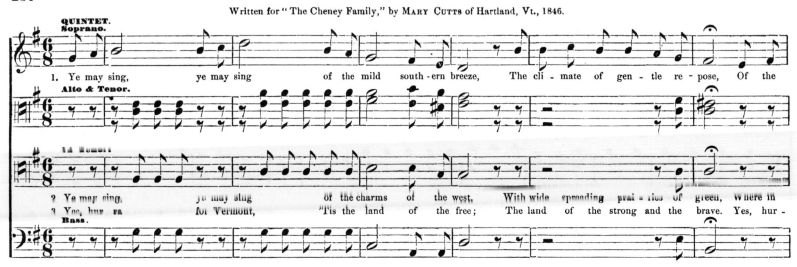

1. Ye may sing, ye may sing of the mild south-ern breeze, The cli-mate of gen-tle re-pose, Of the

2 Ye may sing, ye may sing of the charms of the west, With wide spreading prai-ries of green, Where in

3 Yes, hur-ra for Vermont, 'Tis the land of the free; The land of the strong and the brave. Yes, hur-

land where the vine and the ol-ive u-nite, And the sweet-scent-ed or-ange bud blows. We will tell, we will

in freedom the buf-fa-lo

free — dom the buf — fa-lo rang-es a-long, And the fa-ther of wa-ters is seen. We will tell, we will

'ra for Vermont, ev-er stead-y and true, What foe-man can ev-er de-prave? Her fair are for

in freedom the buf-fa-lo

4, Ah! oth-er bright scenes may on-tice us a-way, In oth-er lands oft we may roam; Yet still will the heart ev-er beat with de-

-light, At the name of its own mountain home, At the name of its own mountain home.   Then hur-ra yet a-gain for our dear na-tive

State, Though oft we may wander a - far, For Vermont, brave Vermont, With her ev - er - green hills, Hurra........ and hur - ra

ra, Hurra........ and hur - ra and hur - ra. Hur - ra, hur - ra, hur - ra,

SOLO. cres. & rit. ad lib. CHORUS. ff ad lib. fff

Hur - ra.......................... and hur - ra and hur - ra. fff

hur - ra and hur - ra. ad lib.

Sir Walter Scott.

O HUSH THEE, MY BABY.

Arthur S. Sullivan.

O hush thee, my ba - by, thy sire was a knight, Thy mother a la - dy both gen - tle and bright, both gen-tle and bright, The woods and the

O hush thee, my ba - by, thy sire was a knight, Thy mother a la - dy both gen - tle and bright, both gen - tle and bright; The woods and the

glens from the tow'rs which we see, They are all be - long-ing, dear ba-by, to thee, They are all be-long-ing, dear ba - by, to thee.

They are all be-long ing to thee, They are all be-long-ing, dear ba - by, to thee. O

glens from the tow'rs which we see, They are all be-long- ing to thee, They are all be-long-ing, dear ba - by, to thee. O

to thee. O hush thee, O

hush thee, my ba-by, O hush thee, my ba-by, O hush thee, my ba - by.

hush thee, my ba-by, O hush thee, my ba-by, O hush thee, my ba - by. O fear not the bugle, though loudly it blows ; It calls but the

staccato.

war-ders that guard thy re-pose, that guard thy repose. Their bows would be bended, their blades would be red, Ere the step of a foeman draws

Ere the step of a

warders that guard thy re-pose, that guard thy repose. Their bows would be bended, their blades would be red, Ere the step of a

that guard thy repose.

near to thy bed, Ere the step of a foe-man draws near to thy bed.   O hush......... thee, my ba - - - -

foeman draws near, Ere the step of a foeman draws near to thy bed.   O hush thee, my ba-by, O hush thee, my ba-by, O hush thee, my ba -

foe-man draws near, Ere the step of a foe-man draws near to thy bed.   O hush thee, my ba-by, O hush thee, my ba-by, O hush thee, my ba -

O hush thee, O hush thee, my baby, O hush thee, my ba-by, O hush thee, my ba -

by.   O hush thee, my ba- by, the time soon will come, When thy sleep shall be broken by trum - pet and drum,   by trum-pet and

by.   O hush thee, my ba- by, the time soon will come, When thy sleep shall be broken by trum - pet and drum, by trum-pet and

drum. Then hush thee, my dar-ling, take rest while you may, For strife............ comes with man - hood, For strife comes with manhood and wa - king with

For strife comes with manhood, and waking with day, For strife comes with manhood and waking with day. O

day,   O hush........ thee, O hush........ thee, O hush...... thee, O hush thee, O hush thee, my ba - by !

day   O hush thee, my ba-by, O hush thee my ba-by, O hush thee my ba-by, O hush thee my babe,   O hush thee, my ba - by !

day.   O hush thee my ba -by, O hush thee my ba -by, O hush thee my ba-by, O hush...... thee, O hush thee, O hush thee, my ba - by !

hush thee, O hush thee my ba- by, O hush thee my ba -by, O hush thee my ba- by, O hush thee my babe,   O hush thee my ba - by !

SWEET HOME. Quintet.   Arranged for " The Cheney Family " by GEORGE KINGSLEY.

Soprano & Alto.

1. 'Mid pleasures and pal - a - ces, tho' we may roam, Be it ev - er so humble there's no place like home ; A charm from the skies seems to hallow us

1st Tenor.

2d Tenor.

? An id ile from home, splendor daz - zles in vain, Oh ! give me my low - ly thatch'd cottage again ; The birds singing gai-ly that came at my

Bass.

there, Which, seek thro' the world is ne'er met with elsewhere. Home, home, sweet, sweet home, There's no place like home, There's no place like home. Home, sweet home.

call, Give me these with the peace of mind, dear - er than all. Home, home, sweet, sweet home, There's no place like home, There's no place like home. Home, sweet home.

Home.....

THE STIFF COLD-WATER MAN.

John G. Saxe.

S. P. Cheney. 1846.
As sung by "The Cheney Family."

2 For science and for books, he said
    He never had a wish,—
No school to him was worth a fig,
    Except a school of fish.
He ne'er aspired to rank or wealth,
    Nor cared about a name,—
For though much famed for fish was he,
    He never fished for fame.

3 All day this fisherman would sit
    Upon an ancient log,
And gaze into the water, like
    Some sedentary frog :
With all the seeming innocence,
    And that unconcious look,
That other people often wear
    When they intend to "hook !"

4 To charm the fish he never spoke,—
    Although his voice was fine ;
He found the most convenient way
    Was just to drop a line !
And many a gudgeon of the pond,
    If they could speak to-day,
Would own with grief, this angler had
    A mighty taking way !

5 Alas ! one day this fisherman
    Had taken too much grog,
And being but a landsman, too,
    He couldn't keep the log !
'Twas all in vain with might and main
    He strove to reach the shore,
Down—down he went, to feed the fish,
    He'd baited oft before !

6 The jury gave the verdict that
    'Twas nothing else but gin
Had caused the fisherman to be
    So sadly taken in ;
Though one stood out upon a whim,
    And said the angler's slaughter,
To be exact about the fact,
    Was clearly gin-and-water !

7 The moral of this mournful tale,
    To all is plain and clear,—
That drinking habits bring a man
    Too often to his bier ;
And he who scorns to "take the pledge,"
    And keep the promise fast,
May be, in spite of fate, a stiff
    Cold water man at last !

SONG OF THE VERMONTERS.

Arranged for " The Cheney Family " by Geo. Kingsley.

1. Ho! all to the bor - ders, Vermonters come down, With your breeches of deer-skin and jackets of brown With your red woollen caps and your

2. Does the old Bay State threaten ! Does Congress complain ? Swarms Hampshire in arms on our bor- ders a-gain ! Bark the war-dogs of Britain a-

moc - ca - sons come, To the gath - er - ing sum-mons of trum - pet and drum. Come down with your ri - fles, let gray wolf and fox Howl

loud on the lake ? Let them come, what they can they are wel - come to take. What seek they a - mong us ? the pride of our wealth Is

on in the shade of their prim . .

comfort, con-tentment, and la - bor and health, And lands which as free-men we on - ly have trod, In - de - pen - dent of all save the mercies of God.

3 We owe no allegiance, we bow to no throne,
Our ruler is law and the law is our own;
Our leaders themselves are our own fellow men,
Who can handle the sword, or the scythe, or the **pen**;
Our wives are all true and our daughters are fair,
With their blue eyes of smiles and their light **flowing hair,**
All brisk at the wheel till the dark even fall,
Then blithe at the sleigh-ride, the husking and ball.

4 And ours are the mountains that awfully rise
Till they rest their green heads on the blue of the **skies;**
And ours are the forests, unwasted, unshorn,
Save where the wild path of the tempest is torn;

And though savage and wild be this climate of **ours,**
And brief be our seasons of fruit and of flowers,
Far dearer the blast round our mountains which **raves,**
Than the sweet summer zephyr which breathes **over slaves.**

5 Then hurra for Vermont, for the land which we **till**
Must have sons to defend her from valley and hill.
Leave the harvest to rot on the field where it grows,
And the reaping of wheat for the reaping of foes.
Come York or come Hampshire, come traitors and **knaves,**
If you rule o'er our land you shall rule o'er **our graves;**
Our vow is recorded, our banner unfurled,
In the name of Vermont we defy all the world.

THE SPRING IS COMING.

S. P. Cheney.

From the New York Tribune, April, 1848.

The Spring is coming, The Spring, the Spring,

1. The Spring is com-ing, it is, it is, The spring is com-ing, it is, it is; The snow is melt-ing a-way, The

2. The flowers will soon...... be here, The

The Spring is coming, The spring is coming,

3. Let ev-ery heart........ re-joice, Let

snow is melt-ing a-way, And birds which fled when sum-mer sped, For fields more bright and gay, Have come a-gain to their

flowers will soon....... be here, With per-fume rare to fill the air, And bid our spir-its cheer; The ver-nal grass.... once

ev-ery heart........ re-joice. Let ev-ery tongue that ev-er sung, Chime in with na-ture's voice: Bid gloom-y care......and

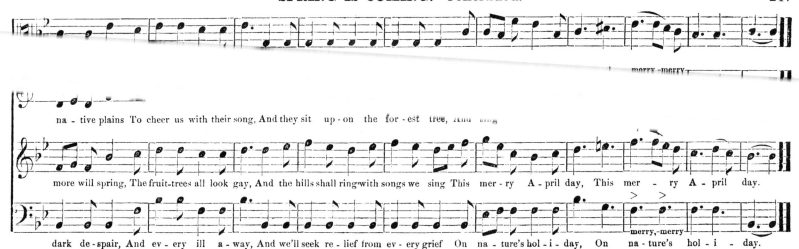

na - tive plains To cheer us with their song, And they sit up - on the for - est tree, And sing

more will spring, The fruit-trees all look gay, And the hills shall ring with songs we sing This mer - ry A - pril day, This mer - ry A - pril day.

dark de-spair, And ev - ery ill a - way, And we'll seek re - lief from ev - ery grief On na - ture's hol - i - day, On na - ture's hol - i - day.

COME SING WITH DO RE MI.*

S. P. CHENEY.

Allegretto.

mf Do re mi do re mi do re mi do re mi do do do do do do si

Do re mi do re mi do re mi do re mi, We all a-gree, And sing in tune and time.

mf Come sing with do re mi, And we will hap - py be, If we can all a - gree, And sing in tune and time.

Do re............ mi do re mi, All a - gree, And sing in tune and time.

*The spirit and movement of this piece were caught from the motion of cars riding from Napa to Napa Junction, Cal.

Do re mi do re mi   do re mi do re mi   do re mi, We almost have a glee in rhyme.   rhyme.

Do re mi do re mi   do   re   mi do re mi   We al-most have   a   glee in rhyme.   rhyme.

Let out the voices free,   And make it plain to see,   We al-most have a glee   in rhyme.   rhyme.   Now

Do re mi do re mi   do re mi do re mi   We al-most have   a   glee in rhyme.   rhyme.

La si do   la si do la si do la si do la   la si do la si do la............ We

La si do   la si do la si do la si do la   la si do la si do la si do la   We

change to la si do,........... And change the move-ment too,........... That all may sure-ly know.......... We

La si do   la si do la si do la si do la   la si do la si do la si do la   We

sing the mi-nor scale, We sing no tale of woe, We on-ly wish to show We're sure to make it go Without fail. fail.

Now sing with la la la la

la la la la la la la la la la la la la la la la Mu-sic hates all war, We must have har-mo - ny.

la la la la la la la la la la la la la la la Mu-sic hates all war, We must have har-mo - ny.

la Look out and make no jar, For mu - sic hates all war, We must have har-mo - ny. Sing now with loud hur-

la la la la la la la la la la la la la la la Mu-sic hates all war, We must have har-mo - ny.

hur-rah,   hur-rah,   hur-rah, with what e - clat sing we, sing we.   And louder still hur - rah,   hurrah, hurrah, hur-

hur-rah,   hur-rah,   Hurrah, with what e - clat sing we, sing we.   hur - rah,

rah,   Hurrah, hur-rah, hur-rah,   hurrah, with what e - clat   sing we, sing we.   And louder still hur - rah,   hurrah, hurrah, hur-

hur-rah,   hur-rah,   Hurrah, with what e - clat sing we, sing we.   hur - rah,

hurrah, |1st.| 2d.   Sing we,......   sing we, sing we.

rah,   Hurrah with what e- clat   sing we. we. With what eclat sing we, With what eclat sing we, sing we, Sing   we,   sing we, sing we

hurrah,   Sing we, sing we,   sing we.

2. Who rightly scans thy beau - ty, A sol-emn word shall read Of love, of truth and du - ty, Our hope in time of need. And I have read them of - ten,

2. Who rightly scans thy beau - ty, A solemn word shall read Of love, of truth and du - ty, Our hope in time of need. And I have read.... them of - ten,

2. Who rightly scans thy beau - ty, A solemn word shall read Of love, of truth and du - ty, Our hope in time of need. And I have read.... them of - ten,

And I have read them often,

Those words so true and clear, What heart that would not soften Thy wisdom to re - vere, What heart that would not soft - en Thy wis - dom to re - vere?

Those words so true and clear, What heart that would not soften Thy wisdom to re - vere, What heart that would not soft - en Thy wis - - - - dom to re - vere?

Those words so true and clear, What heart that would not soften Thy wisdom to re - vere, What heart that would not soft - en Thy wis - dom to re - vere?

soft - en, What heart that would not soft - - en Thy wis - dom to re - vere?

And there the world re - call - ing,

3. Ah! soon must I for - sake thee, My own, my shelt'ring home, In sorrow soon be - take me, In yon vain world to roam, And there the word...... re - call - ing,

3. Ah! soon must I for - sake thee, My own, my shelt'ring home, In sorrow soon be - take me, In yon vain world to roam, And there the word...... re - call - ing,

And there the word recalling,

Thy solemn les -sons teach, 'Mid care and danger fall - ing, No harm my soul shall reach, 'Mid care and danger fall - ing, No harm my soul shall reach

Thy solemn les -sons teach, 'Mid care and danger fall - ing, No harm my soul shall reach, 'Mid care and danger fall - ing, No harm...........my soul shall reach.

Thy solemn les -sons teach, 'Mid care and danger fall - ing, No harm my soul shall reach, 'Mid care and danger fall - ing, No harm my soul shall reach.

fall - - - ing, 'Mid care and danger fall - - - - - ing, No harm my soul shall reach,

Words by T. K. Harvey — English.

TO MY MOTHER IN HEAVEN.

AND THE REPLY, by Lizzie Manchester.

Melody by Sarah Burtis, of Troy.

Harmonized by J. A. Johnson.

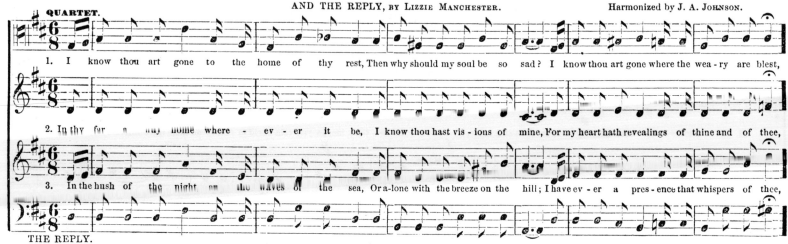

And I hear a low murmur like thine in re-ply, When I pour out my spir-it in prayer. I nev-er look up with a wish to

But the forms of thy darlings come gather-ing nigh, When thou raisest thy spir-it in prayer. Thou never look'st up with a wish to the sky,

But a light like thy beau-ty is there; And I hear a low murmur like thine in re-ply, When I pour out my spir-it in prayer.

The love of thy moth-er to share; But the forms of thy darlings come gath-er-ing nigh, When thou rais-est thy spir-it in prayer.

James Linen. **GROWING AULD. Quartet for male voices.** S. P. Cheney.

1. I feel I'm grow-ing auld, gude wife, I feel I'm growing auld; My steps are frail, my een are bleared, My pow is un - co bauld. I've seen the snows of fourscore

2. I feel I'm growing auld, gude wife, I feel I'm growing auld. Frae youth to age I've kept it warm, The love that ne'er turned cauld. I can - na bear the dreary

3. I feel I'm growing auld, gude wife, I feel I'm grow-ing auld: Life seems to me a wintry waste, The ve - ry sun feels cold. For lang, lang years ye've been to

years O'er hill and meadow fa', And hinney, were it no for you, I'd gladly slip a - wa, And hinney, were it no for you, I'd glad-ly slip a - wa.

thocht, That we maun sindered be; There's naething binds my poore auld heart To earth, gude wife, but thee, There's naething binds my poore auld heart To earth, gude wife, but thee.

me O' world-ly friens the best? Now I'll lay down my weary head, Gude wife, and be at rest; Now I'll lay down my weary head, Gude wife, and be at rest.

4. A king-dom thou seemest, a-lone, Sur-round-ed by moun-tain and sea; Let work be the king on the throne, Till work-men and

world turn to thee; The sound of thy mu-si-cal name Is heard on the ut-ter-most shore, All na-tions are spreading thy fame, In

work cease to be; And ev-er re-mem-ber that God Holds na-tions and worlds in his hand, Will pun-ish all wrong with his rod, And de-

splen - dor ne'er spo - ken be - fore, In splen - dor ne'er spo - ken be - fore. 2. Fairest land of the

fend all the right in the land, And de - fend all the right in the land. 5. But mountain and

fig and the vine, And rich - er than O - phir of old, Thy press - es flow riv - ers of wine, Thy can - yons are cof - fers of gold; The

sea cannot sever Co - lum - bi - a's "Un - ion of states," E plu - ri - bus u - num for - ever, Is the mot - to de - creed by the fates. Then

stand by the Star-Spangled Ban - ner, The Fath - ers trans - mit - ted to thee, And shout as a sa - cred ho - san - na, One land from the.

glo - ri - ous state. O'er the weal of thy glo - ri - ous state.

sea to the sea, One land from the sea to the sea.

3. And thine is the land of the Forest,
   With trees reaching high toward the stars,
   Thrice taller than Lebanon's tallest,
   And graven with centuries' scars ;
   Thy mountains " that awfully rise,"
   And sleep in perpetual snows,
   Hold secrets of God in the skies,
   They never to man will disclose.

A SPRING SONG.

CIRO PINSUTI.

Allegro moderato.

1. I sat beneath the Abeles old, The meads were shot with green and gold, And un-der-neath my feet there roll'd The lit - tle sil - very Gad.

1. I sat beneath the Abeles old, The meads were shot with green and gold, And un-der-neath my feet there roll'd The lit - tle sil - very Gad.

The cuckoo and the thrush were singing, singing, singing, singing, The sheep-bells on the hills were ringing, ringing, ringing, ringing, All life was gay and

The cuckoo and the thrush were sing - ing, singing, The sheep-bells on the hills were ring - ing, ringing, All life was gay and

Larghetto scherzoso.

The cuckoo and the thrush were singing, singing, singing, The sheep-bells on the hills were ringing, ringing, ringing, All life was gay and

The cuckoo and the thrush were singing, singing, singing, sing - ing, The sheep-bells on the hills were ringing, ringing, ringing, ring - ing, All life was gay and

D. P. THOMPSON.

FAREWELL TO MY NATIVE STATE.

* MALE QUARTET.

As sung by "The Chency Family."

1st Tenor.

1st Bass.

2. It was here that the chords of young friendship first bound me, When my youthful af - fec - tions all ar - dent - ly glowed, And

2d Bass.

3. And with pride thy re - mem - brance shall e'er be at - tend - ed, I e'er shall re - spect, tho' I view them no more, Those

beau - ti - ful cas - cades, thy pure gush - ing foun - tains, I bid you for - ev - er, for - ev - er fare - well. Green

here with com - pan - ions all smil - ing a - round me, I joyed in the pleasures that friend-ship be - stowed. Tho'

re - gions where sci - ence and vir - tue are blend - ed, Those mountains where triumphed young free - dom of yore. Green

* *Soprano and Alto voices may sing the* 1st *and* 2d *Tenors, and Tenor voices the* 1st *Bass. If too low, sing in key of* D. *It may be sung in chorus*

land of my youth, of my life's ear-ly dawn-ing, When glad-some I sport-ed in fan-cy's bright ray, When she

dis-tant I wan-der, I still must re-gret thee, To greet thy wild scenes as far on-ward I roam; And

mountains, fare-well, o'er my dim eye is steal-ing, As it rests on thy ver-dure fast fad-ing from view, The

shone o'er my soul like the beams of the morn-ing, And be-guiled my young life in sweet vis-ion a-way, a-way, a-way.

cold be my bos-om be-fore I for-get thee, Be-fore I for-get the en-chantments of home, of home, sweet home.

tear that is wak-ened by an-guish of feel-ing, While I bid you a long and a last-ing a-dieu, a-dieu, a-dieu.

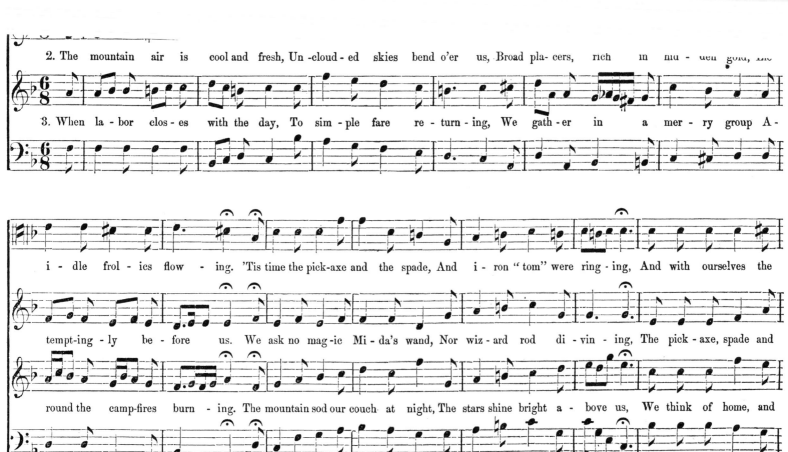

2. The mountain air is cool and fresh, Un -cloud- ed skies bend o'er us, Broad pla- cers, rich in hid- den gold, lie

3. When la- bor clos- es with the day, To sim- ple fare re- turn- ing, We gath- er in a mer- ry group A-

i- dle frol- ics flow - ing. 'Tis time the pick-axe and the spade, And i- ron "tom" were ring- ing, And with ourselves the

tempt- ing- ly be - fore us. We ask no mag- ic Mi- da's wand, Nor wiz- ard rod di- vin- ing, The pick- axe, spade and

round the camp-fires burn - ing. The mountain sod our couch at night, The stars shine bright a - bove us, We think of home, and

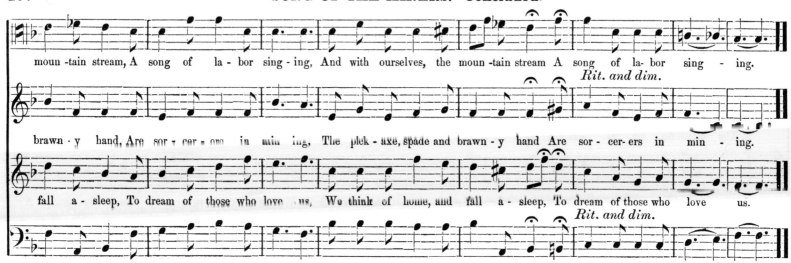

moun-tain stream, A song of la-bor sing-ing, And with ourselves, the moun-tain stream A song of la-bor sing - ing.

brawn - y hand, Are sor - cer - ers in min-ing, The pick-axe, spade and brawn-y hand Are sor-cer-ers in min-ing. *Rit. and dim.*

fall a-sleep, To dream of those who love us, We think of home, and fall a-sleep, To dream of those who love us. *Rit. and dim.*

MY HOME IS THERE. Arranged by Jas. A. Johnson. from an old English Song.

Isle

1. There is an Isle, a bon - - ny Isle, Stands

Sym.

2. Farewell! though oth - er lands may meet My

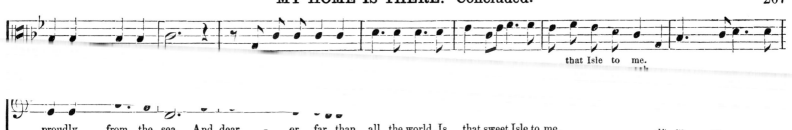

that Isle to me.

proudly from the sea, And dear - er far than all the world, Is that sweet Isle to me.

gaze wher - e'er I look, I shall not find a spot so sweet As my own dear cottage nook. It is not that a -

meads are green, It is not that its hills are fair, But because it is my na - tive land, And my home, my home is there.

lone it stands Where all a-round is fresh and fair, But because it is my na - tive land, And my home, my home is there

MRS. PETER SAXE. **THE STREET CRIER, or "TEENS TOW MENT."** S. P. CHENEY.

2 All his garments are thin, And the breeze enters in,

    As his way through the street he doth wend,

  With his endless refrain, In the sunshine or rain,

        " Teens tow ment."

3 He's no beggar nor shirk, He is willing to work,

    And asks not to borrow nor lend;

  But his heart is not here, While his words sound so queer,

        " Teens tow ment."

4 Ah! he thinks of his home, O'er the ocean's white foam,

    And the dark rolling waves without end;

  And he brushes a tear From his eye while you hear,

        " Teens tow ment."

5 Now he passes your door, And you see him no more,

    As he turns down the street at the bend,

  Whilst the breeze in his track Wafts the faint echo back,

        " Teens tow ment."

After the last verse, " Teens Tow Ment " is to be repeated *ad lib.* and diminished to *ppp*, and at last a voice *in the distance* is to give it as soft as can be distinguished.

THE RECOLLECTIONS OF HOME.

Arranged from a song composed by " The Hutchinson Family."

QUARTET.

1. Ah! why from my own na-tive land did I part, With mountains and val-leys so dear to my heart? Ah ? why did I

2. For oft have I roamed in a far dis-tant clime, I've been in the land of the or-ange and lime ; My footsteps are

3. New Eng-land, thou land of the brave and the free ! My coun-try, my home, I am looking towards thee ; I long for the

leave the en-joy-ments of home, O'er the wide waste of wa-ters a stranger to roam, O'er the wide waste of wa-ters a stranger to roam.

print-ed on ma-ny a shore, Where the sea loud-ly breaks with the deep sullen roar, Where the sea loudly breaks with the deep sul-len roar.

day when a-gain I shall stand On thy rude rock-y soil, but my own na-tive land, On thy rude rock-y soil, but my own na-tive land.

Words by C. L. GOODELL.

Allegretto.

2. The lyre of the po - et, The pen of the sage, The lyre of the po - et, The pen of the sage, May quick - en the spir - it, En - light -en the

3. Then let ev - ery freeman Re - mem - ber with joy, Then let ev - ery freeman Re - mem - ber with joy, The deeds of old E - than, The Green Mountain

nigh; His sword was an ar - my, His presence a host; Who bold - er and brav - er Can chiv-al - ry boast? Who bold-er and braver Can chivalry boast?

age; Still the sword of the he - ro, When drawn for the truth, Is the pride of the a - ged, The glo - ry of youth, Is the pride of the a -ged, The glory of youth.

Boy. From mountain and val - ley Let pa - tri - ots cry, Hur - rah for old E - than, The he - ro of Ti, Hurrah for old Ethan, The hero of Ti.

SUMMER DAYS ARE COMING.

MENDELSSOHN.

1. Song birds warble soft and clear, Bees are i - dly humming; Welcome are the sounds I hear, Summer days are com - ing.

2. Here among these green-wood bowers, I forgot my sadness; Roaming thro' this world of flowers, Wakes my heart to gladness.

THE SUMMER DAYS ARE OVER.

S. P. CHENEY.

1. The sum-mer days are o - ver, But bees are linger-ing still, A - bout the dy - ing clo - ver, No more the whip-poor-

2. The har - vest work is end-ing, The leaves are shad-ing brown, And Au-tumn hues are blend-ing, The for - est hills to

4. Thus sea - son fol-lows sea - son, All teach-ing life is brief; Af - ford-ing still no rea - son For sor - row or for

crown. Oh! Au - tumn, how thy charms Man - tle the world! May long thy col - ors wave, Like ban - ners all un - furled.

grief. Oh! *life!* we cher - ish thee! When thou art o'er, We'll hope for bright - er skies, Up - on the oth - er shore.

3. But Win - ter sends his warn - ing, Be sure he'll do his worst To blast thy world - a - dorn - ing, With snow and wind and

frost.   Blow,   win-ter,   blow thy blast,   Whirl wild the   snow!   Ah,   thou   canst on-ly   last   Till Spring shall bid thee go.

VERMONT WINTER SONG.

Written 1846, by MARY CUTTS, for "The Cheney Family."   "The CHENEY FAMILY."

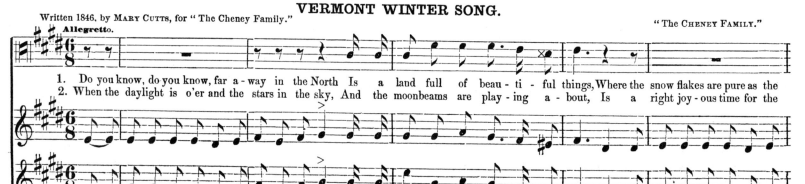

1. Do you know, do you know, far a-way in the North Is   a   land   full   of   beau-ti-ful things, Where the snow flakes are pure as the
2. When the daylight is o'er and the stars in the sky, And   the moonbeams are play-ing a-bout, Is   a   right joy-ous time for the

3. Hark,   hark to the bells, how they jin-gle a-long 'Mid the laugh and the wild note of glee! While the hearts that are beating 'neath
4. And   then when arrived, what a glo-ri-ous sight Is   the cheer-ing, the bright ro-sy fire! How it ri-ses and crackles and
5. How   peaceful the hearth of thy la-bor-ing sons, When the toils of the day-light are o'er, With their warm hon-est hearts and their

bell rings? O! that land hath a charm to all oth-ers unknown, When old

ride o-ver hill, o - ver dale, O - ver

wrap-pers and furs, From all shack-les but true love are free; O! the sleigh-rides they have in the Green mountain state, Do you

bla - zes a - way, As they pile the wood high - er and high-er; O! Vermont, loved Vermont, with thy soft summer charms, With thy

strong hard - y frames, By ex - er - cise taught to en - dure! O! then hail to Vermont, with her wool and her corn, With her

win - ter comes scowling a - long, Old win - ter, the sea - son for pleas - ure and mirth, For the dance and the blithe jol - ly

ice and o'er mountains of snow, "With swift Mor-gan hors - es" as fleet as the deer, Full of fun, full of life, on they

Cres. e Accelerando.

know, do you know what they are? When the pure i - cy crys - tals are all light - ed up By the moon and the glit - ter-ing

wild winds and deep win - ter snows, Dear, dear are thy glad fes - tive sea - sons of joy, And dear are thy scenes of re-

cheese "and all that sort of thing!" Let her snows beat a - way and her win - ter gales blow, Yet hail to Ver-mont, we will

song, For the dance and the blithe jol-ly song, For the dance and the blithe jol-ly song, For the dance and the blithe jol-ly song.
go, Full of fun, full of life on they go, Full of fun, full of life on they go, Full of fun, full of life on they go.

a tempo.

star, By the moon and the glit-ter-ing star, By the moon and the glit-ter-ing star, By the moon and the glit-ter-ing star.
pose, And dear are thy scenes of re-pose, And dear are thy scenes of re-pose, And dear are thy scenes of re-pose.
sing, Yet hail to Vermont we will sing, Yet hail to Vermont we will sing, Yet hail to Ver-mont we will sing.

SLEEP ON.

Arranged from a Quartet for men's voices. As sung by Hermann & Co.

1. Sleep on, sleep on, sleep on, hap-pi-ly on, Sleep on, sleep on,   Un-troubled by the cares of day, While thy free soul wings its way,   Then to me, to
2. Dream on, but dream of me, Dream on, but dream of me;   As all my dreams of dear de-light, Thro' the slumbers of the night,   Are of thee, of

1. Sleep on, sleep on, sleep on, hap-pi-ly on, sleep on, sleep on,   Un-troubled by the cares of day, While thy free soul wings its way,   Then to me, to
2. Dream on, but dream of me,......Dream on, but dream of me;   As all my dreams of dear de-light....Thro' the slumbers of the night,   Are of thee, of

1. Sleep on, sleep on, sleep on, Sleep on, sleep on, sleep on,   Un-troubled by the cares of day, While thy free soul wings its way,   Then to me, to
2. Dream on, but dream of me, Dream on, but dream of me;   As all my dreams of dear delight....Thro' the slumbers of the night,   Are of thee, of

on. Sleep on,.......... sleep on, sleep

me, sleep on, sleep on, sleep hap-pi-ly on, sleep on, sleep on, sleep hap-pi-ly on. on. Sleep on,...... sleep on, sleep
thee, dream on, dream on, but dream of me, dream on, dream on, but dream of me. me.

Sleep on,.......... sleep

me, sleep on, sleep on, sleep hap-pi-ly on, sleep on, sleep on, sleep hap-pi-ly on. on. Sleep on,.................... sleep on, sleep
thee, dream on, dream on, but dream of me, dream on, dream on, but dream of me. me.

on, but dream of me, Sleep on,.... sleep on, sleep on, but dream of me, sleep on, sleep on, but dream of me. Sleep on, Dream on.

on, but dream of me, Sleep on,.......... sleep on, sleep on, but dream of me, sleep on, sleep on, but dream of me. Sleep on, Dream on.

on, but dream of me, Sleep on,...............

Sleep on, Dream on.

on, but dream of me, Sleep on,...... sleep on, but dream of me, sleep on, sleep on, but dream of me.

UNION SONG.

"It was written by the Rev. Dr. Gilman, of Charleston, S. C., and sung at the 4th of July celebration in 1832 by the Union party of that city."

1. Hail, our country's natal morn! Hail our spreading kindred born! Hail, thou banner not yet torn, Waving o'er the free! While this day in festal throng,
2. Who would sever freedom's shrine? Who would draw th' invidious line? Though by birth one spot be dear, Dear is all the rest. Dear to me the south's fair land,

3. By our altars pure and free, By our law's deep-rooted tree, By the past's dread memory, By our Washington, By our country's kindred tongue,
4. Fathers! have ye bled in vain? Ages! must ye droop again? Maker! shall we rashly stain, Blessings sent by thee? No! receive our solemn vow,

Millions swell the patriot's song, Shall not we the notes prolong? Hallow'd jubilee,
Dear the central mountain band, Dear New England's rocky strand, Dear the prairied west:

CRES.. Hallow'd jubilee: Hallow'd jubilee.

By our hopes, bright, buoyant, young, By the tie of country strong, We will still be one.
While before thy throne we bow, Ever to maintain as now, Union, liberty.

GOOD NIGHT.

The CHENEY FAMILY.

Mary Jane Cunningham.

OUR NATIONAL ENSIGN.

S. P. Cheney.

1. Flag of the plan-et gems! Whose sap-phire - cir - cled di - a - dems Stud ev'-ry sea and shore and sky. Oh! can thy chil-dren

2. Flag of the stripes of fire! Long as the bard his loft - y lyre Can strike, thou shalt in - spire our song. We'll sing thee round the

3. Flag of the bird of Jove! Who left his home, the clouds a - bove To point the he - ro's lightning path; Around thee will we

4. Flag of two o - cean shores! Whose ev - er-last - ing thun - der roars From deep to deep in storm and foam, Tho' with the sun's red

gaze Up-on thy sil - ver blaze, Nor kin - dle at thy rays Which led the brave of old to die? Thou banner, thou banner, beautiful and

hearth, We'll sing thee on strange earth, We'll sing thee when we forth To bat-tle go with clar-ion tongue.

stand With glit'-ring sword in hand, And swear to guard the land Which quelled the British Li-on's wrath. Thou banner, thou banner, beautiful and

set Thou sink'st to slumber, yet With him in glo-ry great, Thou ris - est *and shall share his tomb.*

grand, Float thou, Float thou for - ev - er, for - ev - er o'er our land, Float thou for - ev - er, Float thou for - ev - er o'er our land.

JOHN VANCE CHENEY.

WINTER.

S. P. CHENEY.

1. The wea-sel thieves in sil - ver suit, The rab - bit runs in gray, While Pan betakes his frost - y flute To pipe the cold a - way, To pipe the cold a-
2. The flocks are fold - ed, boughs are bare, The sal - mon takes the sea; And O! my fair, that I somewhere Might house my heart with thee, Might house my heart with

way. The wea - sel thieves in sil - ver suit, The rab-bit runs in gray, While Pan betakes his frosty flute To pipe the cold a-

thee. The flocks are fold - ed, boughs are bare, The salmon takes the sea; And O! my fair, that I somewhere Might house my heart with

way, To pipe the cold a - way.

thee, Might house my heart with thee.

1. While Pan be - takes his frost - y flute, his frost - y flute.

2. And O! my fair, that I somewhere, that I some - where,

1. The rab - bit runs in gray, The rab - bit runs in gray, runs in gray.

2. The sal - mon takes the sea, The sal - mon takes the sea, takes the sea.

1. The wea - sel thieves in sil - ver suit, The wea - sel thieves in sil - ver suit, The wea - sel thieves.

2. The flocks are fold - ed, boughs are bare, The flocks are fold - ed, boughs are bare; The flocks are fold-ed.

1. To pipe the cold a - way.

2. Might house my heart with thee.

While Pan be - takes his frost - y flute, To pipe the cold a - way, To pipe the cold a - way, To pipe
And O! my fair, that I somewhere, Might house my heart with thee, Might house my heart with thee, Might house my heart with

a tempo. cres.

f

way, To pipe the cold a - way, To pipe the cold a - way, To pipe the cold a - way.................
thee, Might house my heart with thee, Might house my heart with thee, Might house my heart with thee.................

mp

ff > > > >

EDWIN RANSFORD. **LUNA.** J. BARNBY.

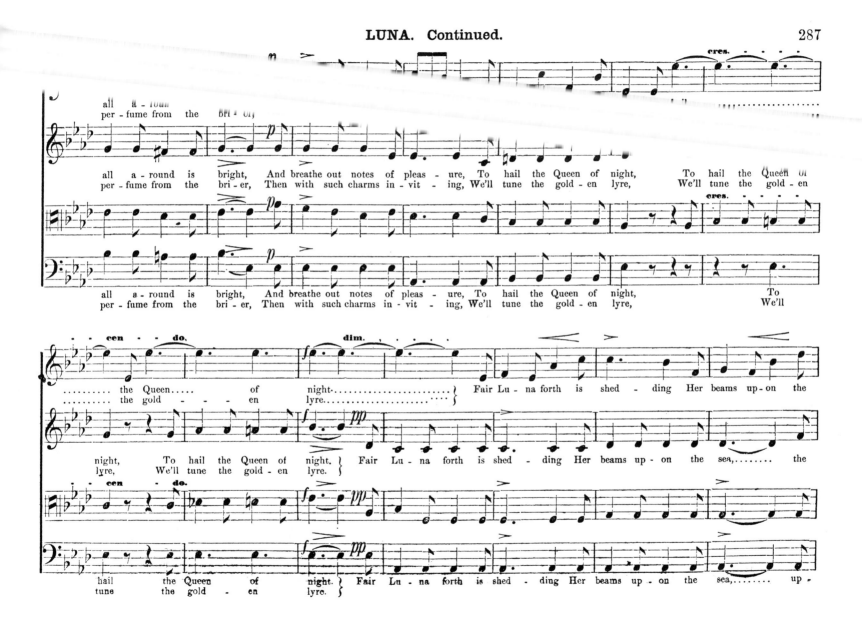

LUNA. Concluded.

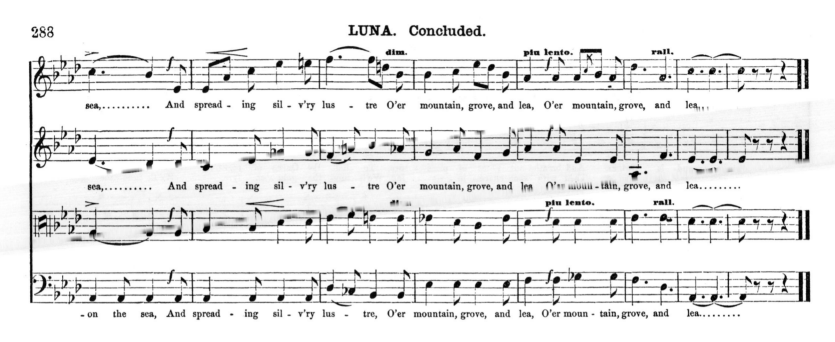

sea,.......... And spread - ing sil - v'ry lus - tre O'er mountain, grove, and lea, O'er mountain, grove, and lea....

sea,.......... And spread - ing sil - v'ry lus - tre O'er mountain, grove, and lea O'er moun - tain, grove, and lea........

-on the sea, And spread - ing sil - v'ry lus - tre, O'er mountain, grove, and lea, O'er moun - tain, grove, and lea........

COME, SING THIS ROUND WITH ME. Glee.

MARTINI.

Come, sing this round with me, And if we all a - gree, We'll laugh right mer - ri - ly, Ha, ha, ha, ha, ha, ha, ha, ha,—We'll

laugh right mer - ri - ly, Come, sing this round with me, And if we all a - gree, We'll sing right mer - ri - ly, Ha, ha, ha, ha, ha,

HARK! 'TIS THE BELLS.

Helen W. Cross.

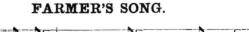

1. Oh! happy

     laid woods and fields.

2. He sows, he reaps, he tills the land, While near

3. A king he is in nature's right, He asks not pow'r or wealth, ha, ha! His sleep is sweet, his heart is light, His days are crown'd with health.

4. A life a-mong the brooks and hills, O, what so glad and free! ha, ha, What changeful joy each sea-son fills; O, a farm-er's life for me.

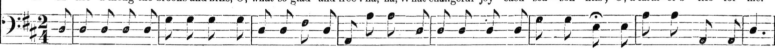

To be whistled the second time.   Soprano and Alto parts only.

CHORUS.

La   la   la   la   la   la   la la   la   la   la   la   la la la la.

La la la la la la la la la la la la la la la la la la la la la la la la la la la la la la la la.

La   la   la   la   la   la   la la la   la   la   la   la   la la la la.

Mrs. THOMAS FITCH, California.   **THE SONG OF THE FLUME.**   S. P. CHENEY.
Accomp. by J. A. JOHNSON.

A - wake!   a - wake! the flam - ing east Is red with the com - ing day; My strug - gling breast dis - dains its rest,....... I haste o'er the hills a -

way....... Up from val - ley and up from plain! Up, up from the tr.........welling

tide, There's wealth in my swell - ing tide.......

QUARTET. Slow.

To the shores of the sounding sea, From the far Si - er - ra's

height, With star-ry breast and foam-capped crest, I leaped in a path of light. They turned me thence thro' winding ways, They fettered me like a

slave, As serfs of old were sold for gold, They bartered my soil-stained wave.

INSTRUMENT.

No stern and war-rior march is mine, With the storm-y trump and drum; No ban-ners gleam...... on

haste;..... In search of gold my drops are sold, And they are too dear to waste, And they are too dear to waste. 4. Awake! Awake! for

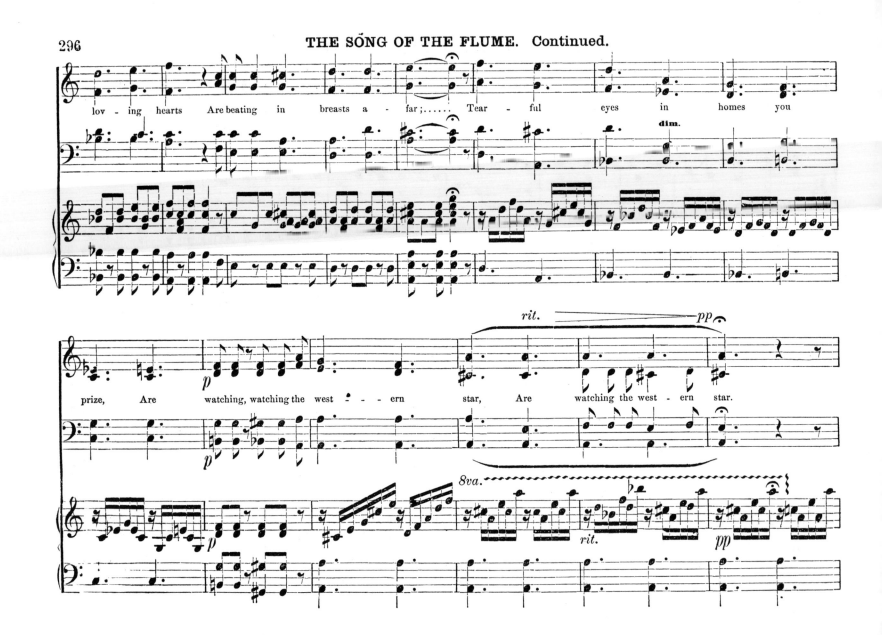

lov - ing hearts   Are beating   in   breasts a - far;......   Tear - ful   eyes   in   homes   you

prize,   Are   watching, watching the west - - - ern   star,   Are   watching the west - ern   star.

up from the riv - er's side!........ With joy - ous song I rush a - long, There's wealth in my swell - ing tide..... With

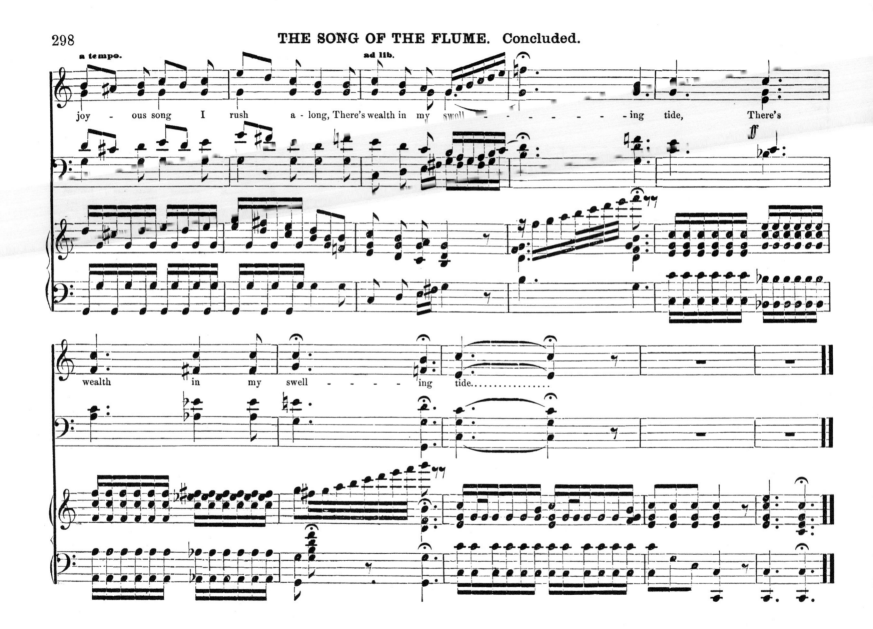

joy - ous song I rush a - long, There's wealth in my swell - - - - - - - - ing tide, There's

wealth in my swell - - - ing tide..................Concluded.

ro - ses? Are her steps on gras - sy Lumon, near the bed of ro - ses? Ah me! ah me! I behold her bow in the

ro - ses? near .... the bed of ro - ses? Ah me! ah me! I behold her bow in the

ro - ses? Are her steps on gras - sy Lumon, near the bed of ro - ses? Ah me! ah me! I behold her bow in the

I be-

hall, I be - hold her bow in the hall. Where art thou, where art thou, beam of light? where art thou, beam of

hall, her bow in the hall. Where art thou, beam of light? where art thou, beam of

hall, her bow in the hall. Where art thou, beam of light? where art thou, beam of

hold her bow in the hall. Where art thou, beam of light? where art thou, beam of

light? where art thou, where art thou, beam of light? where art thou, beam of

light? where art thou, beam of light? where art thou, beam of light? beam of light? beam of light?

light? where art thou, beam of light? where art thou, beam of light? beam of light? beam of light?

Words by CARLOTTA PERRY.

ENCHANTMENT.

Dedicated to Mrs. General FOOTE of Sacramento, Cal.

S. P. CHENEY.

Arranged by ALVIS F. LEJEAL, San Francisco.

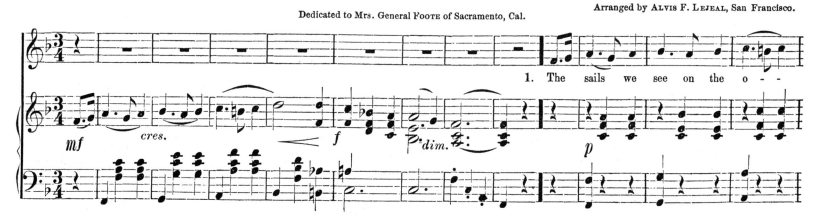

1. The sails we see on the o - -

cean Are white as white can be;........ But nev - er are in the har - bor As white as the sails at

sea .... And the clouds that crown the moun - tains with pur - ple and gold de - light, ...

Turn to cold gray mists and va-pors Ere ev - er we reach the height; Turn to cold gray mists and va - pors Ere

2. The
3. O

mountains wear crowns of glo — ry, When they are seen from a-far,.......... And the sails lose all their white — — —
"distance," thou dear en — chant — er, Still hold in thy mag — ic vail.......... The glo — ry of far off moun — — —

ness, In — side of the har — bor bar............... State — ly and fair is the ves — — — sel That
tains, The gleam of the far-off sail!.............. Hide in thy robes of splen — — dor, O

comes   not   near   our   beach;.......... State - ly   and   grand   the   moun - tain   Whose height we   may nev - er   reach,

moun - tain   cold   and   gray;...... O   sail   in   thy   snow - y   white - ness,   Come not   in - to   port, I   pray; O

State - ly and   grand   the   moun - - tain...... whose   height   we may   nev - er   reach.

sail,   in thy   snow - y   white - - ness,   come   not   in-to

port,............ I pray.

"THE BLUE AND GRAY."

C. A. WHITE.

The words of the following song are an extract from a beautiful poem, read at Memphis, Tenn., on Decoration Day, May, 1875, by Dr. Granger, an old ex-Federal soldier, now residing in Arkansas; it is worthy of being preserved, not only for its poetic merit, but for the noble sentiment which it breathes.

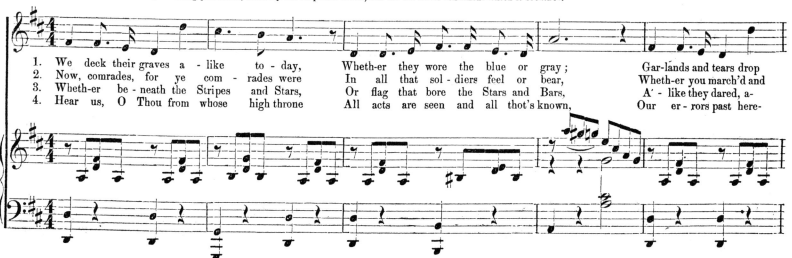

1. We deck their graves a - like to - day, Wheth-er they wore the blue or gray; Gar-lands and tears drop
2. Now, comrades, for ye com - rades were In all that sol - diers feel or bear, Wheth-er you march'd and
3. Wheth-er be - neath the Stripes and Stars, Or flag that bore the Stars and Bars, A' - like they dared, a-
4. Hear us, O Thou from whose high throne All acts are seen and all thot's known, Our er - rors past here-

o'er   each brave   Who fills   a   gal - lant sol- dier's grave ;   Wheth-er with Sher- man to   the sea,   Or   in the
fought,   and died   On mine   or   on the oth - er side,   Hear now our vows as here we stand,   Clasp - ing a-
like   they died   For what   to   them seemed du - ty's side;   On Sem - mes' or   on Winslow's ships,   Wher - ev - er
in   ah solve,   And fill   our   hearts with high re - solve   To   let the "dead past" bur - ied lie ;   And now, with

Wil - der - ness with Lee,   Where'er they fell, by who - so led,   Hon - or to - day our glorious dead.
cross your graves our hands,   Ha - tred and doubt, and mean   dis-trust,   We bur - y now beneath the dust.
death has scaled their lips,   South-born, or North-ern — all   the same,   Theirs still shall be im-mor - tal fame.
hands up - lift - ed high,   We pledge that hence-forth, long   as life,   We join in hard but friendly strife.

Hear us to-day, ye glorious dead, Clasping 'cross your graves our hands; Oh, help us above to ever stand For God, Truth, Right, and Fatherland.

COLBURN. 8s & 7s, 4 lines.

U. C. HILL.

Gent - ly, Lord, O gent - ly lead us Thro' this lone-ly vale of tears, Thro' the changes thou'st decreed us, Till our last great change appears.

URILLA CORELLI HILL. I have had no little difficulty in the search for Mr. Hill's history. From several sources which do not a-gree in all particulars, I settle upon the following as correct.

Mr. Hill was born in Boston, Mass., or Hartford, Conn., in 1808 or 1809. In 1837 he went to Germany, and there studied with Spohr, the great violin teacher and Music Master. On his return to New York, he published Spohr's Violin School, and was considered the best exponent of Classical Music in that city. He was a prominent man in founding The Philharmonic Society in 1843, was its first Pres-ident, and for several years its leader. He was a teacher of singing as well as of instruments. Charlotte Cushman was his pupil.

In 1846 he invented "a tuning-fork Piano." Dr. Hill, so well known as "Yankee Hill," was his younger brother and a man of gen-ius; he was a good Dr., a good writer, a good musician, and on or off "the stage" was the most perfect delineator of Yankee character ever in this country. He was an intellectual, happy, and most *natural* man. "The Cheney Family" will never forget an evening with him and W. E. Robinson, the witty Irish reporter, in Buffalo, in 1846.

U. C. Hill was a composer of sacred music, and this tune of his bears evidence of refined taste and knowledge of harmony. He died in New Jersey in 1876. S. P. C.

[*The above was inadvertently omitted from biographical department.*]

KATIE'S ANSWER.

W. S. Rogers.

Dedicated to Miss K. A Woodward, of Watertown, Conn.

1. O Ka - tie's a rogue, it is true, But her
2. An me heart, ar - rah, now how it bate, For my
3. Then I filt me - self grow ver - y bowld, For I

eyes like the skies are so blue, And her dim - ples so swate, And her an - kles so nate, She dazed and she bothered me
Kate looked so tempt - in' and swate, Wid her cheeks like the ros - es And all the red po - sies That grow in the gar - den so
knew she'd not scold if I towld Uv the love at me heart, That would nev - er de - part, Tho' I lived to be wrinkled and

too; Till one morn - ing we went for u
nate; But I sat just as mute as the dead,
owld; An' I said "If I dared to do so,
4. Then she blushed a more el - li - gant red, As she said

side, The dar - lint she sat Wid the wick - ed - est hat 'Neath a pur - ty gurl's chin ev - er tied.
head, "If I'd known that to - day Ye'd have noth - ing to say, I'd have gone wid me cous - in in - stead."
throw Both arms round your waist An' be stal - in' a taste Uv thim lips that are coax - in' me so."
head, An' her eyes look - in' down 'Neath her lash - es so brown, "Would you like me to dhrive, Mis - ter Ted?"

310

Miss Augusta Browne, of New York, (now Mrs. Garrett, of Washington, D. C.,) is an American composer of note. Wherever or when born, she is of English descent, and early enjoyed the advantage of a scientific musical education; many years ago becoming famous as a composer and as a performer upon the organ and piano-forte. Her compositions, many of them, are for the instruments upon which she performed; but she has written music for songs also, and for sacred compositions; among which, one of the most popular and perhaps the best known in this country, is the "Pilgrim Fathers;" the words being composed by Mrs. Hemans, (Felicia Dorothea Browne,) who was born at Liverpool, Eng., Sept. 25 1700, and who died May 16, 1835, aged 41. The age of Mrs. Garrett is not known; but she was born to adapt the beautiful words of Mrs. Hemans to excellent music; and it is known that besides occupations in such compositions, Mrs. G. has contributed to many magazines, and has published some books; such as "The Young Artist," and "Precious Stones of the Heavenly Foundation;" and her articles on "Church Music" have elicited much interest. *Moore's New Encyclopedia of Music.*

THE PILGRIM FATHERS. Solo and Chorus.

Words by Mrs. Hemans. SUITABLE FOR NATIONAL OCCASIONS. Arranged from Miss Browne, by L. Marshall.

The breaking waves dash'd high, On a stern and rock-bound coast, And the woods against a stormy sky Their gi-ant branches toss'd;

And the heav-y night hung dark, The hills and wa-ters o'er, When a band of ex-iles

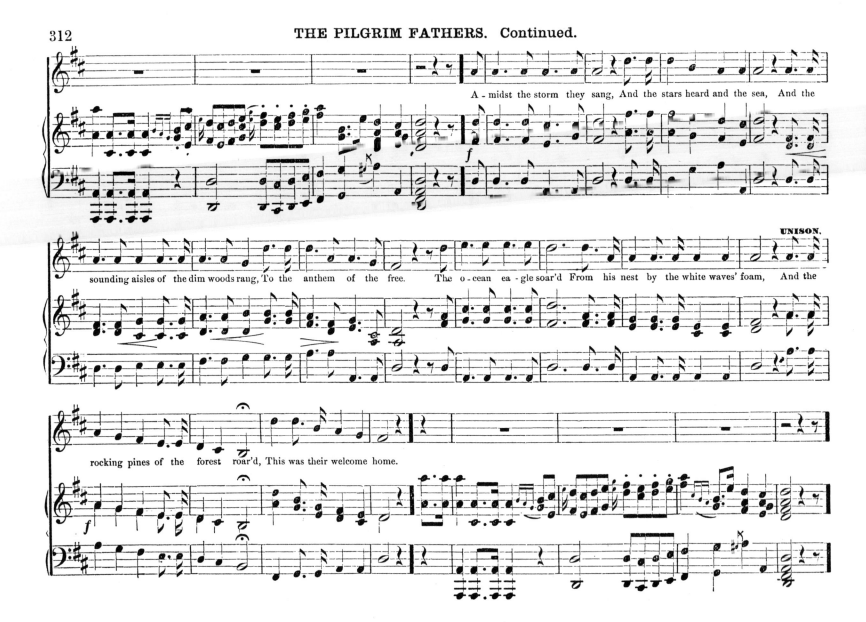

A - midst the storm they sang, And the stars heard and the sea, And the

sounding aisles of the dim woods rang, To the anthem of the free. The o - cean ea - gle soar'd From his nest by the white waves' foam, And the

rocking pines of the forest roar'd, This was their welcome home.

MY SHIP COMES IN.

Words by JOAQUIN MILLER.

Dedicated to Miss MARTHA E. WOODRUFF.
Music by W. S. ROGERS.

1. My ship comes sail - ing in from sea, And I am as glad as glad can be. Oh I have kissed my love to-night, And all life seems one
3. I know full well in my ship's hold Lie nei - ther gorgeous silks or gold, But oh! I know my love loves me, And ask no more of

2. ship comes in, My ship comes in, My ship comes climb - ing up the sea, My ship comes in, My

calm delight. My ship comes in, My ship comes in, My ship comes sail - ing up the sea, My ship comes in, My
land or sea. My ship comes in, My ship comes in, My ship has cross'd the lone - some sea, My ship comes in, My

ship comes in, And land and sea are fair to me

ship comes in, And mo
ship comes in, And I am as glad as glad can be.

now the door Of Par-a-dise is o-pen wide As yon church door for my fair bride, As yon church door for my fair bride. My

WHEN WE MEET THE ANGEL BAND. Song and Chorus.

Words by M.

Music by FRANK E. CRANE.

First four lines may be sung as a duet, using the small notes.

Moderato con espressione.

1 When we hear the music ring — ing, Thro' the bright ce-les-tial dome, When sweet an-gel voi-ces sing — ing,
2. When the ho-ly angels meet us, As we go to join their band, We shall know the friends that greet us,
3. Oh ye wea-ry, sad and tossed ones, Droop not, faint not by the way, Ye shall join the loved and lost ones,

Glad — ly bid us wel-come home, To the land of an-cient sto — ry, Where the spir-it knows no care,
In that glorious spir-it land. We shall see the same eyes shin — ing, On us as in the days of yore,
In that land of per-fect day. Harp-strings touched by an-gel fin — gers, Murmured in my raptured ear,

J. Hawes, Baraboo, Wis.

HE SLEEPS IN PEACE.

Theme by John C. Baker, of "The Baker Family."

A Quartet, sung at the funeral of Julius C. Chandler, at Baraboo, Wis., Aug. 30, 1878.

He sleeps in peace,

Slowly.

1. He sleeps in peace,.......... the sleep of death, To friends and kindred

INTRODUCTION and INTERLUDE. cres.

Pia.

mf dim. p

He sleeps in peace,

2. Nor grief nor pain can e'er intrude Their pangs upon him

ad lib.

mf ad lib. pp

dear,.... While round his form........ we meet to drop the sym-pa-thet-ic tear. He sleeps in peace, He sleeps in peace, He sleeps in peace............ in peace.

mf ad lib. pp

more;.... His rest is found,........ his toils are past, His weary journey o'er. He sleeps, &c.

320   INDEX.

BIOGRAPHICAL DEPARTMENT.